The Directory of Programs for Students At Risk

Thomas L. Williams

Routledge
Taylor & Francis Group
New York London

First published 1999 by Eye On Education

Published 2013 by Routledge
711 Third Avenue, New York, NY, 10017, USA
2 Park Square, Milton Park, Abingdon, Oxon OX14 4RN

Routledge is an imprint of the Taylor & Francis Group, an informa business

Copyright © 1999 Taylor & Francis.

All rights reserved. No part of this book may be reprinted or reproduced or utilised in any form or by any electronic, mechanical, or other means, now known or hereafter invented, including photocopying and recording, or in any information storage or retrieval system, without permission in writing from the publishers.

Notices
No responsibility is assumed by the publisher for any injury and/or damage to persons or property as a matter of products liability, negligence or otherwise, or from any use of operation of any methods, products, instructions or ideas contained in the material herein.

Practitioners and researchers must always rely on their own experience and knowledge in evaluating and using any information, methods, compounds, or experiments described herein. In using such information or methods they should be mindful of their own safety and the safety of others, including parties for whom they have a professional responsibility.

Product or corporate names may be trademarks or registered trademarks, and are used only for identification and explanation without intent to infringe.

Library of Congress Cataloging-in-Publication Data

Williams, Thomas L., 1946—
    Best practices and programs for students at risk / Thomas L. Williams
        p.   cm.
    Includes bibliographical references (p.) and index.
    ISBN 1-883001-74-9
    1. Socially handicapped children—Education—United States. 2. Problem children—Education— United States
LC4091.W55   1999
371.826'94'0973—dc21   99-10542
                                                                                                                              CIP

ISBN: 978-1-883001-74-2 (pbk)

Also Available from EYE ON EDUCATION

Urban School Leadership: Issues and Strategies
by Eugene T. W. Sanders

Data Analysis for Comprehensive Schoolwide Improvement
by Victoria L. Bernhardt

**The School Portfolio:
A Comprehensive Framework for School Improvement**
by Victoria L. Bernhardt

Best Practices from America's Middle Schools
by Charles R. Watson

The Directory of Innovations in Elementary Schools
by Jane McCarthy and Suzanne Still

Transforming Schools into Community Learning Centers
by Steve R. Parson

The Administrator's Guide to School Community Relations
by George E. Pawlas

Performance Standards and Authentic Instruction
by Allan A. Glatthorn

**Performance Assessment and Standards-based Curricula:
The Achievement Cycle**
by Allan A. Glatthorn with Don Bragaw, Karen Dawkins, and John Parker

**The Performance Assessment Handbook
Volume 1: Portfolios and Socratic Seminars
Volume 2: Performances and Exhibitions**
by Bil Johnson

Research on Educational Innovations, 2nd ed.
by Arthur K. Ellis and Jeffrey T. Fouts

Handbook of Educational Terms and Applications
by Arthur K. Ellis and Jeffrey T. Fouts

The School Leadership Library

David A. Erlandson and Alfred P. Wilson,
General Editors

The School Leadership Library, a series of 21 books, shows you what successful principals and other school leaders must know and be able to do. Grounded in best knowledge and practice, these books demonstrate best practices of effective principals. They provide recommendations which can be applied to a school leader's daily work.

Each volume includes practical materials, such as:

- checklists
- sample letters and memos
- model forms
- action plans

What should an effective principal know and be able to do? Members of the National Policy Board for Educational Administration (sponsored by NAESP, NASSP, AASA, ASCD, NCPEA, UCEA, and other professional organizations) developed a set of 21 "domains," or building blocks, that represent the essential knowledge and skills of successful principals. Each volume in this series is dedicated to explaining and applying one of these building blocks.

Contact Eye On Education for more details.

The School Leadership Library

The Functional Domains

Leadership: A Relevant and Realistic Role for Principals Gary M. Crow, L. Joseph Matthews, and Lloyd E. McCleary

Information Collection: The Key to Data-Based Decision Making Paula Short, Rick Jay Short, and Kenneth Brinson, Jr.

Problem Analysis Charles Achilles, John Reynolds, and Susan Achilles

Judgment: Making the Right Calls Jim Sweeney and Diana Bourisaw

Organizational Oversight: Planning & Scheduling for Effectiveness David A. Erlandson, Peggy L. Stark, and Sharon M. Ward

Implementation: Making Things Happen Anita Pankake

Delegation and Empowerment: Leading With and Through Others Michael E. Ward with Bettye MacPhail-Wilcox

The Programmatic Domains

Instruction and the Learning Environment James Keefe and John Jenkins

Staff Development: Practices That Promote Leadership in Learning Communities Sally J. Zepeda

Student Guidance and Development Mary Ann Ward and Dode Worsham

Measurement and Evaluation James McNamara, David Erlandson, and Maryanne McNamara

Resource Allocation: Managing Money and People M. Scott Norton and Larry K. Kelly

The Interpersonal Domains

Motivating Others: Creating the Conditions David P. Thompson

Interpersonal Sensitivity John R. Hoyle and Harry Crenshaw

Oral and Nonverbal Expression Ivan Muse

Written Expression: The Principal's Survival Guide India J. Podsen, Charles Allen, Glenn Pethel, and John Waide

The Contextual Domains

Working in a Legal and Regulatory Environment David J. Sperry

Dedication

This book is dedicated to my mother and father (posthumously) whose unconditional love and devotion nurtured, and inspired me. Also, this book is dedicated to all the educators and parents throughout this great country who *truly believe* that students at risk are capable of:

- learning at the highest levels;
- succeeding in school; and ultimately
- completing high school or college.

Thomas L. Williams

Acknowledgments

Whereas it is impossible to recognize every single person or organization that has contributed to the creation of this book; and

Whereas a book is never the result of the efforts of one person; and

Whereas this book would never have become a reality without assistance, support, and guidance from many people; therefore, the following acknowledgments are made:

First and foremost, I would like to pay tribute to my family. My mother and recently deceased father were my first and best teachers. Their direction and support have been an inspiration and guiding force throughout my entire life. My older brother, Ed, who almost 10 years ago sent me a book about students at risk, which greatly piqued my interest about students at risk, and ultimately led to the development of this book. To my sisters, Charmaine and Faye, you have always been the type of sisters of whom a "big brother" can be proud.

My very sincere appreciation goes to my wife, JoAnn. Her support and insights make the many roles I play possible and the work I do credible and worthwhile. As a fellow educator, her editorial contributions to the development of this book were immeasurable. Her input as a reader, critic, and sounding board was well received. Additionally, her patience, understanding, and support made it all possible during the many months that I was preoccupied with writing this book. Not to be overlooked is my son Justin, who is methodically formulating his plan to make his mark on the professional world. Thanks to all of my family members for hanging in there with me.

My friend and colleague, Dr. Alicia Meza, started the journey with me, but due to circumstances beyond her control, we were not able to finish the journey together. Maybe next time....

I extend my appreciation to Mrs. Beverley Lindfeldt. For almost 15 years, she has helped me get words, ideas, and concepts out of my head, into the computer, and ultimately onto paper. She skillfully and cheerfully represents me to others and has been steadfast in her support of me each time I undertake "another project." Regardless of the project's length, complexity, or time line, she has started and finished the task with exceptional accuracy and has always completed it ahead of schedule. I am absolutely astounded every time I pick up documents which she has word processed for me. Due to her technical skill, the finished products are always greatly enhanced when compared to the draft documents which I delivered to her!

I wish to thank Eye On Education, specifically its president, Robert Sickles. Over the years, Bob has been a counselor, adviser, confidante, and mentor. Without his encouragement and support, I would never have undertaken this project.

Finally, I am indebted to the countless students, parents, educators, and community members with whom I have worked over the years, and who have taught me a great deal. I consider myself privileged to be working in their schools and communities—to be able to observe, learn, and contribute to what happens therein. I hope this book will encourage all of them to continue to put their best foot forward and to assist others in taking their first step.

Foreword

In the midst of the complexities and hurdles confronting educators who work with students at risk, there is good news! There are clear and measurable signs that many of these students are making significant progress.

We can learn from the successes of others and Tom Williams has searched the country for examples. His efforts have resulted in this collection of solid and credible source materials—*The Directory of Programs for Students At Risk*.

This is a wonderful resource book for superintendents, principals, other school leaders, teachers, parents—in fact, for anyone working with students at risk. Within these pages, Tom has summarized a wide variety of programs. While some of the programs in this book focus on an individual student's learning skills, others tackle whole school improvement. There are teacher training and professional development initiatives described here, as well as programs which target parent involvement. I am impressed by the number and diversity of programs identified and summarized by Professor Williams. These profiles, presented in a clearly written, unbiased form, are easy to review and evaluate. The names, addresses, and phone numbers of contact people for each of the programs is included so it is easy to access additional information about those which interest the reader.

Tom Williams has written a practical and realistic book. It is essentially a "directory of hope,"—a highly effective tool in the pursuit of student success.

Rudolph F. Crew, Chancellor
New York City Public Schools

About the Author

Thomas L. Williams, Ed. D., is currently a professor in the Department of Teacher Education at California State University, Sacramento, California. He has been a professor at California State University, Sacramento since August 1990. Additionally, Dr. Williams serves as Senior Research Associate for the California High-Risk Youth Educational and Public Safety Program—SB 1095. This supplementary assignment is held concurrently with his professorial position at California State University, Sacramento. His responsibilities as Senior Research Associate include providing consultative and technical assistance as well as performing research and evaluation duties for county offices of education and for school districts, to help them implement prevention and early intervention strategies for youth who are seriously at risk of becoming chronic, repeat offenders.

Dr. Williams received his Bachelor of Science (B.S.) from Indiana State University, Terre Haute, Indiana, and his Master of Science (M.S.) from Purdue University, Lafayette Indiana. He received his Doctor of Education (Ed. D.) from the University of the Pacific, Stockton, California.

He has served as a Director of Compensatory Education, in addition to having been an elementary and secondary school principal. Other professional activities include working as a consultant to school districts assisting with curriculum development; program planning and implementation; preparation of grant proposals; and policy analysis. Dr. Williams also assists school districts with professional development activities to include school restructuring; program improvement; recruiting, screening, selection and evaluation of administrators and other staff, and so forth.

Dr. Williams' résumé chronicles the rich background of education, teaching and administrative experience that he has amassed over his professional career. His outstanding achievements as a presenter and writer are heightened by his interpersonal skills and are grounded in the firm value system from which he operates. He is self-motivated, decisive, and has a consuming belief in the potential of every child and adult with whom he works. Regardless of the medium he uses, verbal or written, his underlying message is always the same—*You Can If You Think You Can!*

Table of Contents

Acknowledgments ix
Foreword xi
About the Author xii

1 Introduction and Background 1
   An Overview 3
     Placing a Few Things into Perspective 3
     A Personal Perspective 4
     Background, Rationale, and Purpose 6
     Organization of the Remainder of the Book 6
   Background Information Related to Students At Risk 7
     The Purpose of the School 7
     Definition of Dropout 8
     Defining and Calculating Event Dropout Rates Using the
       Common Core of Data 9
     Types of Dropout Rates 10
     The Dropout Problem 11
     Factors that Impact a Student's Decision to Drop Out of School ... 12
       Race-Ethnicity 12
       Income 12
       Age 13
       Geographic Region 13
       Teen Pregnancy 14
   Creating a Professional Learning Community: An Environment That
     Facilitates Student Learning and Achievement of Students At Risk ... 16
   Moving Toward Excellence: Establishing a Positive School Environment ... 20
     Classroom-Related Activities That Foster Learning 26
     Resiliency-Building Class Strategies 33
     Strategies for Reclaiming Black and Hispanic Students 35
   Parental Engagement of Students At Risk 39
     So, Does Involving Parents Really Make a Difference? 42
     An Ending Note—What Parents Want From Teachers 49

2 Program, Instructional, and Curricular Initiatives 51
   Advancement Via Individual Determination (AVID) 53
   The California Mini-Corps 57
   Core Knowledge 63
   Equity 2000 72

Help One Student To Succeed (HOSTS) 76
Higher Order Thinking Skills (HOTS) 80
International Youth Leadership Institute (IYLI) 83
Mathematics, Engineering, Science Achievement (MESA) 85
The (Ronald E.) McNair Program 91
MegaSkills 95
Parent Expectations Support Achievement (PESA) 103
Project Zero 106
SCORE 114
Success for All (SFA) 116

3 Comprehensive School-Improvement Initiatives 121
Accelerated Schools Project 123
The Coalition of Essential Schools (CES) 125
The Developmental Studies Center Child Development Project .. 133
The Edison Project 137
The Efficacy Institute 144
Effective Schools 153
Foxfire 157
Different Ways of Knowing—The Galef Institute 161
The League of Professional Schools 166
The Paideia Program 169
The School Development Program 175
SCORE 180

4 Teacher Training and Professional Development Initiatives .. 187
The Center for the Study and Teaching of At-Risk Students (C-STARS) 189
The National Writing Project 193
Reading Recovery 197
Teach For America (TFA) 207
Teacher Expectations and Student Achievement (TESA) 214
Teachers of English to Speakers of Other Languages, Inc. (TESOL) 218

5 District, State, and National Systemic Initiatives 221
The Center for Educational Renewal 223
The Center for Leadership in School Reform (CLSR) 226
The Center for Research in Human Development and Education (CRHDE) .. 228
The Center for the Study and Teaching of At-Risk Students (C-STARS) 234
The Clearinghouse for Immigrant Education (CHIME) 238
Education Commission of the States 240
The Holmes Partnership 245
The Institute for Urban and Minority Education (IUME) 251
The National Center on Education and the Economy (NCEE) ... 253
The National Coalition of Advocates for Students (NCAS) 262
New American Schools (NAS) 264
The Panasonic Foundation 268
The Urban Education Web 273

Table of Contents

6 Epilogue 277

Bibliography. 281

Appendices 287
    Appendix A: High School Completion Rates 289
    Appendix B: Membership, Dropout Counts, and Event Dropout Rates 291
    Appendix C: Race-Ethnicity and Income 293
    Appendix D: Event Dropout and Persistence Rates 294
    Appendix E: Selected Web Sites 295
    Appendix F: Information About Parental Involvement 296
    Appendix G: New Report Documents Public Engagement 298
    Appendix H: The PTA's National Standards 299
    Appendix I: Schools of Promise 301
    Appendix J: Listen, Discuss, and Act: Recommendations from
        the Education Commission of the States 302
    Appendix K: Resources for Change Schools 303
    Appendix L: Mobilization for Equity Partner Organizations .. 307
    Appendix M: School Choice Resources 310
    Appendix N: Programs At-a-Glance (In Alphabetical Order) .. 311

1
Introduction and Background

Introduction and Background

> *For the purposes of our discussion, we will define the term "student at risk," as a student who, on the basis of several risk factors, is unlikely to graduate from high school (or complete college).*
>
> *Listed in alphabetical order, selected risk factors include, but are not limited to: attendance at schools with large numbers of poor students; child abuse or neglect; delinquent behavior; family conflict and disruption; low achievement; low socioeconomic status; poor school attendance; retention in grade; school conflict and disruption; substance abuse; teen pregnancy; and violence.*
>
> — T. Lloyd Williams

An Overview

Placing a Few Things into Perspective

Using my own definition, I have always considered myself to be a student at risk. (I have met 7 of the 12 risk factors which I previously outlined.) Also, in conjunction with a review of the literature related to students at risk, a great deal of what I have experienced as a teacher, assistant principal, principal, central office administrator, consultant and university professor is reflected in my writing.

In this book, I most frequently used the term *African-American* (note that it is hyphenated) and *Hispanic* to refer to students living in the United States but who are of African, Spanish, or Latin-American origin or descent. Because I tried to incorporate the ideas and concepts of many of my colleagues, you will find little consistency in the usage of these terms throughout the book. The same holds true regarding the use of the term *at-risk student* versus *student at risk* and the capitalization of the words *Black, White, and Hispanic*. Although, some of my colleagues do not capitalize these terms in their writing, I have done so to define racial groups.

As the author-editor, I have tried to remain neutral and have not endorsed any program as being more effective than another. If you perceive some of the program descriptions in Chapters 2 through 5 to be somewhat biased, it may be because most of the descriptions were prepared from materials sent to me by the organization on which I reported. This also explains why some descriptions are much longer than others. If you are interested in the cost of the programs, contact the organization directly because many of the organizations did not provide information relative to program costs.

This book is written for field-based educators who are required to consume large quantities of information in short periods of time. To make the best use of the reader's time, I have synthesized many of the research findings and presented them in a format that is easy to read and understand.

A Personal Perspective

During more that 25 years as an educator, I have never met a student who enjoyed failure; a parent who enjoyed seeing their child fail; or an educator who enjoyed failing to meet the needs of the students. Neither have I ever worked in a school that was proud to be perceived by the school community as being unsuccessful. Therefore, I launched this project based on my personal experiences and on my knowledge of research-based data about increasing student achievement.

For my entire professional career, I have always had an interest in observing and creating classroom environments which enhance student success. My interest was piqued nearly 10 years ago when my older brother Ed sent me a gift. It was a book entitled *School Success for Students At-risk: Analysis and Recommendations of the Council of Chief State School Officers* (1988). The book profiled information about students at risk and outlined information which was designed to increase the success of students at risk. Close scrutiny of that book's contents, coupled with my personal desire to have access to current information pertaining to students at risk ultimately lead to the development of this book.

Regardless of your role—whether educator, parent, or concerned community member—you will find the information herein useful as you develop and embellish school programs, strategies, and activities that are designed to meet the needs of students at risk. Take this information and customize it to your students' needs. Use this body of information as a foundation upon which you can build a repertoire of best practices for your school site(s). If my efforts in any way positively influences your school improvement efforts, then this endeavor was not in vain. I am grateful to assist you and, most importantly, your students.

Writing this book has been both challenging and exciting—not to mention time-consuming. The project was undertaken as an attempt to help educators meet the challenge of educating *all* children in diverse settings—ethnically, culturally, socioeconomically, and cognitively. It contains valuable information that educators need to know to expose students at risk (or any student for that matter) to opportunities, educational and otherwise, which will increase their chances of graduating from high school.

Introduction and Background

Educators seeking to ascertain whether any program in this book would be appropriate and effective in their school or district will find a wealth of information embedded in the detailed description of each of the programs. The information and the programs can be adapted to meet the identified needs of specific schools (from the most privileged to those with the most limited resources) willing to try new strategies to address long-standing and ongoing educational issues. However, educators must never forget that the success of any program is dependent upon the effort of those charged with the implementation of the program—keeping in mind that no program can be designed in such a manner as to be *people proof*.

Early in my career, I learned there is no magic program, practice, or initiative that works for all children and at all schools. Currently, there are a myriad of programs available which hold promise for public schools seeking to meet the challenge of educating all children. I have attempted to present the reader with a description of programs that can help them determine which program will be helpful in their quest to increase student achievement; deliver a well-defined, appropriate curriculum; and graduate a higher percentage of students.

Many scholars have analyzed school reform proposals made by different governmental and private entities which are designed to address the needs of students at risk (e.g., *A Nation at Risk*, 1983; *Becoming a Nation of Readers*, 1985). That notwithstanding, their analyses may not address the issues at the heart of *at-riskness*—race-ethnicity, diversity, and the socioeconomic status of the student populace as opposed to that of those teaching them. These are not the only factors that negatively impact schoolage children. However, I strongly suggest that educators need to consider the implications of these factors when adopting or implementing programs or practices. Prior to initiating new strategies to meet the needs of students at risk, educators must consider the extent to which these initiatives will positively impact or address the following:

- The needs of members of diverse ethnic groups;
- The needs of students from families with low incomes;
- The achievement gaps that have been identified among the various student groups (ethnic, sociological, etc.);
- The assessed needs of the staff; and
- The school's overall curriculum design and established curriculum delivery system.

My recommendation is to pay particularly close attention to students from diverse ethnic groups and students from families with low incomes, and to how they interface with the school's curriculum and delivery systems.

Background, Rationale, and Purpose

For a multitude of reasons, far too many students fail to graduate from high school. I wrote this in an effort to provide pre-K through college-level educators with easy-to-access information about programs, practices, and initiatives that show promise as a means of meeting the needs of students at risk—those students whose participation in school is marginal and who may ultimately fail to satisfy their graduation requirements.

This book helps educators accomplish the goal of providing for pupil learning and of delivering a well-defined and appropriate curriculum to all students—including students at risk. By examining selected program critiques and information about restructuring and improving schools, you can ascertain what will work for your school's population.

Organization of the Remainder of the Book

The Directory of Programs for Students At Risk is organized into five chapters. Each program's description is placed under specified chapter headings in Chapters 2 through 5. However, some of the programs were multifaceted and did not clearly fit under the predetermined chapter headings. Therefore, I simply placed the program's description in the chapter that I deemed most appropriate.

Chapter 1: Introduction and Background provides discussion related to students at risk and practices that can help educators implement programs and initiatives that better address the needs of students at risk and, ultimately, to decrease school dropout rates and increase college *going* rates. Chapter 1 is further subdivided into four sections:

- Background Information Related to Students At Risk
- Creating a Professional Learning Community: An Environment that Facilitates Learning and Achievement for Students At Risk
- Moving Toward Excellence: Establishing a Positive School Environment
- Parental Engagement of Students At risk

Chapter 2: Program, Instructional, and Curricular Initiatives details school improvement approaches that are:

Introduction and Background

- Student focused;
- Designed to assist students in the learning process; and
- Structured to strengthen their learning skills.

Chapter 3: Comprehensive School-Improvement Initiatives describes schoolwide approaches that detail improvement strategies and provide students with the academic support they need to reach high levels of achievement in challenging academic courses.

Chapter 4: Teacher Training and Professional Development Initiatives profiles programs that focus on professional development. Although the programs vary widely, each emphasizes ongoing professional development for school personnel to raise their expectations of all students, and to help them use varied instructional strategies.

Chapter 5: District, State, and National Systemic Initiatives outlines district, state, and national systemic change initiatives that are designed to positively affect districtwide policy changes and, ultimately, to lead to increased academic achievement of students at risk.

Chapter 6: The Epilogue concludes the discussion related to enhancing the successes of students at risk.

Background Information Related to Students At Risk

A discussion about students at risk is logically initiated by sharing information concerning the existence and purpose of the school, and pertinent information about school dropouts including such key components as defining *dropout*, defining and calculating dropout rates, specifying types of dropout rates, and identifying some of the factors that impact a student's decision to drop out of school.

The Purpose of the School

The purpose of the school is to promote pupil learning. To achieve this purpose, the school must have and deliver a well-defined and appropriate curriculum. In addition, the school must strive to develop an environment that maximizes learning and minimizes conditions which interfere with learning. The degree to which a school accomplishes these objectives is the measure of its degree of "wellness." (Ogden and Germinario, 1988, p. 1).

A "well" student is defined as one who is achieving at a rate commensurate with his or her ability, has a positive attitude toward self, teachers, and school, has positive relationships with peers, and does not demonstrate destructive behaviors. A "well" school is one that has assessed its learning environment and has taken action to reduce or eliminate impediments to learning (Ogden and Germinario, 1988, p. 1). It is a school in which students of all types, including students at risk, are achieving academically. The degree to which students at risk benefit from attending school is dependent on the how well principals, teachers, counselors, support staff, and parents create school environments that maximize learning and minimize conditions that interfere with learning. In tandem with school personnel and parents, the school's curriculum and program offerings must enhance the learning environment to ensure that students at risk learn how to learn, increase their ability to resist involvement in destructive activities, and promote positive involvement with peers and society (Ogden and Germinario, 1988).

Definition of Dropout

There are variations in how *dropout* is defined in the existing data sources, including the Current Population Survey (CPS), the High School and Beyond Study (HS&B), and the National Education Longitudinal Study of 1988 (as cited in U.S. Department of Education, 1997). In addition, the age or grade span examined and the type of dropout rate—status, event, or cohort—varies across the data sources. Furthermore, there were potentially significant changes in CPS procedures in 1986, 1992, and 1994.

The dropout collection through the National Center for Education Statistics (NCES) Common Core of Data (CCD) is designed to be consistent with the current CPS procedures. However, the CCD collection includes all dropouts in grades 7 through 12 versus only grades 10 through 12 in CPS; it is based on administrative records rather than on a household survey as in CPS; and it counts anyone receiving a GED outside of a regular (approved) secondary education program as a dropout as opposed to the CPS approach of counting GED certificate holders as high school completers. One of the concerns addressed in the NCES CCD data collection on dropouts is the development and implementation of a nationally consistent definition of a dropout to be used in school districts and state departments of education.

Prior to gathering data for this book, I thought that I had a very clear understanding of who was and who was not a school dropout. Perhaps it was too simple, but I considered a dropout as a student who left school prior to graduating from high school (or college). In fact, as you read on, you, too, may have some difficulty interpreting which students meet the criteria for being classified as a dropout and which students meet the criteria for being classified as a graduate.

Introduction and Background

To further confuse the problem, there is considerable variation across local, state, and federal data collection agencies on such issues as:

- Whether those below the legal school-leaving age are identified as dropouts;
- Whether those who complete a grade and drop out over the summer are attributed to the grade completed or to the next grade;
- Whether students entering correctional institutions are dropouts;
- Whether those in GED programs or with an equivalency certificate are dropouts;
- Whether those not graduating with their class (but not leaving school) are dropouts; and
- Whether those leaving high school early to enter college are dropouts.

Until there is agreement on these issues, some disagreement will continue about who is and who is not a dropout and some discontinuities in dropout reporting will continue.

Defining and Calculating Event Dropout Rates Using the Common Core of Data

The Common Core of Data (CCD) administered by NCES is an annual survey of the state-level education agencies in the 50 states, the District of Columbia, and the outlying areas. Statistical information is collected on public schools, staff, students, and finance. The CCD defines dropout as an individual who was enrolled in school at *some* time during the previous year, was not enrolled at the beginning of the current school year, had not graduated from high school or completed an approved educational program, and did not meet any of the following exclusionary conditions:

- Death;
- Temporary absence due to suspension or illness; or
- Transfer to another public school district, private school, or state- or district-approved education program.

Supporting data related to the CCD definition include:

- A school year is the 12-month period of time beginning with the normal opening of school in the fall, with dropouts from the previous summer reported for the year and grade for which they fail to enroll;

- An individual has graduated from high school or completed an approved education program upon receipt of formal recognition from school authorities; and

- A state- or district-approved education program may include special education programs, home-based instruction, and school-sponsored GED preparation (National Center for Education Statistics).

Types of Dropout Rates

Depending on the graduation and completion data being collected, different dropout rates may be reported. Event, status, and cohort dropout rates are commonly used, and they provide a different perspective on the student dropout population. The National Center for Education Statistics includes definitions and data for each type of dropout rate in order to provide a detailed profile of dropouts in the United States. Those definitions follow:

- *Event rates* describe the proportion of students who leave school each year without completing a high school program. This annual measure of recent dropout occurrences provides important information about how effective educators are in keeping students enrolled in school.

- *Status rates* provide cumulative data on dropouts among all young adults within a specified age range. Status rates are higher than event rates because they include all dropouts, regardless of when they last attended school. Because status rates reveal the extent of the dropout problem in the population, this rate also can be used to estimate the need for further education and training that will help dropouts participate fully in the economy and life of the nation,

- *Cohort rates* measure what happened to a cohort of students over a period of time. This rate is based on repeated measures of a group of students with shared experiences and reveals how many students starting in a specific grade drop out over time. Typically, cohort rates from longitudinal studies provide more background and contextual data on the students who drop out than are available through the Current Population Survey (CPS) or Common Core Data (CCD) data collections.

The Dropout Problem

Charting dropouts and reporting dropout rates is a daunting task because students leave school in alarming numbers for a variety of reasons. The following data illuminate the magnitude of the dropout problem:

- Five of every 100 young adults enrolled in high school in 1995 left school before October 1996 without successfully completing a high school program. This estimate of 5 percent is on par with those reported over the last 10 years.

- A larger percentage of Hispanic students, compared with White students, leave school short of completing a high school program. However, the 6.7 percent rate for Black students falls between the rate of 9.0 percent for Hispanics and 4.1 percent for Whites.

- In 1996, young adults living in families with incomes in the lowest 20 percent of all family incomes were 5 times as likely as their peers from families in the top 20 percent of the income distribution to drop out of high school.

- Ninety-six percent of young adults in families with high incomes held high school credentials in 1996, while only about 75 percent of youths from low income families reached this goal.

- In 1996, there was nearly a 20-percentage-point gap between the dropout rates of youths from the highest and lowest income levels.

- Students who remain in school after the majority of their age cohort has left, drop out at higher rates than their younger peers.

- Although dropout rates were the highest among students age 19 or older, about 75 percent of the current year dropouts were ages 15 through 18; moreover, 43 percent of the 1996 dropouts were 15 through 17 years of age.

- In October 1996, some 3.6 million young adults were not enrolled in a high school program and had not completed high school. These youths account for 11.1 percent of the 32.4 million 16- through 24-year-olds in the United States in 1996.

- Forty-four percent of Hispanic young adults born outside the 50 states and the District of Columbia are counted as high school dropouts. Although the dropout rates of Hispanics with one or both parents born in the United States are lower, they are higher than the dropout rates of Whites and Blacks.

- The status dropout rates in the Southern and Western regions of the country are 1.5 times those in the Northeast and Midwest (National Center for Educational Statistics, 1996).

These data reveal that our work is cut out for us. Far too many students leave school prior to obtaining their high school credentials. Each young adult who leaves school prior to graduation is placed in a perilous position and will undoubtedly face many and varied hardships.

Factors that Impact a Student's Decision to Drop Out of School

There are a number of factors that play an important role in student decisions to drop out of school. A few examples are the student's race-ethnicity, income level of his or her parents, the student's age, the geographic region in which the student resides, and teen pregnancy. Analyses of specific interactions among intervening variables that impact a student's decision to drop out of school are beyond the scope of this book. Therefore, this section presents a review of selected primary factors that are associated with higher event-determined dropout rates including a discussion related to race-ethnicity, income, age, and geographic region and culminates with information relative to teen pregnancy.

Race-Ethnicity

The 1996 CPS data are consistent with earlier reports of a strong association between race-ethnicity and dropping out of school. Data from the U.S. Department of Commerce, Bureau of the Census, October 1996 Current Population Survey repeat this pattern, showing an event dropout rate of 9.0 percent for Hispanic students, higher than the rate of 4.1 percent for White students. The estimated rate for Black students (6.7 percent) falls between the rates for Hispanics and Whites, but the differences are not significant (National Center for Educational Statistics, 1996).

Income

Socioeconomic background and home environment often have an impact on the decisions of young adults to drop out of school. In 1996, 11.1 percent of students from families in the lowest 20 percent of the income distribution dropped out of high school. By way of comparison, 5.1 percent in the middle 60 percent of the income distribution dropped out, and 2.1 percent of students from families with incomes in the top 20 percent dropped out. (National Center for Educational Statistics, 1996).

There was a 5.7 percentage-point difference between the rates for Blacks and Whites, which is, in part, due to the differences evident in the dropout rates for White and Black youths at the low income levels; but the size of this gap is also driven by differences in the population distribution across the income levels. Relatively more White than Black youths live in families in the highest income group (28.6 percent versus 9.7 percent), while a larger share of Black than White youths live in families in the lowest income group (35.7 percent versus 13.3 percent). As a result, a larger portion of Black youths are at the increased risk of dropping out observed in the low income group (21.9 percent for Blacks) and a larger portion of White youths experience the decreased risk of dropping out observed in the high income group (2.0 percent for Whites) (National Center for Educational Statistics, 1996, p. 19).

Age

In October of 1996, only 1 of every 10 youths ages 15 through 24 enrolled in school was over age 18, but dropouts from this older group of students accounted for 1 of every 4 high school dropouts in 1996. Thus, students who pursue a high school program beyond the traditional ages are at an increased risk of dropping out of school. While the event dropout rates for younger enrollees are substantially lower (for example, only 3.5 percent for 15- and 16-year-olds and 3.4 percent for 17-year-olds), it is important to understand that 43 percent of all young adults who left school between October of 1995 and October of 1996 were ages 15, 16, and 17 in October of 1996. These youths left school short of a projected normal school completion (National Center for Educational Statistics, 1996).

Geographic Region

Historically, geographic regions have been another area of interest in efforts to understand patterns and trends in dropout rates. Similar to findings in 1995, the high status dropout rates of 13.0 percent in the South and 13.9 percent in the West are at least 1.5 times the rates of 8.3 percent in the Northeast and 7.7 percent in the Midwest. When these dropout rates are reviewed across regions for each racial-ethnic group, the dropout rates for Hispanics exceed the national dropout rates in each region, but there is no clear pattern for Hispanics across regions. The rates for Black youths are on a par with the national average in each region except the West. Black youths in the West have dropout rates lower than the national average and lower than the dropout rates for Black youths in each other region of the country. The rates for White youths are lower than the national averages in each region. But the rates for White youths in the South are higher than the rates experienced by White youths in each of the regions. The South is the only region in which the dropout rate for White youths exceeds the national dropout rate for White youths (10.0 percent versus 7.3 percent) (National Center for Educational Statistics, 1996).

Teen Pregnancy

Despite the recent decline in teen pregnancy, the teen birthrate in the United States remains much higher than that of other industrialized countries, running about 57 births per 1,000 15- to 19-year-olds compared to 29 in Great Britain, 11 in Germany, and 4 in the Netherlands (Black, 1998b). Statistics related to teen sex and pregnancy are alarming as reflected in the following:

- About 1 million teenagers, 11 percent of 15- to 19-year-old girls, become pregnant each year. Of those 1 million pregnant teenagers, more than 530,000 give birth.

- Thirteen percent of all U.S. births are to teens.

- Eighty-five percent of teen pregnancies are not planned.

- Twenty-five percent of all teenage mothers have a second child within two years of their firstborn.

- About 3 million teens contract sexually transmitted diseases each year.

- Fifty-six percent of girls and 73 percent of boys have sexual intercourse by age 18.

- Seven of 10 girls who had sex before age 14 report having had sex involuntarily.

- Fifty-five percent of sexually active 15- to 17-year-old girls have had 2 or more partners; 13 percent have had at least 6 partners.

- A sexually active teenage girl who does not use contraception has a 90 percent chance of becoming pregnant within one year.

- About 75 percent of teens use some method of contraception, usually a condom, the first time they have sex.

- Among sexually experienced teens, about 8 percent of 14-year-olds and 18 percent of 15- to 17-year-olds become pregnant each year.

Introduction and Background 15

- About 50 percent of pregnant teens give birth, 40 percent have abortions, and 10 percent have miscarriages each year.
- Every 26 seconds, a U.S. teenager becomes pregnant; every hour, 56 children are born to teenagers
- Eighty-three percent of teens who give birth each year are from poor and low-income families.
- Eighty percent of teen mothers will live in poverty and rely on welfare; 50 percent will not graduate from high school.
- Teen mothers have 24 percent more children, but, over time, are 50 percent less likely to marry.
- Teen mothers have 50 percent more low birth weight babies who are more likely to be afflicted with blindness, deafness, chronic respiratory problems, cerebral palsy, retardation and mental illness, dyslexia, hyperactivity, and other learning disabilities.
- Daughters of teen mothers are 83 percent more likely to have a baby before age 18.
- Sons of teen mothers are three times more likely to receive a prison sentence.
- Children of teen mothers more often repeat grades and drop out of high school (Black, 1998b).

It is imperative school personnel implement special programs designed to change teens' attitudes toward having sex and risking becoming pregnant. Handing out simulated, pretend babies as part of a one-week school assignment, which creates the illusion of being a parent, simply is not enough. Educators are obligated to provide learning activities for students which will help them understand that a few minutes of pleasure may lead to a lifetime of pain. They need to place an emphasis on implementing programs which will help students participate fully in the economy and life of the nation. Also, educators need to focus on increasing academic achievement and subsequently engage students in activities such as: mentoring, counseling, goal-setting, goal-attainment, visioning, and building self-esteem.

Creating a Professional Learning Community: An Environment That Facilitates Student Learning and Achievement of Students At Risk

To improve [schools], one must invest in people, support people, and develop people.

Phil Schlecty
Schools for the 21st Century

Sokoloff (1998) stated that there are two broad strands of thought in the current school reform movement. One strand, which includes such strange bedfellows as Ted Sizer and E. D. Hirsch, starts from the assumption that school reform must focus on what happens within the school walls. We need to change what's taught, how it's taught, how it's assessed, how we prepare and supervise teachers, and so on. For those advocates, school reform can proceed without trying to change the communities in which schools exist.

The second strand of thought related to school reform starts from the assumption that the problems in schools mirror crises in society: The breakdown of communities and the disconnect between schools and communities are behind the failures and loss of legitimacy of our public schools. Advocates of this position include those who argue for charter schools and vouchers, as well as those of us (Sokoloff, 1998) who argue that we must rebuild the public for public education and that school reform must be linked to changing the relationship between schools and their communities.

As an academician, educational consultant, and sometimes practitioner, I find myself vacillating between the two strands of thought dependent upon factors such as the location of the school, the competency of the staff employed at the school, the extent of participation of the parents and community members in school activities, and the level of desire of the students to get the best possible education. Generally, I lean toward the second strand of thought. In addition, I believe that to reform a school, educators must focus on investing in, supporting, and developing, to the fullest extent, all of the human resources affiliated with a specified school.

Introduction and Background

I firmly believes that to facilitate learning and achievement of students at risk, educators must invest time and money, and support the people who are employed by educational institutions. Investing in, supporting, and developing people must be a priority and should be done in tandem with implementing comprehensive school improvement strategies. Ongoing evaluation and assessment of the people and the school reform initiatives should be a priority and be linked to a continuous school improvement process which looks beyond the at risk population and examines the performance of the entire school populace.

The key to school improvement is people improvement (Du Four and Eaker, 1992). Attention to professional development must be the cornerstone of any initiative to enhance the effectiveness of schools. This adapted list of strategies is recommended to ensure proper attention to this critical aspect of school improvement:

- Review the efforts and resources devoted to the professional development of staff in the past year. List the efforts made to develop the human resources in your school.

- Develop a list of ideas for enhancing the efforts of your school to develop its human resources.

- Meet in small groups to assess the barriers to change in your school. Attempt to reach consensus as to the degree those barriers are present in your school.

- Discuss an innovation that was attempted in your school without success. Identify the factors that led to its demise and speculate as to what might have been done to ensure its success.

- Create a consumer validation group to identify and implement a classroom innovation.

- Develop a proposal to use peer coaching frequently in your school.

Fulton (1998) offers suggestions as to what improves student achievement and provides a process for evaluating initiatives that are put in place to increase student achievement and simultaneously decrease the number of students at risk who drop out of high school prior to graduation. Fulton suggests that staff engage in a series of assessments and questioning activities that includes:

- Insist on well-documented evidence or results in student achievement before investing in or expanding education initiatives.

- Ask tough questions about suggested reforms and those already in place.

- What are the intended goals of a strategy, and how can we know if they are achieved?

- How do we gauge progress along the way?

- What do we do if we seem to be off track?

- How long do we allow a program to operate before deciding whether to continue, expand, or abandon it?

- How do we build in rigorous, periodic evaluation to measure the progress and impact of education initiatives on our students?

- Put together a diverse package of initiatives combining the best of the old with the most promising of the new. Judiciously mix better-researched approaches, such as early emphasis on reading, with more cutting-edge initiatives, such as using technology, to improve teaching and learning.

- Be sure any initiative includes rigorous plans to evaluate progress and measure success.

- Keep your eye on a comprehensive, long-term plan that focuses on improving teaching and learning. Commit yourself to "staying the course" with plans to improve student learning in your schools (Fulton, 1998).

A valuable resource in the research base that should underlie a school improvement initiative is found in the studies of organizations outside of education. Research findings on such topics and organizational climate, organizational effectiveness, personnel development, leadership, and organizational change provide a portrait of a healthy, vital organization and are often applicable to schools (Du Four and Eaker, 1992).

One of the most widely read descriptions of common characteristics of excellent companies is *In Search of Excellence* (1982) by Thomas Peters and Robert Waterman (as cited in Du Four and Eaker, 1992). This study of the factors that have contributed to the success of America's best-run companies is rich with information on leadership and organizational climate that can be readily applied to schools. The ideas in this book and others like it should be made available to those attempting to describe an excellent school. These ideas can serve as an effective catalyst for discussions of those characteristics, other than academic achievement, that are important ingredients of excellence. The following material summarizes the conclusions reached by Peters and Waterman:

- The best-run companies show a bias for action, for getting things done.

Excellent companies get quick action because their organizations are fluid. These companies are characterized by a vast network of informal, open communications.

- The best companies stick close to the customer.

    Excellent companies learn from the people they serve. These companies are good listeners and get many of their best ideas from their customers.

- Excellent companies encourage autonomy and entrepreneurship.

    Outstanding companies foster many leaders and innovators throughout the organization. Managers in these companies do not launch a new project unless an individual zealot or champion volunteers to embrace that project and becomes personally committed to its success.

- The best-run companies achieve productivity through people.

    Managers in excellent companies realize that a prime motivational factor is the individual's perception that he or she is doing well. Consequently, these companies set goals that most people can reach and let employees know when they are doing well. These firms celebrate success with ceremony and hoopla.

- The best companies are hands-on, value-driven organizations.

    In excellent companies, top management stays close to the action —walking plant floors, visiting stores, and so on. These leaders believe in "management by wandering about." And they continually remind employees of the organization's values and mission.

- Excellent companies *stick to their knitting*.

    The best-run companies stay with the basics rather then diversifying their goals or tasks.

- The best-run companies maintain a simple form and a lean staff.

    The best-run corporations have a structure that is "elegantly simple." Top-level staffs are lean.

- Excellent companies are simultaneously *"loose"* and *"tight."*

    Even as they encourage individual initiative and autonomy ("looseness"), the best companies also demand rigid adherence ("tightness") to a few core values that drive and give direction to everyone in the organization.

Moving Toward Excellence: Establishing a Positive School Environment

To establish school environments that are conducive to meeting the needs of students at risk, educators should refer to the abundant research related to effective schools, establishing positive school environments, and implementing programs which met the needs of the student clientele. It is important to recognize the contribution research can play in describing an excellent school. Research findings can provide a frame of reference for thinking about characteristics consistently associated with effective schooling. These findings should be viewed not as a simple recipe for reform, but rather as a theoretical framework around which a plan for school improvement can be developed (Du Four and Eaker, 1992).

Edmonds' research (1979 study cited in Du Four and Eaker, 1992) on school effectiveness may have contributed more than any other study to the widespread recognition that what schools do, does affect the achievement of students. These characteristics were consistently found in effective schools:

- Safe and orderly environment
- Clear and focused school mission
- Instructional leadership
- High expectations
- Opportunity to learn and high time on task
- Frequent monitoring of student progress
- Positive home-school relations

The Northwest Regional Educational Laboratory (1990 study cited in Du Four and Eaker, 1992) provides a useful synthesis of the research on effective schools. This synthesis, which focused on studies that identified schooling practices and characteristics associated with measurable improvements in student achievement and behavior, provides this snapshot of an effective school:

- Everyone emphasizes the importance of learning.
- The curriculum is based on clear goals and objectives.
- Students are grouped to promote effective instruction.

Introduction and Background

- School time is used for learning.
- Discipline is firm and consistent.
- There are pleasant conditions for teaching and learning.
- Strong leadership guides the instructional program.
- Teachers and administrators continually strive to improve instructional effectiveness.
- Staff engage in ongoing professional development and collegial learning activities.
- There are high expectations for quality instruction.
- Incentives and rewards are used to build strong student and staff motivation.
- Parents and community members are invited to become involved.
- Learning progress is monitored closely.
- Students at risk of school failure are provided programs to help them succeed.

Purkey and Smith (1983 study as cited in Du Four and Eaker, 1992) conducted a review of the research on school effectiveness and identified organizational and structural variables, and process-form variables—variables which they believe are the most important characteristics of effective schools. The organizational and structural variables include:

- School site management
- Leadership
- Staff stability
- Curriculum articulation and organization
- Staff development
- Parental involvement and support
- School site recognition of academic success
- Maximized learning time
- District support

The process-form variables associated with school effectiveness are:

- Collaborative planning and collegial relationships

- Sense of community
- Clear goals and high expectations that are commonly shared
- Order and discipline

Researchers may disagree about a particular finding or a particular research methodology, but research on effective schools does provide a surprisingly clear and consistent picture of school practices and characteristics associated with student achievement. Although the findings are not a recipe for quick success, they do form a useful framework for thinking about and planning for school improvement (Du Four and Eaker, 1992).

Du Four and Eaker (1992) posited that research on effective schools, school improvement, studies of outstanding businesses, analysis of leadership and the specific practices and procedures from a number of fine schools was remarkably consistent and offered a framework for a systematic approach to significant school improvement. This edited version of their observations is offered to those interested in moving toward excellence:

- The key to school improvement is a commitment to people improvement.

   A school improvement effort grounded in disdain or disregard for the professional staff is doomed to failure. It should be self-evident that the real key to improvement of any school is a commitment to the nurturing and professional development of its practitioners because, in reality, they are the school.

- Excellent schools have a clear vision of what they are attempting to accomplish, what they are trying to become.

   One of the most consistent findings of the research on effective organizations is that they have a vision that provides a sense of purpose, direction, and ideal future. In fact, the importance of vision has been cited so often that it has become something of a cliché.

- The day-to-day operation of an excellent school is guided by a few shared central values.

   Effective organizations have shared values that reflect the vision of the organization. These values help individuals to understand how they are expected to behave and serve as a mechanism for sanctioning or proscribing behavior.

Introduction and Background 23

- Excellent schools have principals who are effective leaders.

  They must be forceful and aggressive promoters and protectors of the vision and values of their schools, and at the same time, provide their teachers with the freedom and autonomy to satisfy personal and professional needs. They must be strong instructional leaders, and at the same time, encourage teachers to become comfortable with a new and emerging definition of the principalship. The research on effective schools often portrays the principal in heroic terms, but the key to improving schools is not so much principals who are heroes, but principals who make heroes.

- The shaping of organizational culture and climate is critical to the creation of an excellent school.

This norm represents shared expectations for behavior and serves as a guide for what is to be done, how it is to be done, and by whom. Some of the conditions found to be present in schools that have been successful in bringing about significant improvements are a safe and orderly environment conducive to learning, high expectations for both students and staff, professional relationships characterized by collaboration, and a willingness to experiment.

- The curriculum of an excellent school reflects the values of the school and provides a focus that helps teachers and students *stick to the knitting*.

  To ensure a sharp focus within the organization, many successful companies operate according to the premise that "to have more than one goal is to have no goals at all." Schools, on the other hand, tend to suffer from curriculum overload. As Phillip Schlecty observed, "Much of what we now do in schools probably doesn't need to be done and much that should be done cannot be done so long as we keep doing what we have always done." An excellent school develops and offers a curriculum that reflects or fits the values of the school and helps to focus the attention of teachers and students on what learning is considered most significant.

- Excellent schools monitor what is important.

  Studies of effective leaders consistently conclude that these leaders communicate what the organization values by paying attention to the factors that reflect those values. An excellent school focuses on results rather than on activity because a results-oriented culture is essential to school improvement. This means that procedures must be developed to enable teachers and administrators to acquire valid and useful information regarding student achievement. Furthermore, because the classroom represents the very heart of the educational enterprise, excellent schools must monitor teaching and develop procedures to promote the planning, effective instructional strategies, and reflective characteristics of good teaching.

♦ In an excellent school, teachers are expected to act as leaders within their classrooms.

Teaching is multidimensional. Good teachers have the knowledge, strategies, and skills essential to effective instruction. Furthermore, they approach their tasks in the classroom in much the same way that effective leaders conduct themselves within their organizations.

♦ Excellent schools celebrate progress toward their vision and the presence of their core values with ceremonies and rituals.

Effective organizations create systems that are specifically designed to produce lots of winners and to celebrate winning when it occurs. These celebrations recognize and promote the values upheld by the organization. The celebration of values is an area that has generally been neglected by schools. Educators have been quick to advise parents of failure and slow to recognize success. Rituals and celebrations have tended to focus on athletic accomplishment or exemplary effort.

♦ An excellent school is committed to continual renewal.

A key to the ongoing effectiveness of any organization is its ability to renew itself—to seek and find better ways of fulfilling its mission and responding to change. However, there is a tendency in schools to accept things as they are. Perhaps the largest barrier to school improvement is the perception of the professional staff that the leadership will not sustain the initiative to see improvement through. Remembering how often they have been called on to embrace a new program only to see the interest of the district wane and the program sputter and die, teachers are likely to respond to yet another improvement program with the ho-hum attitude of "This too shall pass." (Du Four and Eaker, 1992).

Too many educators are looking for interventions that will better enable them to meet the needs of the students, staff, and parents with whom they work. While looking for those interventions, they often fail to refer to the literature which consistently highlights the fact that good schools, structures, and organizations are made great by the people, the human infrastructure. Able, creative, positive, thoughtful people are the fundamental building blocks of strong, surviving organizations (Harvey and Drolet, 1994). Educators who are seeking to implement programs, practices, and policies which meet the needs of their student clientele, would be wise to build upon the strengths of the staff, implement an effective curriculum, and refer to the literature to ascertain what is currently working well in their colleagues' schools.

Jones (1998) has outlined some of the favorite methods for improving student achievement. Following are excerpts from Jones' work related to what educators should do to meet the needs of students:

- Start early

    Research shows students' home backgrounds are responsible for roughly half of their school achievement. You can't control who has babies, of course, but you can step in early with initiatives that give a young child a better start.

- Focus on reading and math

    Educators applaud President Clinton's goal of making sure every child can read well by the third grade. But researchers say the critical time comes even earlier: Kids who aren't reading at grade level by the end of first grade face 8:1 odds against ever catching up.

    Research indicates schools should test kindergartners for their ability to recognize sounds (one of six can't), and check again in the middle of first grade to make sure kids are reading independently.

- Bring in trained tutors

    Several dozen studies indicate that early one-on-one intervention with a trained tutor can set kids on the right academic track and can, in the long run, save schools money by drastically reducing the number of students who later need special education and remedial services.

- Invest in teachers

    There's no denying the importance of good teaching—or the price of poor teaching.

- Shrink the size of classes—and schools

    For years, the research has gone back and forth on the impact of class size on student achievement. Now it seems to be settling on the side of smaller classes, especially in early grades and in inner-city schools.

- Increase the amount of time spent learning
- Set goals and assess your students' progress

    Almost every state has set academic standards for its students, and many districts have added their own goals to the mix, but all of this doesn't mean much if you don't check to see how students are doing in pursuit of those goals.

    Assessment can be as simple as a three-minute test to check on a kindergartner's awareness of the sound made by letters, or it can involve something complicated enough to qualify as a Westinghouse science project. (Assessment specialists explain the difference between standardized test and diagnostic assessments by pointing to mountains: A standardized test compares mountain climbers to each other, but a diagnostic assessment tells the climbers and their coaches where they are on the mountain.)

- Support teachers' professional development

    Research indicates that the most effective professional development programs are the ones teachers seek out or develop themselves.

- Adopt a whole-school curriculum

    There is another advantage to ready-made programs. Their curriculum is usually more rigorous than what an individual teacher—or a group of teachers—can come up with alone.

    Researchers, many of whom are associated with one of these programs, are careful not to identify *the perfect curriculum program*, but they do caution schools to make sure that they choose a program that is backed by solid research and enthusiastically supported by the staff. Most companies selling a research-based curriculum refuse to sign on with a school unless the faculty approves overwhelmingly.

Classroom-Related Activities That Foster Learning

Teaching a class of so-called average students is formidable; however, teaching a class of students at risk is even more difficult. Preparing teachers to teach in classrooms with high percentages of students at risk is a task not taken lightly by teacher training institutions, but continues to be a challenge that leaves much to be desired. In short, there is much that still needs to be done to better

Introduction and Background 27

prepare teachers to teach students at risk. Everyone needs to realize that there are requisite skills, attitudes, and behaviors that teachers need to exercise prior to and during their engagements with students at risk. What is most essential, however, is that teachers truly believe they can teach all students effectively.

Most college professors, school administrators and teachers agree there is requisite preparation that all teachers should have, but for those teachers entering schools comprised heavily of minority students, more than the standard or traditional preparation is necessary (Hill, 1989). Following is an abbreviated version of Hill's recommendations as they relate to teaching students at risk or minority students (this is not intended to imply that all students at risk are minority or vice versa).

- Be prepared to teach educationally underprepared students.

  A large percentage of minority students are educationally underprepared. This means that you may have to develop skills to handle compensatory, remedial, and developmental learning needs. Be mindful though, that educationally underprepared minority students show as wide a range in learning ability as any other group. In fact, many will eventually receive scholarships to Yale, Berkeley, Michigan, Harvard, Hampton, and other excellent institutions.

- Develop a second language skill.

  It is very helpful for a teacher to be able to speak a second (or third) language. Spanish is of value to all teachers. An understanding of regional dialects and slang is also helpful. Well-developed and varied language skills are at the heart of the communication process with students.

- Develop *street smarts*.

  Know what *ribbin'*, *jivin'*, and *playin' the dozens* are about. (These are verbal sparring games in which the players trade verbal insults.) These games eventually come up in the classroom, corridors, cafeteria, and elsewhere at school. Teachers must play tough, otherwise these games can be psychologically devastating. Such games are especially hard on the nonminority teacher who may be the only one in the classroom unaware of or unable to understand a remark that has been made to him or her by a student.

- Be aware of cultural and ethnic history.

  It is imperative that teachers be knowledgeable about the cultural and ethnic history of all minority students in their classroom. If in-depth information of this kind is not yet known, the teacher must acquire it quickly. Important historical dates must be understood and recognized by the teacher and, where possible, celebrated.

- Ethnic literature must be used in teaching whenever possible.

References can be made to minorities and their many contributions to education, the arts, music, literature, the sciences, and other facets of life. Teachers should include materials relevant to the minority groups they are teaching as a necessary balance to the regular curriculum.

- Intercultural differences or idiosyncrasies must be examined and understood.

It is expected that teachers of minority students will have completed formal courses in urban education and multicultural understanding during their initial teacher certification program, or, if not then, as requirements for a master's degree. If such courses are not completed at some point, a serious void will exist in the teacher's academic background.

- Find a mentor.

If you know someone who is experiencing success in teaching minority students, confide in her or him that you need assistance. When a genuine friendship with someone is established before mentoring begins, the likelihood is greatest that favorable results will be realized and students will benefit. A teacher's race does not determine success in classrooms where minority students comprise the largest enrollment. There are cases on record where nonminority teachers have had greater success in teaching minority students than have minority teachers.

Hill concluded his discussion related to skills essential to teaching students at risk or minority students by stating that teachers must be academically competent; must be personable, but not overly friendly; and must have a considerable repertoire of teaching methods at his or her disposal.

Hill also recommended that when teaching students at risk or minority students, role modeling can prove to be a key to student learning. Role models are sorely needed in classrooms because students at risk or minority students need teachers who can act out life patterns familiar for them. By being aware of this, teachers can display consistently positive and mature behavior for students to emulate.

Introduction and Background

Included in those mature behaviors that teachers want students to emulate are interpersonal skills. Some interpersonal skills that teachers may use in facilitating learning with minority students are:

- Accepting students' ideas and feelings. Students have the right of ownership relative to their ideas and feelings.

- Knowing your students' names. Avoid getting the attention of students with "you," "Hey you, in the blue dress," a pointed finger, and so forth.

- Believing that every child is a winner. Everyone is good at something; seek that something in students.

- Including your students in the lesson-planning process.

- Maintaining an *integrated* personality. Be open and sensitive to the needs of students. Also, show a concern for personal growth and development (Hill, 1989).

One thing we know about educating students at risk is that many of the traditional modes of instruction do not work. Educators need to examine other instructional modes and strategies when teaching students at risk. Marzano's Dimensions of Learning Model (1992) should be given consideration because it is an instructional program that grew out of the comprehensive research- and theory-based framework on cognition and learning called Dimensions of Thinking. Dimensions of Learning translates the research and theory explicated in Dimensions of Thinking into a practical model that K-12 teachers can use to improve the quality of teaching and learning in any content area. Implicit in the Dimensions of Learning Model are six basic assumptions:

- Instruction must reflect the best of what we know about how learning occurs.

- Learning involves a complex system of interactive processes that includes five types of thinking—the five dimensions of learning.

- What we know about learning indicates that instruction focusing on large, interdisciplinary curricular themes is the most effective way to promote learning.

- The K-12 curriculum should include explicit teaching of higher-level attitudes and perceptions and mental habits that facilitate learning.

- A comprehensive approach to instruction includes at least two distinct types of instruction: one that is more teacher-directed and another that is more student-directed.

- Assessment should focus on students' use of knowledge and complex reasoning rather than on their recall of low-level information (Marzano, 1992).

The Dimensions of Learning program includes a variety of components designed to help educators fully understand how these six assumptions affect the teacher's work in the classroom. Implicit in the Dimensions of Learning Model is the belief that teachers help students feel accepted in the classroom through seemingly trivial, yet very important, behaviors. For instance, the Teacher Expectations and Student Achievement (TESA) Program advocates that teachers can engage in classroom activities that can enhance students' perceptions of their acceptance in many ways:

- By making eye contact with each student in the class, being sure to pay attention to all quadrants of the classroom.
- By calling all students by their first or preferred name.
- By deliberately moving toward and staying close to learners.
- By touching students in appropriate and acceptable ways.

Marzano also reminds teachers not to forget the basics—something which is done all to often soon after completing the teaching credential program. To some, these actions may seem insignificant, but they send powerful messages to students. Here are a few basic but powerful behaviors:

- Providing wait time—pausing to allow a student more time to answer instead of moving on to another student when you don't get an immediate response.
- Dignifying responses—giving credit for the correct aspects of an incorrect response.
- Restating the question—asking the question a second time.
- Rephrasing the question—using different words that might increase the probability of a correct response.
- Providing guidance—giving enough hints and clues so that the student will eventually determine the correct answer. (Marzano, 1992).

Armstrong approaches the task of teaching children from a rather nontraditional perspective. He asks teachers to view every student as a genius. By doing so, he believes that teacher and student interactions are enhanced. To define the *genius*, he went back to the origins of the word itself. According to the *Compact Oxford English Dictionary* (1991, p. 664, as cited in Armstrong, 1998), the *genius* derives from Greek and Latin words meaning *to beget, to be born,* or *to come into being* (it is closely related to the word *genesis*). It is also linked to *genial*, which means, among other things, *festive, conducive to growth, enlivening,* and *jovial.* Armstrong felt that combining these two sets of definitions comes closest to the meaning of genius that he uses most frequently—giving birth to one's joy.

From the standpoint of education, genius means essentially *giving birth to the joy in learning.* Further, he suggests that this is the central task of all educators. It is the genius of the student that is the driving force behind all learning. Before educators take on any of the other important issues in learning, they must first have a thorough understanding of what lies at the core of each student's intrinsic motivation to learn, and that motivation originates in each student's genius (Armstrong, 1998). Imagine what could happen in classrooms across America if teachers were to approach all students as if the students were geniuses instead of low-achieving students, average students, high-achieving, gifted students, learning disabled students, or students at risk. Labeling and tracking students undermine the premise that every student is or can be a genius.

Armstrong also believes that genius is a symbol for an individual's potential—all that a person may be that lies locked inside during the early years of development. So, when he says that as educators we want to help students to develop their potential, he is essentially saying that we want to assist them in finding their inner genius and support them in guiding it into pathways that can lead to personal fulfillment and to the benefit of those around them (Armstrong, 1998).

Armstrong provides a structure for educators that can make the concept of genius useful. He has expanded his meaning to include 12 basic qualities: curiosity; playfulness; imagination; creativity; wonder; wisdom; inventiveness; vitality; sensitivity; flexibility; humor; and joy. He also offered the following partial list of activities that might start you on this journey to the center of your own genius. Many (but not necessarily all) of these activities are appropriate for students and can help them enhance their social and academic skills:

- Reading for pleasure
- Keeping a journal
- Writing poetry or stories
- Listening to music
- Taking up a musical instrument
- Learning to paint or draw
- Joining a choir
- Traveling

- Building furniture
- Designing and sewing clothes
- Attending concerts or lectures
- Taking courses at a local college
- Listening to books on tape
- Learning how to meditate
- Learning calculus through computer software
- Joining a book club
- Doing volunteer work at a community center
- Engaging in nature study
- Building electronics from kits
- Running for office in your community
- Learning a competitive sport such as tennis or golf
- Watching classic movies
- Studying a particular historical period
- Taking up photography
- Solving mathematical puzzles or brainteasers
- Following current developments in science
- Starting or joining an investment club
- Studying art, history, or literature
- Backpacking in the wilderness
- Learning a new language
- Watching how-to videos to learn a new skill
- Starting a classical music collection
- Joining a theatrical production
- Joining an interest group on the Internet
- Cultivating your spiritual life
- Planning a garden
- Studying philosophy

Introduction and Background

- Starting a business
- Joining Toastmasters or another speaking group
- Starting a collection (e.g., stamps, old posters)
- Learning how to fix things around the house
- Inventing something and then patenting it
- Taking dance classes
- Writing a column for a newsletter or newspaper
- Creating a special-interest club
- Taking up stargazing
- Attending a retreat
- Creating a video in an area of interest
- Learning a new style of cooking

Resiliency-Building Class Strategies

The term *resiliency* is frequently used in educational circles. It is one of those survival skills that students at risk must have, or teachers must help them acquire in order for the students to be successful in school or in their personal lives. The role of the teacher is to establish a classroom environment steeped in social support activities which promote the development of students' coping mechanisms. These provide opportunities for students to cope with the stresses of daily life, and, ultimately, to learn to overcome them.

Although I don't have a stack of research data to backup my hunch (or perhaps I should say hypothesis), I believe that all of us have an innate ability to withstand, adjust to, or recover from adverse environmental circumstances. For students at risk, some of those adversities are what have been previously called risk factors. The risk factors to which I most commonly refer and that students at risk most commonly face are:

- Attendance at schools with large numbers of poor students
- Child abuse or neglect
- Delinquent behavior
- Family conflict and disruption

- Low achievement
- Low socioeconomic status
- Poor school attendance
- Retention in grade
- School conflict and disruption
- Substance abuse
- Teen pregnancy
- Violence

According to Sagor (1996, as cited in Pikes, Burrell, and Holliday, 1998) and Wang, Haertel, and Walberg (1995, as cited in Pikes, Burrell, and Holliday, 1998), schools can provide support to students, particularly those at risk, through resilience-building experiences that focus on five themes:

- Competency (feeling successful)
- Belonging (feeling valued)
- Usefulness (feeling needed)
- Potency (feeling empowered)
- Optimism (feeling encouraged and hopeful)

Teachers should always focus on classroom academics, but should also consider incorporating classroom activities that encompass resilience-building experiences that focus on the foregoing five themes.

While developing and implementing, educational resiliency-building experiences may seem like just one more thing to do, many of these techniques are already part of an educator's repertoire (Sagor, 1996, as cited Pikes, Burrell, and Holliday, 1998). Teachers can infuse the five themes of resilience into everyday academic instruction across subject areas, either as repeated learning experiences or as themes for long-term group and class projects. For example:

- Shared reading activities can center on stories in which the major characters exhibit resilience.
- Topics for journal writing can include factual narratives and personal reflections related to resilience.
- Scientific experiments can provide visible and tangible examples of resiliency.

Strategies for Reclaiming Black and Hispanic Students

When developing programs designed to meet the needs of students at risk, educators must ensure that they implement activities and strategies which are specifically designed for African-American and Hispanic students—two ethnic groups that are particularly at risk. Teachers have to remember that their students are always tuned into radio station WIFM (that is an acronym for What's In It For Me). Students need to be told, and reminded on a daily basis, why it is important to attend and complete school so that they can take their rightful place in society. Overall, they must have hope for better lives, and know that a high school diploma, and ultimately a college degree, can improve their status in life and their general prosperity.

Establishing an environment for students at risk to obtain the best education possible has always been a my personal and professional goal. Perhaps that is because I have always understood that the better the education one receives, the more money he or she is able to make; and the more money one makes, the better the quality of life that he or she is able to experience. Students at risk need to be constantly reminded of the benefits of staying in school and getting a good education. My hypothesis was recently borne out in an article in the *Sacramento Bee* newspaper (1998) in which details of a U.S. government report discussed why it pays to get a good education and why it pays to be rich.

The findings were detailed in a special section of the annual report entitled "Health, United States, 1998." The study is the most comprehensive to date of socioeconomic status and health. It offers the strongest proof yet that health discrepancies exist within racial and ethnic groups. The National Center for Health Statistics in a report entitled "Health, United States, 1998," surprised even its authors by showing how powerful money and education are in shaping Americans' health. Following are selected excerpts from the article:

- The authors found a stairstep pattern from rich to poor that holds true for virtually every health risk factor, for every disease, whether a chronic illness such as cancer, or a communicable disease such as AIDS, and for every cause of death.

- The economic ladder is also evident: Wealthier African-Americans not only fare better than middle-class and poorer African-Americans, but they also report that their health is better than middle income and poor whites.

- Still the report shows that, on average, African-Americans and Latinos often have poorer health and less access to care than Whites.

Poverty is a large part of the reason: The poverty rate for African-American and Latinos is three times that of Whites.

- For the population as a whole, researchers reported that the life expectancy has increased to 76.1 years for a baby born in 1996. The gender gap in life expectancy between men and women in the United States has narrowed to six years—the lowest in a generation—largely because women are posting stubbornly high rates of smoking-related illnesses.

- Meanwhile deaths from heart disease, cancer, and firearms are on the decline. Infant mortality is at a record low, although the gaps among Whites, African-Americans, and Latinos remain wide. But the rosy statistics are true only for those in the middle- and upper-income brackets. Those in lower socioeconomic groups still lag farther behind.

- Money can lengthen a person's life. A 45-year-old White man who makes at least $25,000 can expect to live 6.6 years longer than a White man of the same age making less than $10,000. For African-American men, the difference in life expectancy between the middle class and the poor is 7.4 years.

- Education, too, can add years. The 1995 chronic disease death rate for men with less than a high school education was 2.5 times that for men with more education. For infectious diseases other than AIDS, the death rate for those least educated was three times that of the most educated.

- Lower-income men and women also are more likely to lead sedentary lives, have hypertension, and suffer from diabetes. The death rate from diabetes for poor women was three times that of wealthier women and each increase in the educational level is associated with a decline in the percent of women who are overweight.

- Lower income children between the ages of one and five years were seven times as likely to have elevated levels of lead in their blood than higher-income children. High lead levels has been linked to cognitive and behavioral problems.

- Poor children between the ages of one and fourteen were more than twice as likely to be hospitalized for asthma than higher-income children—a fact that suggests they might have been unable to receive preventive care. Higher asthma rates also have been associated with poor and unsanitary living conditions.

Introduction and Background

Based on these finding, and other related data, educators need to work diligently to implement programs that meet the needs of the students, while ensuring that each of them is in a position to take advantage of life to the fullest, to live a healthy and productive life.

When teachers are unmotivated and don't believe in themselves, it is often difficult to instill positive beliefs within their students with reference to school-related tasks. Unfortunately, a classroom atmosphere that is mired in disbelief is one that breeds inattention, misbehavior, poor communication, and overall lack of academic achievement—an atmosphere in which many Black and Hispanic youth see themselves as trapped in a society with limited or nonexistent opportunities to achieve significant and legitimate upward mobility. The current existence of a growing underclass of Black and Hispanic youth is an indication that many of these youth see an absence of opportunity for significant change in income, social roles, and social class status. The end result is often predictable—they give up and ultimately drop out of school.

Kuykendall (1992) reported that there are many things educators can do to rekindle the excitement of Black and Hispanic students. She uses the term *rekindle* because she says that she has yet to hear of a kindergartner who was not excited about starting school. Black and Hispanic youth are just like all other children who want so much to please and to learn.

Educators must be willing to learn and grow with their students. Following are Kuykendall's *Ten Tips for Teaching Terrific Children*. They are provided to help teachers rekindle student motivation and academic success; and, in the process, derive greater gratification from the teaching profession:

- Develop *strong bonds* with diverse students.
- Identify and build on the strengths of all students.
- Help students overcome fear of failure.
- Help students overcome rejection of success.
- Set short- and long-term goals with and for your students.
- Develop teaching styles that are more congruent with the learning style preferences of Black and Hispanic students.
- Use homework and television to your advantage.
- Communicate so that your real intentions are understood.
- Establish a climate where children receive the ongoing support and encouragement they need to succeed.
- Strengthen relations between the home and school (Kuykendall, 1992).

(For a more detailed description of Kuykendall's *Ten Tips for Teaching Terrific Children* refer to her book.)

Keeping that information in mind, educators must be mindful that girls, particularly African-American girls are often left out of the educational equation in the disciplines of mathematics and science. In no academic area does the nexus between race and gender claim more casualties than in the area of mathematics and science—and no group has been more excluded than African-American girls. Research has consistently identified this population as virtually invisible when messages are aimed at motivating young people to pursue study in mathematics, science, and engineering (Adenika-Morrow, 1996).

Adenika-Morrow stated that one of the reasons African-American females do not pursue careers in the sciences is that they lack the tools to negotiate the racism and sexism that undermine their belief that the can succeed in the sciences. A second, more powerful obstacle, is a world view in the African-American community that stresses the pragmatism of obtaining immediate employment. The reality has been that African-American girls must go to work early and be practical in career selection. Certain occupations (service and clerical workers, teachers, nurses, and other low-paying, female-dominated occupations) have become traditional choices (Adenika-Morrow, 1996).

Practitioners must work with community groups and churches to ensure that African-American females are given the tools, skills, and practical knowledge to make academic choices that maximize their educational opportunities and eliminate as many obstacles to career entry as possible. Without intervention, many African-American females will continue to select only the safest career choices.

The teacher's personal belief system is crucial. How their teachers view themselves and the world around them is very important to student success. Correspondingly, students who see themselves as persecuted will probably experience the classroom as oppressive; while students who view themselves as competitors will probably experience the world as challenging, A personal view of *conqueror* yields a world view of *spoils* (Rousell, 1996). Rousell also reported that it is equally true that how we experience the world can affect how we experience ourselves. Although one factor generates the other, Piaget believed, as do I, that the factors co-evolve.

Educators seeking to meet the needs of students at risk, particularly students of color, with targeted assistance to African-American females, must acknowledge the strength of the African-American world view as crucial to improving academic choices of females. Also, they need to realize that respecting diversity means being willing to explore that world view as it operates within the community.

Parental Engagement of Students At Risk

Research has shown again and again that parental involvement is the most important factor in a child's success. It is important to all of us as well. I encourage you to talk to your children about school, make homework a high priority, limit television and entertainment activities, and promote reading. I know that these things are not easy for today's busy families, but they really will make a difference for your child.

David W. Gordon, Superintendent
Elk Grove Unified School District
Elk Grove, California

Joyce Epstein, one of the most frequently cited authors in the literature related to parental involvement, is director of the Johns Hopkins University Center on Families, Communities, Schools, and Children's Learning, in Baltimore. Epstein and Dauber (1991) described six types of parental involvement that include both home-based and school-based activities. When attempting to engage parents of students at risk, educators should develop comprehensive parent involvement programs that include each of these types of involvement:

- *Basic obligations of families* include providing for children's health and safety; developing parenting skills and child-rearing approaches that prepare children for school and that maintain healthy child development across the grades; and building positive home conditions that support school programs (and other forms of education, training, and information giving).

- *Basic obligations of schools* include communicating with families about school programs and children's progress. This includes the memos, notices, phone calls, report cards, and conferences that most schools conduct and other innovative communications with parents that some schools create. Schools vary the forms and frequency of communications and greatly affect whether the information sent home can be understood by all families.

- *Involvement at school* includes parent and other volunteers who assist teachers, administrators, and children in classrooms or in other areas of the school. It also refers to family members who come to school to support student performances, sports, or other events. Schools can improve and vary schedules so that more families are able to participate as volunteers and as audiences. Schools can improve recruitment and training so that volunteers are more helpful to teachers, students, and to school improvement efforts.

- *Involvement in learning activities at home* includes requests and guidance from teachers for parents to assist their own children at home on learning activities that are coordinated with the children's class work. Schools assist families in helping their children at home by providing information on skills required of students to pass each grade. Schools provide information to families on how to monitor, discuss, and help with homework and on when and how to make decisions about school programs, activities, and opportunities at each grade level so that all students can be more successful in school.

- *Involvement in decision making*, governance, and advocacy includes using parents and others in the community in participatory roles, in the parent-teacher association/organization (PTA/PTO), advisory councils, Title I programs, or in other committees or groups at the school, district, or state level. It also refers to parents as activists in independent advocacy groups in the community. Schools assist by training parent leaders and representatives in decision-making skills. They also assist by showing parents ways to communicate with all of the parents they represent and by providing information needed by community groups for school improvement activities.

- *Collaboration and exchanges with community organizations* includes connections with agencies, businesses, and other groups that share responsibility for children's education and future successes. This includes school programs that provide children and families access to community and support services, including after-school care, health services, and other resources and that coordinate these arrangements and activities to support children's learning. Schools vary in how much they know and share about their communities and how much they draw on community resources to enhance and enrich the curriculum and other experiences of students.

This information can be helpful to educators who are analyzing their school's practices and implementing new programs. Although the six types of parental involvement are not *pure* and involve some aspects that overlap, most practices that schools use to involve families in their children's education fall under one of the six types.

Schools with programs that include the six types of involvement help parents build home conditions for learning; help parents understand communications from the schools; help parents become productive volunteers at school; help parents share responsibilities for their children's education in learning activities related to the curriculum at home; and include parents' voices in decisions that affect the school and their children.

Getting parents involved in their child's education is a movement that is sweeping the nation (Black, 1998a). In Kentucky, the state reform plan expects schools to enlist parents in large-scale restructuring efforts. In Hawaii, all schools are required to use a *school/community-based management system* that grants parents roles ranging from *executive* to *advisory* in areas such as school policy, personnel, budget, facilities, and curriculum. Other states, including California, Missouri, Tennessee, Minnesota, and Florida, also mandate some form of parent involvement.

At the federal level, Congress added "increased parent involvement in schools" to the list of national education goals in 1994. When states submit plans under the Goals 2000: Educate America Act, they must show how they intend to raise levels of parent participation in schools. And as part of the Improving America's Schools Act, Title I requires local schools and districts to adopt three types of parent-involvement strategies: including parents in developing school policies; forming school-parent compacts to raise students' academic performance; and establishing school-parent partnerships to work on collaborative improvement projects. (Schools are permitted to use Title I Part A funds, combined with other federal education funds, to upgrade the school's entire educational program rather than to deliver federally supported services only to identified Title I students.)

At the district level, nowhere is the push for parent involvement felt more keenly than in Chicago, where a sweeping school reform law gives parents strategic decision-making power in each of the city's 533 schools. As part of the *decentralization process*, in their neighborhood schools parent groups hire and fire principals, plan curriculum content and teaching methods, and authorize budget expenditures. In most school districts, parents tend to be involved on a less grand scale. However, Black also reported that, for better or worse, involving parents in their children's education seems to be part of every educator's job description (1998a). The problem though, is that when something is everybody's job, it sometimes turns out to be nobody's job, or nobody does it.

So, Does Involving Parents Really Make a Difference?

Trying to educate a child without involving his or her parents and the community in which they live can be time-consuming, and, in some cases, counterproductive. Hatch (1998) reported that something mysterious happens when community involvement contributes to improvements in student achievement. Further, the power of community involvement for improving learning may come from a number of different sources. Beyond changes in curriculum or improvements in self-esteem, meaningful community involvement sets in motion a chain of events that transforms the culture of the school and often that of the community the school serves.

The role the community plays with reference to educating the children of that community is significant because, in addition to addressing some of the children's social, emotional, and recreational needs, the community, to some degree, can make contributions to increasing students' academic achievement. Hatch (1998) says that the community can make a difference; but the most important factor in producing rapid increases in test scores is difficult to pin down. Common patterns among schools suggest that community involvement contributes to improvement in:

- The physical conditions, resources, and constituencies that support learning;
- The attitudes and expectations of parents, teachers, and students; and
- The depth and quality of the learning experiences in which parents, teachers, and students participate.

Henderson and Berla (1996) reported in *A New Generation of Evidence: The Family is Crucial to Student Achievement* that the positive role parents play related to their child's education is now beyond dispute. They divided their findings into two areas of research: changes in family structure and their effect on student achievement; and the contributions of families to their children's general development.

Henderson and Berla stated that when schools work together with families to support learning, children tend to succeed not just in school, but throughout life. In fact, the most accurate predictor of a student's achievement in school is not income or social status, but the extent to which that student's family is able to:

- Create a home environment that encourages learning;

Introduction and Background

- Express high (but not unrealistic) expectations for their children's achievement and future careers; and
- Become involved in their children's education at school and in the community.

Taken together, the studies summarized in this report strongly suggest that when schools support families to develop these three conditions, children from low-income families and diverse cultural backgrounds approach the grades and test scores expected for middle-class children. They also are more likely to take advantage of a full range of educational opportunities after graduating from high school. Even with only one or two of these conditions in place, children do measurably better at school.

The studies summarized by Henderson and Berla document these benefits for students:

- Higher grades and test scores
- Better attendance and more homework done
- Fewer placements in special education
- More positive attitudes and behavior
- Higher graduation rates
- Greater enrollment in postsecondary education.

Families benefit, too. Parents develop more confidence in the school. The teachers they work with have higher opinions of them as parents and higher expectations of their children. As a result, parents develop more confidence not only about helping their children learn at home, but about themselves as parents. Furthermore, when parents become involved in their children's education, they often enroll in classes to continue their own education.

Schools and communities also profit. Schools that work well with families have:

- Improved teacher morale
- Higher ratings of teachers by parents
- More support from families
- Higher student achievement
- Better reputations in the community

When parents are involved in their children's education at home, their children do better in school. When parents are involved at school, their children go farther in school, and the schools they attend become better.

Henderson and Berla also reported data about the relationship between parent involvement and student achievement from the family perspective by assessing how family background and behavior influence children's development. They reported on these themes related to parent involvement:

- Family background and student achievement

    The socioeconomic status (SES) or cultural background of a home need not determine how well a child does at school. Parents from a variety of cultural backgrounds and with different levels of education, income, or occupational status can and do provide stimulating home environments that support and encourage the learning of their children. It is what parents do in the home rather than their status that is important (Kellagan, Sloane, Alvarez, and Bloom, 1993, as cited in Henderson and Berla, 1996).

- Families as learning environments

    The way that time is spent can have a powerful influence on what and how much children learn. Henderson and Berla (1996) reported on the types of family interactions and behavior associated with high-achieving students, and compared them to families with low-achieving students. They highlighted Reginald Clark's findings about African-American 12th-graders in Chicago, and Hispanic, Asian, African-American, and Anglo elementary, middle, and high school students in Los Angeles, which reported that high-achieving students typically spend approximately 20 hours a week engaged in a *constructive learning activity* after school. Clark's finding were reported in his 1990 article entitled "Why Disadvantaged Students Succeed: What Happens Outside School is Critical."

    Additionally, descriptions of families whose children who are doing well in school repeatedly mention many of these characteristics and examples:

    - Establishing a daily family routine—providing time and a quiet place to study, assigning responsibility for household chores, being firm about times to get up and go to bed, having dinner together.

- Monitoring out-of-school activities—setting limits on television watching, checking up on children when parents are not home, arranging for after-school activities and supervised care.

- Modeling the value of learning, self-discipline, and hard work —communicating through questioning and conversation, demonstrating that achievement comes from working hard, using reference materials and the library.

- Expressing high but realistic expectations for achievement—setting goals and standards that are appropriate for children's age and maturity, recognizing and encouraging special talents, informing friends and family about successes.

- Encouraging children's development and progress in school—maintaining a warm and supportive home, showing interest in children's progress at school, helping with homework, discussing the value of a good education and possible career options, staying in touch with teachers and school staff.

- Reading, writing, and discussions among family members—reading, listening to children read, and talking about what is being read; discussing the day over dinner; telling stories and sharing problems; writing letters, lists, and messages.

- Using community resources for family needs—enrolling in sports programs or lessons, introducing children to role models and mentors, and using community services.

♦ Class and cultural mismatch

Although parenting styles that produce high achievement can be found in families from all backgrounds, better performance is still strongly associated with more education and greater income. Low-SES students whose parents provide a strong home learning environment and stay involved with school still do not do as well in school as high-SES students from similar home environments. (Eagle, 1989, as cited in Henderson and Berla, 1996).

The differences in how families relate to school are rooted not only in class divisions, but also in ethnic diversity. In her review of research on families with different cultural and language backgrounds, Lily Wong Fillmore noted a profound mismatch between how low-income and minority children are raised and the background children require to prosper in American schools.

Wong Fillmore suggested (as cited in Henderson and Berla, 1996) that children from mainstream and Chinese-American families earn higher grades and test scores because the middle-class values and the ways learning is promoted at home match those at school. Working-class Black and White children, and Mexican-Americans tend not to perform as well, because their families have emphasized good behavior, not literacy; because they are taught to learn by observation and imitation, not by direct instruction; and because their parents have encouraged an individual pace of development rather than pushed them to keep up with other children.

When parents and schools collaborate to help children adjust to the world of school, bridging the gap between the culture at home and the mainstream American school, children of all backgrounds tend to do well. The research on family processes reveals that the home environment has a powerful influence not only on how well children do, but also on how far they go in school. If the family's approach to life and learning is very different from that of the school, children have difficulty integrating the two experiences and may drop out. On the other hand, culture or background does not rigidly determine a child's fate. What parents do at home to support learning has a strong, independent effect on children's achievement. But parents are in a much better position to assist their children if they are kept informed about how they are doing in school and the best ways to encourage them (Kellaghan, et al., as cited in Henderson and Berla, 1996).

In getting parents involved in the educational lives of their students at risk, it is noteworthy that schools, school staff, and curricular programs can only do so much—no matter how effective. Neither families nor schools can do the job alone. For students at risk to receive the optimum education, school staff must work in tandem with the students' parents. The role of the teacher is to teach the students as much as possible in a predetermined time line; and the role of parents is to offer school staff and their child encouragement and support. The findings of Mitrsomwang, and Hawley (as cited in Henderson and Berla, 1996) support the belief that parents and families need to encourage and support students to ensure the student's success. In their study of Southeast Asian high school students, Mitrsomwang and Hawley found that families needed to provide three supports before their children performed above average at school:

♦ Hold strong, consistent values about the importance of education.

Introduction and Background

- Be *willing* to help children with schoolwork and to be in contact with the school.

- Be *able* to help children with school work and to communicate successfully with teachers and administrators.

Reaching out to families and helping them become more involved in their children's education at home and school can have a powerful impact on student achievement. Effective efforts to involve parents must have these three qualities:

- Comprehensive—reaching out to all families, not just those most easily contacted, and involving them in all major roles, from tutoring to governance;

- Well-planned—specific goals, clear communication about what is expected of all participants, training for both educators and parents; and

- Long-lasting—a clear commitment to the long-term, not just to an immediate project.

Involving parents is an essential component of any reform strategy, but it is not a substitute for a high-quality education program or thoughtful, comprehensive school improvement. Getting parents involved is merely a means to an end—it is not the destination. Moreover, involving parents will not compensate for a curriculum that does not meet the students' needs; nor will parent involvement compensate for poor instruction, any more than public relations campaigns will disguise poor instruction.

To implement and institutionalize an effective parent education plan, school staff have to reach out to parents in ways they have not done before. Staff have to be trained; they have to make home visits instead of waiting for the parents to show up at the school; and parents have to be involved in the decision-making process. Staff may, for the first time, have to hold meetings outside the school in less intimidating and more accessible places, such as churches, community centers, or someone's home. Also, material may have to be translated into languages other than English, and school-related meetings may have to be held at a time other than the one hour time slot immediately following the end of school.

Communities in Schools believes that all young people need and deserve four basics: a personal, one-on-one relationship with a caring adult; a safe place to learn and grow; a marketable skill to use after graduation; and a chance to give back to peers and community.

In 1997, Communities in Schools and America's Promise—The Alliance for Youth joined forces philosophically and practically. The principles of Communities in Schools now form the core of America's Promise.

Local Communities in Schools are independently incorporated, nonprofit public-private organizations. Each local program has a board of directors, an executive director, and a project director; and each promotes partnerships that span communities, cities, or counties to meet local needs. Each organization obtains the funding and resources for its activities. Some programs establish academies; some offer classes and after-school programs at schools, churches, or community centers; some bring doctors, nurses, and mentors into schools; some bring help to the places children and their families live; and some take children into the community for service-learning projects. Each program works to get students to stay in school and make positive life choices. Communities in Schools serves as a broker to bring partners together to meet varying community needs.

Henderson and Berla (1996) digested 66 studies, reviews, reports, and analyses of books related to getting parents involved in their child's education. Their major findings follow and serve as the conclusion to this chapter. During their study on the contributions families make to their children's success, and the supports families need from school and community sources to guide their children successfully through the system, several themes emerged again and again:

- First, the family makes critical contributions to student achievement, from earliest childhood through high school. Efforts to improve children's outcomes are much more effective if they encompass their families.

- Second, when parents are involved at school, not just at home, children do better in school and they stay in school longer.

- Third, when parents are involved at school, their children attend better schools.

- Fourth, children do best when their parents are enabled to play four key roles in their children's learning. Those roles are teacher, supporter, advocate, and decision-maker:

  - As teachers, parents create a home environment that promotes learning, reinforces what is being taught at school, and develops the values and life skills children need to become responsible adults.

Introduction and Background

- As supporters, parents contribute their knowledge and skills to the school, enriching the curriculum, and providing extra services and support to students.

- As advocates, parents help children negotiate the system and receive fair treatment, and work to make the system more responsive to all families.

- As decision-makers, parents serve on advisory councils, curriculum committees, and management teams, participating in joint problem-solving at every level.

♦ Fifth, the more the relationship between family and school approaches a comprehensive, well-planned partnership, the higher the student achievement.

♦ Sixth, families, schools, and community organizations all contribute to student achievement; the best results come when all three work together (Henderson and Berla, 1996).

An Ending Note—What Parents Want From Teachers

Dorothy Rich is the founder and president of the Home and School Institute, and the MegaSkills Education Center of the Home Institute, located in Washington, DC. Rich (1998) has identified three consistent parent concerns:

♦ How well teachers know and care about teaching;

♦ How well teachers know and care about their children; and

♦ How well the teachers communicate with parents.

Unity

I dreamed I stood in a studio,
And watched two sculptors there.
The clay they used was a young child's mind,
And they fashioned it with care.

One was a teacher—the tools he used
Were books, music and art.
The other, a parent, worked with a guiding hand,
And a gentle heart.

Day after day the teacher toiled with touch
That was deft and sure,
While the parent labored by his side,
And polished and smoothed it o'er.

And when at last their task was done,
They stood proud of what they had wrought,
For the things they molded into the child
Could neither be sold nor bought.

And each agreed they would have failed,
If each had worked alone.
For behind the teacher stood the school,
And behind the parent, the home.

Anonymous

2

Program, Instructional, and Curricular Initiatives

Advancement Via Individual Determination (AVID)

Advancement Via Individual Determination (AVID) is a comprehensive middle school through senior high school reform program designed to prepare educationally disadvantaged, underachieving students who have demonstrated potential for success in a rigorous secondary school curriculum for four-year college eligibility. The program also restructures the teaching methodology of an entire school to make the college preparatory curricula accessible to almost all students. Advancement Via Individual Determination has developed a comprehensive professional development program. The program has received the Showcase of Excellence award from the National Council of States on In-service Education. Mary Catherine Swanson, AVID Founder and Director, won the prestigious Charles A. Dana Foundation Award for Pioneering Achievement in Education. She is the only K-12 educator to receive the award.

Advancement Via Individual Determination focuses on the following:

- Students

    AVID students are students who are capable of completing college. AVID students enroll in rigorous academic classes and in the AVID elective class, where they receive academic support. Their self-image improves, and they become academically successful leaders and role models for other students. They are proud to be in the program.

- Curriculum

    The AVID curriculum is based on rigorous standards. It is developed by middle and senior high school teachers in collaboration with college professors, and emphasizes teaching pedagogy which allows college preparatory classes to be accessible to all students.

- Faculty

    One key to a successful AVID Program is a site coordinator/teacher who meets this criteria:

    - Is a respected site instructional leader who works well with secondary school students, college students, and faculty;
    - Can organize curriculum as well as activities; and
    - Is committed to serving the needs of students in the AVID elective classes.

- Site team

  The AVID site team is the key to gaining schoolwide improvement through the implementation of AVID. This team meets regularly to examine site practices that enhance or inhibit the academic progress of all students. As the key leader of the site team, the AVID coordinator works with colleagues in all subject areas to implement methodologies used in AVID. In addition, the program provides tutors to help in implementing these techniques. The coordinators work with counselors to schedule students into college preparatory courses. Counselors assist in college-entry test-taking preparation and in the college and financial aid processes. A site team consisting of an administrator, counselor, AVID coordinator, and subject area teachers makes AVID goals a reality throughout the school. The site team may also include AVID students, tutors, and parents.

- Tutors

  Tutors are available in the AVID elective class, where they lead structured tutorials to facilitate student access to rigorous curriculum. As students from colleges and universities, tutors also serve as role models. AVID students who continue their education in college often return to the program as tutors. AVID tutors receive extensive training through a 16-hour tutor certification program.

- Parents

  Parents encourage their students to achieve academically, participate on an advisory board and in AVID parent and site team meetings, and maintain regular telephone contact with the AVID coordinator. Many parents and students participate in AVID Family Workshops which are part of the AVID curriculum.

- Colleges and Universities

  Colleges and universities demonstrate their support of AVID Programs in many ways. They may provide guest speakers, offer college credit courses to AVID high school students, include AVID students in residential, academically-oriented summer bridge programs, and follow the progress of AVID students during their college careers. Colleges and universities also support AVID by providing speakers and summer apprenticeships for AVID students. An AVID Alumni Association is in place to provide student mentoring and college scholarships.

Program Costs

Costs of the AVID Program vary from state to state. In California, AVID is a state-funded program with resources provided for 11 regional centers. The initial cost of the program is under $2.00 per student per day in year one, declining to under $1.00 per student per day in year three. Outside California, initial costs per student are typically under $3.00 per day, with year three costs declining to under $1.00 per day.

Scope of Implementation

As of 1998, AVID has been implemented at 750 middle schools and high schools in 13 states, including California, Nevada, Texas, Colorado, Kentucky, Tennessee, Virginia, North Carolina, South Carolina, New Jersey, Illinois, Georgia, and Maryland. Advancement Via Individual Determination also serves the Department of Defense Dependents Schools (DoDDS) with 55 sites in Europe and the Pacific.

Results

Advancement Via Individual Determination has been thoroughly studied through independent research. A well-developed AVID program improves schoolwide standardized test scores, advanced-level course enrollments, and the number of students attending college. In *Constructing School Success* (Cambridge University Press, 1996), Dr. Hugh Mehan and colleagues studied eight AVID high schools and found that AVID graduates outperformed their ethnic groups in college enrollment. This research team from the University of California, San Diego, also discovered that 89 percent of the AVID graduates were still in college after 2 years. Mehan et al. also discovered that 92 percent of all AVID graduates enrolled in college, a rate 75 percent higher than the overall student population. The Advancement Via Individual Determination national office —The AVID Center—has collected data indicating that 85 percent of AVID's graduates complete four-year college requirements and that over 60 percent of AVID's graduates enroll in college.

Contact

Mary Catherine Swanson, Executive Director
Advancement Via Individual Determination
(AVID) Center
McConaughy House
2490 Heritage Park Row
San Diego, CA 92110
Voice: (619) 682-5050
Fax: (619) 682-5060
mcsavid@sdcoe.k12.ca.us
www.avidcenter.org

The California Mini-Corps

Background

The California Mini-Corps Summer Indoor Migrant Teacher Assistant Program came into being in 1967. The California Mini-Corps School Year Program is an outgrowth of the California Mini-Corps Summer Indoor Migrant Teacher Assistant Program and was developed in 1974 to meet the need to provide adequate role models and institutional support for students from migrant backgrounds.

Through the summer and school-year programs, Mini-Corps students provide services to the migrant children of California. The Mini-Corps students use their talent and dedication to work in migrant impacted classrooms, and simultaneously serve as the link between the migrant community and the schools. They get personally acquainted with each child and child's family and often share their hopes and frustrations. Most importantly, they act as role models for the migrant students and will hopefully help to raise their aspirations. At the same time, participants serve as a potential pool of teachers who are sensitive to the unique needs of a predominantly rural, bilingual, migrant student population and their families.

The objectives of the California Mini-Corps are twofold:

- Work to provide direct categorical services to migrant children; and
- Work to increase the number of professionals who are sensitive and committed to the needs of migrant children.

The California Mini-Corps affords program participants the opportunity to gain valuable experience working in an actual classroom—an experience often inaccessible to many migrants; and to help migrant children improve their oral and written skills in English. As a result of program involvement, a significant percentage of participants in the California Mini-Corps Program have gone on to become successful educators who are sensitive to the needs of migrant children and their communities.

The California Mini-Corps Program is comprised of five major components. The program includes the Summer Indoor Migrant Teacher Assistant Program; the School Year Program; the Outdoor Education Program; the Health Corps Program; and the Puppetry Program. Following is a description of these program components.

Summer Indoor Migrant Teacher Assistant Program

In 1967, 14 college students were recruited and participated in a 2-week preservice training course at Chico State College. The 14 corpsmen lived and worked in Gridley, CA. Today, Mini-Corps students continue to share their talents with migrant children. A sense of dedication and commitment is still required of the corps of young people. These students provide extracurricular activities at the school and migrant camp centers that make the school's education meaningful to migrant children and their families. Some Mini-Corps students are assigned to live in the migrant labor centers where they work with the migrant community. These young people possess the enthusiasm and devotion to provide services above and beyond what is expected of them.

From the modest beginning of 14 Mini-Corps young people, the program has grown to include 1,000 teacher assistants trained on college sites to provide services to migrant children and their families in at least 32 counties in the state. The summer of 1998 marked the thirty-first summer during which the California Mini-Corps college students provided service for the needs of thousands of migrant students. During the summer months, instructors engage Mini-Corps participants in activities which include, but are not limited to the following:

- Training, staff/professional development, and curriculum development;
- Participating in special projects which are sponsored by the Migrant Education Region;
- Coordinating and organizing after-school activities;
- Reinforcing the concept that stakeholders must play an active role in program development and decision making;
- Identifying migrant children;
- Engaging in program coordination and program improvement activities;
- Conducting home visits and participating in parent conferences;
- Reinforcing the process of focusing on services to migrant children; and
- Participating in puppetry activities.

The School Year Program

The need for migrant students to receive tutorial assistance from bilingual role models gave birth to the idea of recruiting a corps of young people who were from a similar rural background to work in the summer schools and during the regular school year. This idea was put into action in 1974. The Mini-Corps students were assigned to work in migrant-impacted classrooms and were an important link between the migrant community and the school community. They were mentors to:

- Migrant students who needed assistance in developing their literacy skills in the primary and secondary language, and in other academic areas as needed; and

- Migrant students, K-12, who needed tutorial assistance in all the academic areas so that they could graduate from high school.

The kinds of direct services migrant students receive in the School Year Program from Mini-Corps students include, but are not limited to, these:

- Career awareness
- Extended-day tutoring
- ESL or bilingual instruction
- Home tutoring
- Individual tutoring
- Postsecondary awareness
- Tutorial instruction in academic subjects

In the School Year Program, approximately 400 Mini-Corps students work a minimum of 10 to 15 hours per week under the supervision of a classroom teacher. Six hours of in-service time is provided by the college supervisor on a monthly basis. The Mini-Corps students help the classroom teacher better understand the migrant child and the migrant culture. The Mini-Corps students also function as mentors/tutors in the classroom, enabling them to encourage migrant children to continue in school.

The Mini-Corps students receive training in writing objectives, lesson plans, and developing instructional strategies which are designed to help them meet the academic need of the migrant students with whom they work. Second language acquisition and developing career portfolios are among the topics taught during the School Year Program. An underlying theme of the School Year Program, as is the case with all of the Mini-Corp programs, is to engage Mini-Corp students in activities that will help them better understand and address the issues that face migrant families.

The School Year Mini-Corps Programs are held on 24 college sites. Each site has a coordinator who also serves as the site program supervisor. The college coordinators administer the program and work in conjunction with regional staff in the placement of Mini-Corps students. They also perform other related duties as deemed necessary.

Outdoor Education Program

Concordant with California Mini-Corps Program objectives, the Outdoor Education program is a component of the Mini-Corps summer program. The objectives of this program are:

- To provide migrant students the opportunity to experience education outside of the classroom, where students are able to construct meaning that leads to thinking, sharing, exploring, questioning, and developing their own understanding of lessons provided by the instructors.

- To teach migrant children science concepts in a natural setting that will foster students' understanding of their life-sustaining relationship with planet earth, and emphasize the commonalities and connections among human beings and ecology, plant life, earth science, physical science, and so on.

- To teach migrant children a respect for nature, thus developing an understanding of how nature works and how human beings affect the environment. (By teaching migrant students respect for nature, strategies are introduced that further develop their thinking concerning their personal expectations, goal setting, and general leadership skills.)

- To provide Mini-Corps students an opportunity to work in an educational environment where they can further develop their instructional skills.

Mini-Corps teacher assistants serve as bilingual lead instructors and advisors to the migrant students. They receive training that prepares them to work with the migrant students who are actively engaged in learning about the natural world when they are at camp. The Mini-Corps teacher assistants learn to apply the five senses to the learning of science in an outdoor setting, exposing the migrant students to *live science*, while helping them to enjoy and respect nature.

The students are also introduced to *active learning* via readings, listening, and discourse that allow them to make new associations from one week at camp. The migrant students are able to use scientific investigation in their everyday learning activities. Science in the Outdoor Education Program is enjoyable and full of learning opportunities. Migrant students are also provided with diverse learning activities such as rope courses, overnighters, survival, wilderness leadership development, nature walks and hikes. Furthermore, teaching strategies have evolved to include social skill development, collegial support, cooperating group work and projects, as well as, explicitly attempting to build a community of learners.

Health Corps Program

The Health Corps program is a component of the California Mini-Corps Program which focuses on health. Health Corps participants are former migrant students who have continued their education, graduated from college and are pursuing a career in a health-related field. The Health Corps students provide direct health education awareness to the migrant students via classroom presentations. They work with migrant students in preschool through grade 12, and depending on the Migrant Education region, can be assigned to many schools or to one school.

The health field is recognized as one of the areas where there is a lack of bilingual professional health providers. Many social agencies have overlooked the unique lifestyle and health needs of the migrant student. Thus, the services they are provided have been less than adequate.

As a result of the lack of bilingual health educators, a yearly effort is made to recruit young people with more than one year of college in a health-related field, and with the experiential knowledge of the migrant lifestyle, who will use their skills and dedication to:

- Provide health education classes to migrant children and their families in these areas:
  - Preventative medicine and dentistry;
  - Nutrition;
  - First aid; and
  - Pesticide safety.
- Provide awareness to existing health service agencies of the migrant child's special needs and the agencies' responsibilities to meet these needs.

- Assist local agencies in developing programs to meet the health needs of migrant children and their families.
- Serve as the link between the migrant community and health and welfare service agencies.
- Identify and confront existing and potential health problems that might impede the education of the migrant child.

Puppetry Program

The California Mini-Corps Puppetry program's objectives are:

- To provide direct categorical services to migrant children and their families; and
- To increase the number of professional educators who are especially trained, experienced and committed to work with migrant children.

Through the use of puppets and well-orchestrated puppet programs, Mini-Corps participants are trained in how to engage migrant students and their parents in discussions and activities that reinforce the "say no to drugs" approach at school, home, in social activities, and in their work environment, thereby enhancing the importance of a healthy body, healthy self-esteem, safety, and other important topics.

Contact

Maria Avila
California Mini-Corps
510 Bercut Drive, Suite Q
Sacramento, CA 95814
Voice: (916) 446-4603
Fax: (916) 446-9271
Mavila@bcoe.butte

Core Knowledge

Background

The Core Knowledge Foundation is an independent, nonprofit, nonpartisan organization. The Foundation conducts research on curricula, develops books and other materials for parents and teachers, offers workshops for teachers, and serves as the hub of a growing network of Core Knowledge schools. The primary document offered through the Foundation is the Core Knowledge Sequence. It outlines topics in each subject and grade from preschool through grade eight. Teaching these topics in yearly sequence provides participation of all children in classroom instruction. The Sequence serves as the planning document in Core Knowledge classrooms. Its high level of specificity is useful when planning lessons and when communicating with parents. The assignment of specific topics to specific grade levels helps avoid serious gaps and needless repetitions in a student's early education. Other useful publications from the Foundation include the Core Knowledge Series (*What Your Kindergartner–Sixth Grader Needs to Know*), as well as a quarterly newsletter, *Common Knowledge*, which features updates on new resources, events in Core Knowledge schools, and the annual National Conference. It also discusses issues related to implementing the Core Knowledge Sequence. Its homepage—www.coreknowledge.org—is another helpful source of information about Core Knowledge. It is frequently updated with new information on upcoming events, job opportunities, lesson plans, new test data, and related topics. The Core Knowledge movement grew out of ideas first expressed in *Cultural Literacy: What Every American Needs to Know* (1987) and developed in *The Schools We Need & Why We Don't Have Them* (1996), both by E. D. Hirsch, Jr., a professor of education and humanities at the University of Virginia.

In *Cultural Literacy: What Every American Needs to Know,* Professor Hirsch demonstrated that true literacy requires not only the ability to "decode" or sound out the words on a page but also familiarity with a broad range of background knowledge taken for granted by writers and speakers in the United States. "To be truly literate," Professor Hirsch noted, "citizens must be able to grasp the meaning of any piece of writing addressed to the general reader." Those who possess this shared background knowledge can, for example, understand a reference in a newspaper to an "appellate court decision" or "trading competition from the Pacific Rim," or a sportscaster's account of the rise of an unlikely champion as "a Cinderella story." But those who lack the assumed knowledge are excluded from understanding many messages in various media and are thus excluded from full participation in national life.

"If shared background knowledge is necessary for full participation in the larger national society," then, Professor Hirsch says in *The Schools We Need & Why We Don't Have Them*, "the same reasoning must also hold for full participation in a smaller social group, and most especially that of the classroom itself....Every classroom is a little society of its own, and its effectiveness and fairness depend on the full participation by all program participants, just as in the larger society. Such universal participation cannot occur unless (students) all share a core of relevant background knowledge."

This emphasis on knowledge, however, goes against many ideas that have long dominated American education. These ideas—expressed in such phrases as *child-centered schooling, critical thinking skills,* and *multiple intelligences*—have resulted in a widespread prejudice against factual knowledge in schooling. In *The Schools We Need & Why We Don't Have Them*, Professor Hirsch analyzes the sources of these antiknowledge theories and argues that we must cast them aside, taking instead a pragmatic look at the most fair and effective educational practices around the world, especially the compelling evidence that "every nation that manages to achieve universal readiness in the early grades for all its children...does so by following grade-by-grade standards. In large, diverse nations, as well as small, homogeneous ones, a common core curriculum appears to be the only practical means for achieving universal readiness at each grade level."

Core Knowledge is:

- An idea that for the sake of academic excellence, greater fairness, and higher literacy, elementary and middle schools need a solid, specific, shared core curriculum to help children establish strong foundations of knowledge, grade by grade.

- A guide to specific, shared content as outlined in the Core Knowledge Sequence (a grade-by-grade guide to important knowledge) and supported in Core Knowledge resources, including the *What Your Kindergartner–Sixth Grader Needs to Know* book series.

- A school reform movement taking shape in hundreds of schools where educators have committed themselves to teaching important skills and the Core Knowledge content they share, within grade levels, across districts, and with other Core Knowledge schools across the country.

Benefits of Core Knowledge

- For students
  - Provides a broad base of knowledge and a rich vocabulary
  - Motivates students to learn and creates a strong desire to learn more
  - Provides the knowledge necessary for higher levels of learning and helps build confidence
- For the school
  - Provides an academic focus and encourages consistency in instruction
  - Provides a plan for coherent, sequenced learning from grade to grade
  - Promotes a community of learners—adults and children
  - Becomes an effective tool for lesson planning and communication among teachers and with parents
  - Guides thoughtful purchases of school resources
- For the school district
  - Provides a common focus to share knowledge and expertise
  - Decreases learning gaps caused by mobility
  - Encourages cooperation among schools to provide quality learning experiences for all students
  - Provides a strong foundation of knowledge for success in high school and beyond
- For parents and the community
  - Provides a clear outline of what children are expected to learn in school
  - Encourages parents to participate in their children's education both at home and in school
  - Provides opportunities for community members to help obtain and provide instructional resources

Knowledge Builds on Knowledge

Students learn new knowledge by building on what they already know. Students in Core Knowledge schools know a lot because they are offered a coherent sequence of specific knowledge that builds year by year. For example, in sixth grade they should be ready to grasp the law of the conservation of energy because they have been building the knowledge that prepares them for it, as shown in the following selection from the physical science strand of the Core Knowledge Sequence:

- Kindergarten
  - Magnetism, the idea of forces we cannot see.
  - Classify materials according to whether they are attracted to a magnet.
- First Grade
  - Basic concept of atoms.
  - Names and common examples of the three states of matter.
  - Examine water as an example of changing states of matter in a single substance.
  - Properties of matter: measurement.
- Second Grade
  - Lodestones: naturally occurring magnets.
  - Magnetic poles: north-seeking and south-seeking poles.
  - Magnetic fields (strongest at the poles).
  - Law of attraction: unlike poles attract, like poles repel.
- Fourth Grade
  - Atoms: all matter is made up of particles too small to see.
  - Atoms are made up of even smaller particles: protons, neutrons, electrons.
  - Concept of electrical charge: proton has positive charge; electron has negative charge; neutron has no charge.
  - "Unlike charges attract, like charges repel" (relate to magnetic attraction).

Program, Instructional, and Curricular Initiatives

- Properties of matter: mass, volume, and density.
- The elements: basic kinds of matter.

♦ Fifth Grade

- Atoms are in constant motion; electrons move around the nucleus in path called shells (or energy levels).
- Atoms form molecules and compounds.
- The Periodic Table: a tool that organizes elements with common properties.
- Energy transfer: matter changes phase by adding or removing energy.
- Expansion and contraction.
- Three ways energy is transferred: conduction, convection, and radiation.

♦ Sixth Grade

- Kinetic and potential energy: types of each.
- Heat and temperature.
- Energy is conserved in a system.

The Core Knowledge Sequence

Content Guidelines for Grades PreK-8

The Core Knowledge Sequence is a detailed outline of specific content to be taught in language arts, history and geography, math, science, and the fine arts. As the basis of at least 50 percent of a school's curriculum, it can provide a solid, coherent foundation for learning, while allowing flexibility to meet local needs.

A Sampling of the Sequence

♦ Kindergarten: Visual Arts

Relate children's art activities to a variety of artists and works of art, including:

- Painting: line and color in such works as Matisse's *The Purple Robe*, Picasso's *Le Gourmet*, Mary Cassatt's *After the Bath*, Henry O. Tanner's *The Banjo Lesson*, and Diego Rivera's *Piñata*
- Sculpture: Statue of Liberty, Mount Rushmore, mobiles of Alexander Calder, Northwest American Indian totem pole

♦ First Grade: World History

Early Civilizations: Ancient Egypt

- Importance of the Nile River
- Pharaohs, pyramids, and mummies
- Animal gods
- Hieroglyphics

♦ Second Grade: American History

Civil Rights

- Women's rights and roles: Susan B. Anthony, Eleanor Roosevelt
- Equality regardless of color: Mary McLeod Bethune, Jackie Robinson, Rosa Parks, Martin Luther King, Jr., Cesar Chavez

♦ Third Grade: Math

Fractions

- Recognize fractions to one-tenth
- Identify numerator and denominator
- Write mixed numbers
- Recognize equivalent fractions (for example, $\frac{1}{2} = \frac{3}{6}$)
- Compare fractions with like denominators using the signs <, >, and =

Geometry

- Identify lines as horizontal, vertical, perpendicular, parallel
- Identify polygons: pentagon, hexagon, and octagon
- Identify angles: right angle; four right angles in a square or rectangle
- Compute area in square inches and square centimeters

Program, Instructional, and Curricular Initiatives

- Fourth Grade: Science

  Electricity

  - Electricity as the flow of electrons
  - Static electricity: Electric current
  - Electric circuits: closed, open, and short circuits
  - Simple circuit (battery, wire, bulb, filament, switch)
  - Conductors and insulators
  - How electromagnets work
  - Using electricity safely

- Fifth Grade: American History and Geography

  Westward Exploration and Expansion

  - Daniel Boone: Cumberland Gap and Wilderness Trail
  - The Louisiana Purchase: Lewis and Clark, Sacajawea
  - Land routes: Santa Fe Trail and Oregon Trail
  - Water routes: Erie Canal; Mississippi, Missouri, Ohio, Columbia Rivers
  - American Indian resistance: Tecumseh attempts to unite tribes to defend their land
  - "Manifest Destiny" and conflict with Mexico

- Sixth Grade: Language Arts

  Stories

  - Dr. Jekyll and Mr. Hyde
  - The Iliad and the Odyssey
  - Julius Caesar
  - The Secret Garden

  Writing a Research Essay

  - Organizing with an outline
  - Quoting materials from secondary sources
  - Summarizing and paraphrasing
  - Acknowledging sources and avoiding plagiarism
  - Preparing a bibliography

The Common Ground for Uncommon Success

Core Knowledge is:

- Solid

   Many people say that knowledge is changing so fast that what students learn today will soon be outdated. While current events and technology are constantly changing, there is nevertheless a body of lasting knowledge that should form the core of a K-8 curriculum. Such solid knowledge includes, for example, the basic principles of constitutional government, important events of world history, essential elements of mathematics and of oral and written expression, the periodic table of elements, widely acknowledged masterpieces of art and music, and stories and poems passed down from generation to generation.

- Sequenced

   Knowledge builds on knowledge. Children learn new knowledge by building on what they already know. Only a school system that clearly defines the knowledge and skills required to participate in each successive grade can be excellent and fair for all students. For this reason, the Core Knowledge Sequence provides a clear outline of content to be learned grade by grade (K-8). This sequential building of knowledge not only helps ensure that children enter each new grade ready to learn, but also helps prevent the many repetitions and gaps that characterize much current schooling (repeated units, for example, on pioneer days or the rain forest, but little or no attention to the Bill of Rights, or to adding fractions with unlike denominators).

- Specific

   A typical state or district curriculum says, "Students will demonstrate knowledge of people, events, ideas, and movements that contributed to the development of the United States." But which people and events? What ideas and movements? In contrast, the Core Knowledge Sequence is distinguished by its specificity. By clearly specifying important knowledge in language arts, history and geography, math, science, and the fine arts, the Core Knowledge

Sequence presents a practical answer to the question, "What do our children need to know?"

◆ Shared

Literacy depends on shared knowledge. To be literate means, in part, to be familiar with a broad range of knowledge taken for granted by speakers and writers. For example, when sportscasters refer to an upset victory as "David knocking off Goliath," or when reporters refer to a "threatened presidential veto," they are assuming that their audience shares certain knowledge. One goal of the Core Knowledge Foundation is to provide all children, regardless of background, with the shared knowledge they need to be included in our national literate culture.

Contact

Constance Jones
Core Knowledge Foundation
801 East High Street
Charlottesville, VA 22902
Voice: (804) 977-7550
Fax: (804) 977-0021
coreknow@coreknowledge.org
.coreknowledge.org

Equity 2000

Background

Established in 1990, Equity 2000 is a research-based, field-developed, districtwide, K-12 education reform model. The goal is to close the gap in the college enrollment and success rates between minority and nonminority, advantaged and disadvantaged students, through a series of school district policies, practices, and programs, including the elimination of low-level curriculum tracks.

By having school districts set goals of 100 percent enrollment in algebra I or higher for all ninth graders, and a 100 percent enrollment in geometry or higher for all tenth graders, Equity 2000 aims to end the process by which students are *tracked* into watered down courses that limit their future before they can define it for themselves. Through a series of comprehensive professional development approaches and policy interventions, the program seeks to change the manner in which teachers, counselors and administrators approach teaching and learning as a way to improve educational achievement for *all* students. These components comprise the framework of the Equity 2000 model:

- Districtwide policy changes, to end low-level tracking and raise standards for all students, beginning with the completion of algebra by ninth grade and geometry by the tenth grade, and including reform of the curriculum to reflect standards set by the National Council of Teachers of Mathematics and other discipline-based organizations;

- Ongoing professional development for teachers, counselors, and principals to raise their expectations of all students; to help them use varied instructional strategies to reach all students; and to help them master the content required in the new standards;

- Student academic enrichment *safety nets*, such as Saturday Academies that provide students with the academic support they need to-reach high levels of achievement in rigorous courses;

- Parent and family involvement initiatives that empower all parents to be effective advocates for their children's education at school and create a consistent climate for learning at home;

- Partnerships between the school district, postsecondary education institutions, businesses, and community organizations to gain broad-based support for the goal of academic excellence for all students; and

- Effective use of disaggregated student enrollment and achievement data to drive decisions and monitor progress toward reform goals.

Equity 2000 Workshops

Workshops and training opportunities are designed to support pre-K to 16 educational policy and practice leaders who desire to increase their understanding of the Equity 2000 body of knowledge and to become skilled in its application to school reform. These leaders will have opportunities to contribute to the ongoing expansion and refinement of this body of knowledge and practice.

Workshops are offered periodically throughout the calendar year in two-day formats. Their purpose is to offer *best practices* based on the Equity 2000 Pilot Years and beyond. These workshops are available in a practical hands-on format that supports the implementation of Equity 2000. They feature educators from Equity 2000 school districts across the country.

Examples of workshops are: Using Mathematics as a Lever for Reform; Planning Mathematics and Guidance Institutes for Elementary, Middle, and High School Teachers and Counselors; Implementing a New Vision of Guidance Counseling for the Twenty-first Century; and Effective Use of Data to Drive Decisions and Monitor Reform.

Equity 2000 Adoption Institutes

Equity 2000 Adoption Institutes are interactive five-day learning, planning, and team-building experiences designed to equip a five-member district leadership team with the knowledge, skills, and abilities to begin a district implementation of Equity 2000 that is tailored to the needs of the district. Institutes are conducted for up to five school district teams at a time, and are facilitated by nationally known school reform leaders and seasoned practitioners from the original Equity 2000 sites.

Equity 2000 Advanced Institute: A Renewal Process

The Equity 2000 Advanced Institute is offered to school districts that have already taken part in the initial Equity 2000 Adoption Institute. Teams of up to five policy and practice leaders from the school district join with teams from other districts to build on previous knowledge and to expand their skills for implementing school reform. The fee for the three-day institute includes a follow-up site visitation.

Field Development

More than 700 schools and over half a million students across 14 school districts, including Fort Worth, Texas; Milwaukee, Wisconsin; Nashville, Tennessee; Prince George's County, Maryland; Providence, Rhode Island; and San Jose, California (a consortium of nine districts) have helped develop and demonstrate the effectiveness of the Equity 2000 model. Recently, 11 other school districts have adopted Equity 2000.

Impact

Recent data from a six-year summative evaluation illustrate that Equity 2000 has had an important impact at the pilot sites. By the end of the pilot period, the 1995-96 school year, more students were enrolled in and successfully completing algebra or higher mathematics by grade nine and geometry or higher by grade ten than were even enrolled in those courses at those grades at the start of the pilot. Data also reveal that participation in PSAT/NMSQT, SAT, ACT, and AP programs increased significantly; the percentage of students indicating that they plan to attend college after graduation from high school was substantially higher; and students were enrolled in higher mathematics such as algebra 2, trigonometry, pre-calculus, and calculus at levels significantly greater than the national average.

Adoption Process

School district adoption of Equity 2000 takes place when a school district leadership team of up to five members completes a five-day Adoption Institute leading to a formal district commitment to implement a three- to five-year plan for closing achievement and college enrollment gaps, according to Equity 2000 principles and guidelines.

Rationale for Adoption

- Equity 2000 provides a framework that aligns programs, policies, and resources around a core mission of preparing all students for college eligibility, enrollment and success.

- Equity 2000 has a solid track record of increasing student enrollment in college preparatory mathematics courses at its pilot sites.

- Equity 2000 demonstrates effectiveness in the first steps toward helping school districts dismantle the low-level academic grouping policies and practices that limit the opportunities of many students and the potential of the school district.

- Equity 2000 provides school districts with access to a national network of hands-on experts and representatives from existing Equity 2000 sites who have already grappled with the policy and program issues that arise during implementation of the model.

- Equity 2000 develops talent and leadership within school districts through its extensive professional development activities and through the opportunity to collaborate with partner districts and the other programs of the College Board.

Contact

Vinetta C. Jones, Executive Director
Equity 2000
The College Board
1233 20th Street, NW, Suite 600
Washington, DC 20036-2304
Voice: (202) 822-5930
Fax: (202) 822-5939
equity@collegeboard.org
http://www.collegeboard.org

Help One Student To Succeed (HOSTS)

Background

Help One Student To Succeed (HOSTS) is a structured mentoring program (Readiness-Adult) in language arts/reading, mathematics, and/or Spanish language arts. Help One Student To Succeed is neither a curriculum nor is it computer-assisted learning; it is an instructional strategy tailored to a state's, district's, and school's language arts/reading objectives and philosophies. The HOSTS database and software programs align the school's and district's curricula with its performance outcomes, whether they are locally or state designed. The HOSTS structured mentoring program has won numerous prestigious educational awards for improving student performance.

HOSTS Readiness Learning Center Program

HOSTS Readiness is targeted towards very young learners. The eight-part instructional plan includes language development, shape and letter formation and recognition, and objective reinforcement. The set of HOSTS activities will match the objectives set for each student during assessment, and will work to reinforce classroom instruction. HOSTS Readiness can be effectively implemented in pre-K with four-year-olds, and in K-3 classrooms. The program can be delivered with one-on-one, small group, or large group instruction.

Host Language Arts Learning Center Program

HOSTS matches students with trained parent, business, and community volunteer mentors who work to strengthen students' reading, writing, vocabulary development, study skills, and higher-order thinking skills. Mentors provide role models of successful people who motivate, support, and provide individual student attention.

The school's HOSTS team reviews each student's progress through communication with the student's classroom teacher, observation of the student during reading, writing, and vocabulary work in the HOSTS environment, or through diagnostic testing or district outcomes. Once the strengths/weaknesses have been identified, activities specific to the child's needs are integrated with the reading, writing, and vocabulary work already in process with the HOSTS mentor. The school's HOSTS team designs and plans, along with the classroom teacher, a specific instructional program for each child, using the HOSTS database of curriculum aligned materials. The lesson plans in the programs are tailored to each student's learning style, reading level, and motivational interest and needs. The plans are organized in a learning packet for each child. The mentor and the child work through the lesson together. At the end of each session, the mentor makes comments in the folder about the lesson. This not only helps the teacher in preparation and modification of the following day's lesson, but the work becomes a portion of a portfolio for authentic assessment of the student.

HOSTS Math Learning Center Program

HOSTS Math is a supplemental math strategy which focuses on students who need assistance in mathematics. The strategy provides students the opportunity to: learn to value mathematics; become confident in their own abilities; become mathematical problem solvers; learn to communicate mathematically; and learn to respond mathematically. Help One Student To Succeed is not a curriculum nor is it computer-assisted learning; it is an instructional strategy that is tailored to a state's, district's, and school's mathematics curriculum objectives and philosophies.

HOSTS Math is a supplemental program based on the belief that students need to learn mathematics in a way that is meaningful to them. The use of manipulatives and involving the students in the learning process are highly stressed. HOSTS Math provides for the assessment of students' needs and the creation of a long-range plan that summarizes this information and other assessment data (i.e., state proficiency; classroom teacher). Based on the National Math Standards, the HOSTS Math Profile of Objectives meets teachers' needs by providing the framework for this direction. A progression from concrete to symbolic instruction follows assessment.

Because many instructors are faced with the complexity of the students' math needs, HOSTS helps simplify this process by providing lesson plans that provide examples of how to teach with manipulatives, keeping in mind the students' needs. These lesson plans are found in each strand's *Support Guide*. Also, within the *Guide* are vocabulary sections to help introduce students to the language of mathematics and the words that they will encounter in problem-solving situations throughout their lives.

Teachers also have the ability to access the computerized Resource Database that allows them to match quality materials available to the teacher, including literature, to their students' needs through the use of the prescription program. The Math Problem Generator (MPG) program allows teachers to create problems or reviews for individual students or small groups, adding to the commercial materials available in each center.

HOSTS Spanish Language Arts Learning Center Program

HOSTS Spanish Language Arts is a structured mentoring program in language arts. The program targets students in grades K-3 who speak little or no English and read little or no Spanish. Modeled after the successful HOSTS Language Arts Program, the Spanish program is developmental, diagnostic, prescriptive, and individualized. Using a rich array of colorful manipulatives and Spanish literature, blended with the best techniques for language arts instruction, Spanish Language Arts bathes the child in Hispanic culture and language while building the foundation to rapidly learn to read English.

HOSTS Spanish Language Arts matches students with trained bilingual parent, business and community volunteer mentors who work to strengthen the students' reading, writing, vocabulary development, and critical-thinking skills. Mentors provide role models of successful bilingual people who motivate, support and provide individual student attention.

Each student in the program is assessed using HOSTS Spanish assessments. Based on the assessment results and input from the regular classroom teacher, a personalized plan is developed for each child that includes literature, vocabulary, objective reinforcement, writing, and critical thinking. The HOSTS Database then identifies and prints a list of specific resources that match the student's reading level, interest level, and learning style with supplemental resources available on site. At the end of the session, the mentor makes comments in the folder about the lesson.

Most importantly, the Spanish-speaking student learns that he or she can learn to read. This confidence gained in Spanish can then be transitioned into learning English much earlier than is normally accomplished. HOSTS Spanish Language Arts includes assessment, reinforcement, literature selections, core vocabulary, alphabet activities, and activities to reinforce basic reading skills. These materials are provided in both English and Spanish so that students can flip flop between the two languages when it is appropriate.

Contact

Chad R. Woolery
1349 Empire Central, Suite 520
Dallas, TX 75247
Voice: (214) 905-1308 or (888) 380-9117
Fax: (214) 905-1176
cwoolery@.hostscorp.com
www.hostscorp,com

Higher Order Thinking Skills (HOTS)

Higher Order Thinking Skills (HOTS) is an award-winning, special thinking skills program designed for Title I and mildly impaired, learning disabled students in grades 4 to 8. The Higher Order Thinking Skills program is being used successfully in approximately 2,000 schools.

The Higher Order Thinking Skills Project treats these students as gifted and replaces all existing special services provided to them. Instead of reteaching the information the students did not previously learn, HOTS provides the types of thinking skills that students need to learn classroom content the first time it is taught. The intellectually challenging and stimulating HOTS activities simultaneously accelerate a wide variety of abilities and learning. Higher Order Thinking Skills students make dramatic gains in thinking and social interaction skills while substantially outperforming national averages for basic skill gains in reading and math. Nearly 15 percent of the students previously identified as Title I make the school honor roll.

The Title I, Higher Order Thinking Skills Project is an alternative approach to Title I for grades 4 to 8 in which the compensatory services consist solely of systematically designed higher-order thinking activities. Traditional drill and practice activities and content instruction are eliminated. The two years of thinking activities are designed to generate the gains in basic skills expected from Title I programs, while also improving thinking ability and social confidence. By learning how to learn, students are able to learn content the first time it is taught in the classroom. The program is conducted in a computer lab, with a detailed curriculum and a teacher trained in Socratic dialogue techniques. The curriculum is designed in accordance with information processing theories of cognition.

Higher Order Thinking Skills has been a member of the National Diffusion network since 1988. During that time, the approach has remained the same, but the methods have been refined as a result of additional experience and research. In addition, newer technology has been incorporated, and it is currently available for Windows and Macintosh computers. Additionally, there are also some schoolwide elements and options, and some activities for parents.

Higher Order Thinking Skills is one of the programs recommended by The Northwest Regional Education Laboratories, The Mid-Atlantic Regional Education Laboratory at Temple University, and the STAR Center in Texas. It is a creative program designed to build the thinking skills of educationally disadvantaged students in grades 4 to 8. It combines the use of computers, drama, Socratic dialogue, and a detailed curriculum to stimulate thinking processes.

Program, Instructional, and Curricular Initiatives 81

Computers are not used to present content, but rather to intrigue students and get them involved. Drama, in the form of teacher playacting—sometimes in costume—also stimulates students' interest and curiosity. Some days the teacher may present a lesson as a mysterious situation for which the students' help is needed. However, HOTS is foremost a program built on Socratic dialogue, creative and logical conversation between teacher and students. While most teachers ask simple questions of educationally disadvantaged students and are content with one-word responses. Higher Order Thinking Skills teachers are trained to ask questions that require students to explain and elaborate their answers at length. The combination of detailed training, curriculum, and software form a complete system which enables this sophisticated form of instruction to be consistently effective on a large scale.

At first, most students are resistant to expressing their ideas. The computer helps overcome this resistance by building a bridge between the familiar passive visual learning offered by television; and the active verbal learning expected in HOTS and the regular classroom. It provides an interactive means for students to test their ideas before verbalizing them. Over time, the teacher's expectations, combined with interesting program activities, result in a highly conversational environment in which students begin to discover that they are good at thinking and explaining ideas. With this confidence, they embrace intellectual challenges rather than run from them; and most will agree that embracing intellectual challenges enhances children's social, emotional, and academic development.

The HOTS curriculum consists of detailed, 35-minute, daily lessons that coordinate computer activities with class conversations. It is designed to ensure that teachers ask the kinds of questions that enhance brain development and thinking skills. The HOTS learning activities involve tasks that are complex but fun, and students' success at these tasks leads to their realization that thinking and persevering can accomplish the seemingly impossible; and though the HOTS program is a pullout divorced from the formal classroom curriculum, there is a surprising transfer of success to basic learning—as well as to thinking skills and classroom grades.

Program Logistics

- HOTS requires a very good teacher. A weak teacher simply cannot be successful. The pedagogical techniques are very sophisticated. (The ideal teacher is someone who is very bright, energetic, flexible yet organized, and who, above all, loves to get kids to talk. A computer background is not needed.)

- Teacher/pupil/computer ratios

    A teacher can handle up to about 10 students at a time with 10 computers. A teacher and paraprofessional can handle up to 12–14 students at a time with 12–14 computers. Other pupil:teacher ratios with various combinations of personnel can be considered; e.g., for schools wishing to use HOTS as a schoolwide model. Higher Order Thinking Skills project staff will assist in identifying other possible combinations.

- Student selection

    While HOTS helps the vast majority of Title I and learning disabled students, some need other forms of help. Selection guidelines are provided.

- Student scheduling

    When used during the school day, elementary school students should be scheduled for at least 40 minutes per day, 4–5 days per week for 2 years. Middle school students should be scheduled 1 period per day (at least 35 minutes) for a time period of 1½–2 years. In an after-school setting, students should be served from 2 to 4 times per week for a total of 150 minutes per week.

- Students should ideally be kept in the program for 1½–2 years, even if they test out at the end of the first year. (This recommendation is made in keeping with the Title I guidelines.) Extra time in the program often allows students to automate their new problem solving skills. First and second year HOTS students should be in separate classes. However, appropriately selected Title I and learning disabled students can be served together.

Contact

Laurie Dagostino
The HOTS Program
Education Innovation
PO Box 42620
Tucson, AZ 85733
Voice: (520) 795-2143
Fax: (520) 795-8837
info@hots.org
www.hots.org

International Youth Leadership Institute (IYLI)

The International Youth Leadership Institute (IYLI) helps African-American and Latino high school students contribute to their community and to the broader society. IYLI is cosponsored by the Institute for Urban and Minority Education at Teachers College, Columbia University, and the International Youth Leadership Fund, an affiliate of the Phelps-Stokes Fund.

The International Youth Leadership Institute conducts academic, cultural, and leadership development programs that focus on local and international issues. These programs include seminars, community service, and study in Africa and Latin America. The International Youth Leadership Institute Fellows also utilize the Institute to network with other youth leaders and to explore and pursue post secondary and career opportunities.

Seminars Program

Biweekly seminars focus on current, global issues. Additionally, they increase Fellows' knowledge of foreign affairs and their relevance to local conditions and challenges. During these sessions, Fellows acquire an informed perspective on foreign and public policy using a framework of history, culture, geography, and environment. Placing global phenomena in context, rather than seeing them as abstract or isolated events, affords a deeper understanding of local and international challenges. Through these seminars, Fellows:

- Develop critical thinking, problem solving and communication skills;
- Exchange viewpoints, ideas, and resources with peers who share their interests and initiative; and
- Meet and interact with role models in business, education, international relations, and public policy.

Community Service and Development Program

The Community Service and Development Program (CSDP) allows Fellows to directly apply their knowledge of global issues and their developing leadership skills in a variety of structured settings. They gain firsthand knowledge of important social concerns while simultaneously providing a valuable service to several of New York City's many community-based organizations.

Fellows also create a *service project* in cooperation with their placement supervisor. The project incorporates each Fellow's own vision for change while addressing the needs of the community. Fellows also participate in CSDP for a minimum numbers of hours per week. After successfully completing the program, Fellows receive an honorarium.

Opportunities for Overseas Study Through IYLF

The International Youth Leadership Fund sponsors two overseas study programs. These programs provide firsthand, cross-cultural experiences that broaden students' knowledge of community development and international issues. Fellows play a significant role in the programs by facilitating seminars and workshops. They also complete research projects that incorporate interviews and observations of the daily fabric of life. Both programs emphasize how history, culture, geography, and environment have influenced the development of the host nation.

Each winter IYLF conducts the Winter Institute, a week-long, Spanish language immersion program conducted in a Latin American country. Previous programs and themes have included: Dominican Republic—Agriculture and Rural Development; and Mexico—Olmec Culture of Pre-Colombian America

During the summer, IYLF offers the Summer Fellowship Program, a month-long study program in Africa. Students investigate modern and traditional aspects of Africa as reflected in the cities and villages, markets and museums, and through immersion in a rural setting. Students meet with youth and professionals working in government, business, education, and international development.

Contact

Sandra Epps
The International Youth Leadership Institute
Box 11
Teachers College, Colombia University
New York City, NY 10027
Phone (212) 678-3295
Fax: (212) 678-4137

Mathematics, Engineering, Science Achievement (MESA)

Background

Mathematics, Engineering, Science Achievement (MESA) is one of the country's oldest and best-known programs. It produces highly trained technological professionals to enter the workforce and assume leading positions in industry. MESA has been profiled in Science magazine as one of the top programs in the nation that is successfully producing science professionals of color. The program, established in 1970, serves educationally disadvantaged students and, to the extent possible by law, emphasizes participation by students from groups with low eligibility rates for four-year colleges. MESA works with over 21,000 students throughout California from elementary through university levels. MESA is funded by the state legislature, corporate contributions, and various grants. It is a program of the University of California. MESA activities involve students in a rigorous enrichment environment that includes MESA classes, academic advising, peer group learning, career exploration, parent involvement, and other services for students from elementary school through the college level.

The MESA Schools Program (MSP) oversees 19 centers that serve close to 400 elementary, junior and senior high schools. The MESA Success Through Collaboration (MESA STC) Program operates at 12 sites to bring MESA to rural and urban-based American Indian students. The MESA California Community College Program (CCCP) is located on 11 campuses, geared to increase the number of math, engineering, and science majors who successfully transfer to and receive degrees from four-year institutions. The MESA Engineering Program (MEP) supports engineering and computer science students in 23 California colleges and universities.

The success rate of MESA students is outstanding. Over 90 percent of MESA high school graduates in 1996-97 went on to a college or university; in the same year, MEP students comprised 90 percent of California's underrepresented students who attained bachelor degrees in engineering. And over a five-year period, MESA's community college program has produced nearly 90 percent of the underrepresented students who successfully transferred from 11 community colleges to four-year institutions and majored in science, engineering, or math.

MESA's success is based on an active partnership with parents, industry, and educators. This active partnership enables MESA to effect positive change for educationally disadvantaged students and their communities to contribute to the technological needs of California's economy, and to offer insights into education reform efforts—all of which are valuable contributions that extend far beyond the number of students directly served by the program.

Meeting the Needs of Students, Parents, and Communities

MESA is not remedial. It poses a rigorous set of academic standards and challenges students to meet them. The program is open to all educationally disadvantaged students interested in math and science who are willing to work hard and aim for college. MESA is the first opportunity for many students to shake off the low achiever label and begin to seriously consider higher education as part of their future.

In many local communities, MESA has set off a chain reaction of achievement. The program offers role models of local students who, through hard work, have become successes. Many of these students are the first in their family—and community—to attend college. These students provide inspiration for younger brothers and sisters, as well as neighbors and friends, to aspire to higher education.

A key ingredient for this success is parent involvement, especially on the precollege level. Many parents want to support their children but do not know how to do so, particularly if they have limited educational backgrounds themselves. MESA shows parents how to encourage academic achievement, explains the importance of college, and offers different ways to overcome financial barriers. These activities help parents increase their involvement in the education system. MESA is planning to expand its model of parent involvement to groups throughout the state, thus positively affecting thousands more families.

Meeting the Needs of Industry

From electronics to aerospace to agriculture, California's technology-based industries have always required a highly educated workforce. As industry is confronted with increasing competitive challenges on a global level, this need for well-trained technological professionals, especially those familiar with diverse cultures and languages, grows even more urgent.

MESA's rigorous academic training has established the program as a well-known source for such a labor pool. Companies realize that MESA alumni are not only academically prepared to take leading roles in technological fields, but are trained to integrate quickly into the corporate environment. They value how MESA teaches students to work within a collaborative team—a skill not often taught in academia but sought by companies to gain a competitive edge.

The program's demand for individual achievement has created an orientation among MESA graduates to constantly seek self-improvement and find creative answers to difficult challenges. Industry needs professionals with such an approach who can learn to harness rapidly-changing technology.

Because of these attributes, companies look toward MESA as a rich source of reliable and hard-working interns who will fully use their experience to learn from—and produce results for—their sponsor. They realize that internships and summer job experiences with MESA students are efficient methods of early recruitment for the most promising graduates.

Companies also recognize how MESA is changing the environment in many low-income communities and in education. They encourage their employees to become MESA volunteers because they will make a difference. Industry representatives who help students with math or science projects, judge competitions, speak to a classroom of students, or serve on advisory boards, all contribute to MESA's broader effort.

Industry has long recognized that participation in MESA results in a win-win situation for everyone involved. Students have a chance to attain an early introduction to career options and role models, and also have an opportunity to observe professionals conducting real-life applications of math and science concepts. Industry is given a chance to identify promising new employees whose diverse backgrounds and technological preparedness enhance a company's competitive edge.

In 1978, a major initiative to garner industry support for MESA was launched by presidents and board chairs of nationally prestigious corporations including ARCO, Bechtel, Chevron, Fluor, Hewlett-Packard, Lockheed, Northrop, PG&E, Pacific Bell, Rockwell, Southern California Edison, and TRW. Since then, industry support for MESA has continued to expand, representing such fields as computer technology, communications and aerospace.

Meeting the Needs of Teachers and Educational Institutions

More and more educators are using MESA to reshape the teaching environment in entire school districts. MESA teachers receive special training that they use to benefit all students, not just MESA students. In other activities, teachers (mostly from schools with high numbers of disadvantaged or underrepresented students) who receive training then teach other educators, creating a ripple effect whereby all math and science teachers from their school districts ultimately benefit from MESA.

Student Service Components

MESA operates four student service components that provide academic support for students enrolled in elementary through university levels.

- ♦ The Mathematics, Engineering, Science Achievement Schools Program (MSP) provides support for precollege students at elementary, junior, and senior high schools. A new effort, the MESA Agriculture Initiative introduces rural precollege students to high-tech opportunities in agriculture. Elements of the MSP model include:

  - Individual Academic Plans (IAPs) so MESA counselors can monitor individual student progress;

  - Academic Excellence Workshops where students are scheduled in core classes and taught how to maintain high academic standards through group study;

  - MESA periods provide regular designated time during the school day for MESA advisors (usually math or science teachers) to implement The New MESA Model components;

  - SAT/PSAT preparation for MESA students

  - Study skills training so students at all levels learn the most effective techniques for academic achievement;

  - MESA Day where students compete for awards in hands-on math, science, and English activities at local and regional levels;

  - Career and college exploration through field trips to industry and college sites, opportunities to hear guest speakers from industry, and so forth;

  - Incentive awards where students receive cash and noncash awards for outstanding academic achievement, participation, and leadership;

  - Parent leadership training where parents learn how to become effective advocates for their children's academic success; and

  - Extracurricular intensives including Saturday Academies and activities between sessions (for year-round schools) to stimulate excitement for mathematics, science and academic achievement.

- MESA Success Through Collaboration (MESA STC) was established in 1991 as a partnership with American Indian tribes and educators to reach students located in remote rural areas as well as in urban centers.

  MESA Success Through Collaboration includes organized group study, academic enrichment, academic and financial aid advising, career exploration, teacher training, and family involvement. Success Through Collaboration also provides culturally relevant activities based on traditional American Indian concerns such as preservation of the environment and respect for nature.

- MESA Engineering Program (MEP) provides support to university-level students enrolled in colleges of engineering and computer science. Elements of the MEP model include:
  - Student Study Center, a dedicated, multipurpose space which serves as a home away from home, where MEP students can study;
  - Academic Excellence Workshops where students are scheduled in core classes, including labs, and taught how to maintain high academic standards through group study;
  - Clustering, where students are bunched in core math classes with the same instructor in the same course sections so they can study and review the material more effectively;
  - Orientation courses for freshmen and transfers that immediately establish close contact with incoming students to instruct them about college survival as engineering/computer science majors and to help students bond;
  - Career advising for students to learn specifics about engineering fields; field trips, job shadowing exercises and links to mentors are available to students;
  - Links with student organizations like the American Indian Science and Engineering Society (AISES), National Society of Black Engineers (NSBE), Society of Hispanic Professional Engineers (SHPE) and Society of Women Engineers (SWE), professional organizations whose members act as mentors and guest speakers and who offer industry tours;

- Professional development workshops that include résumé preparation, interview skills, development of part-time, full-time, and summer employment, and mock job fairs;

- Industry advisory board, a valuable connection between students and the industry leaders who may later hire them, through which industry participates directly to the program's success; the board provides scholarships, offers special summer internships, hosts field trips, and contributes resources; and

- Personal advising to address the non-academic issues that may interfere with students' schooling.

♦ MESA California Community College Program (CCCP), established in 1991 and greatly expanded in 1993, is based on the MEP model and offers many of the same elements to community college students including a freshman orientation class, a study center, clustering, Academic Excellence workshops, and professional development opportunities. The CCCP also provides important support to assist math or science majors to successfully transfer to four-year institutions. Future plans include strengthening links between CCCP and MEP Centers to provide additional support to transfer students.

Contact

Michael Aldaco
Mathematics, Engineering, Science Achievement
University of California
300 Lakeside Drive, 7th floor
Oakland, CA 94612-3550
Voice: (510) 987-9337
Fax: (510) 763-4704
michael.aldaco@ucop.edu
www.mesa.edu

The (Ronald E.) McNair Program

Program Description

The Ronald E. McNair Program is one of the many programs sponsored by the United States Department of Education. Because the author is most familiar with the Ronald E. McNair Program at California State University, Fresno, this critique highlights that program. For more information about The Ronald E. McNair Program, contact the United States Department of Education or the staff at California State University, Fresno. The phone numbers and addresses are listed at the end of this critique.

The Ronald E. McNair Post-Baccalaureate Achievement Program is a program designed to encourage low-income individuals who are first-generation college students and/or traditionally underrepresented in graduate education to pursue doctoral study. The McNair Program, funded by the U.S. Department of Education, proposes to motivate and prepare promising undergraduate students for graduate study. Named for the *Challenger* space shuttle crew member, the Ronald E. McNair Program serves as a living memorial to a man who overcame seemingly insurmountable odds to be awarded his Ph.D. in physics and to later realize his dream of becoming an astronaut for NASA.

At California State University, Fresno, Ronald E. McNair Scholars commit to a calendar-year involvement. The McNair Program is divided into four components:

- One-week Winter Interim Session of orientation to the McNair Program and to graduate study;
- Spring Semester Lecture and Meeting Series for McNair Scholars designed to enhance knowledge about graduate school requirements and to refine research skills;
- A ten-week paid Summer Research Project under the guidance of a faculty mentor at California State University, Fresno; and
- Fall semester followup geared toward the completion and filing of graduate school applications.

As a result of participating in the McNair Program, McNair Scholars gain:

- Demonstrable research skills;
- Valuable knowledge about graduate education and how to access it;

- Increased chances of applying for and being successful in doctoral study;

- Familiarity with the research environment of a major university; and

- A supportive network of scholarly professionals and peers.

McNair Scholars are responsible for the completion of a carefully planned research assignment for which they will receive a stipend of $2,400 to defray costs of participation in various activities of the program. Upon completion of the program, McNair Scholars continue to enjoy access to McNair seminars, lectures, and assistance with the graduate application process.

The Ronald E. McNair Program at California State University, Fresno, benefits from the joint-sponsorship of the Division of Graduate Studies and the Division of Student Affairs. The facilities of both offices are made available to McNair Scholars to ensure their continued educational advancement. McNair Scholars are entitled to special publications of the Graduate Studies Office and are alerted to funding opportunities and potential contacts in graduate education. In addition, McNair Scholars benefit from student support services offered through the Division of Student Affairs, such as counseling, career development, reentry, and disabled student services.

Eligibility Requirements

- Applicants must be either low-income individuals who are first-generation college students, and/or members of a group traditionally underrepresented in doctoral education as defined by the U.S. Department of Education. Applicants must have completed 60 academic units. Applicants must be enrolled at CSU, Fresno as full-time students.

- Applicants must have a minimum cumulative GPA of 2.75.

- Applicants must be U.S. citizens or permanent residents of the United States.

- Applicants must be considering graduate study.

Selection is made on a competitive basis from those applicants who best meet the purposes of the program as defined by the U.S. Department of Education. Specifically, two-thirds of the individuals participating in the McNair project must be low-income individuals who are first-generation college students. No more than 10 percent of the participants can be enrolled in a graduate program of study at the time of their participation in the McNair project. Applicants who meet the federally-mandated guidelines are selected on the basis of having the greatest potential for pursuing doctoral studies.

Awards and Benefits

McNair Scholars will:

- Be matched with a faculty mentor whose research interests resemble those of the student.

- Participate in a ten week summer research project under the direction of a faculty mentor from approximately June 1 through August 10.

- Receive a $2,400 stipend for participation in the McNair Program.

- Write an abstract and paper based on summer research findings that will be published in the *McNair Scholars' Journal* and presented at the annual McNair Research Symposium.

- Be eligible for individualized tutorial assistance.

- Attend seminars designed to introduce participants to the nature of graduate education, and to successful role models who have obtained doctoral degrees.

- Attend workshops on research skills, the graduate school application process, Graduate Record Examination preparation, and resources for funding graduate education.

- Receive assistance in defining, setting, and realizing educational goals, as well as in applying to graduate programs of choice.

- Benefit from a supportive network of McNair Scholars, who are working toward a graduate degree.

- Have the opportunity to attend a professional meeting or conference with faculty mentor or to visit selected institutions for research purposes with faculty mentor.

- Benefit from ongoing support from faculty mentors and program staff dedicated to ensuring student advancement.

Contact

For more information about the Ronald E. McNair Program at California State University, Fresno:

>Millie Byers
>Ronald E. McNair Program
>Division of Graduate Studies and Division of Student Affairs
>Lab School Building, Rm137
>5048 N Jackson Ave., M/S 67
>Fresno, CA 93740-8022
>Voice: (559) 278-2946
>Fax: (559) 278-7460
>mcnair_csuf@csufresno.edu

For more information about the Ronald E. McNair Program:

>United States Department of Education
>600 Independence Avenue, SW
>The Portals Building, Suite 600D
>Washington, DC 20202-5249
>Voice: (202) 708-4804

MegaSkills

Background

The need for school/family involvement to enable children to achieve has never been greater. At the same time, schools are challenged as never before to accomplish more with diminishing resources and to work more closely with families and communities. The nonprofit Home and School Institute is committed to meeting these needs. The unique dimension of the MegaSkills Process is that it develops the synergistic educational relationships between the school and the home in support of all children's achievement. Uniting the head and the heart—that's what makes this program truly different.

MegaSkills Workshops have been successfully conducted for over 100,000 families including African-American, Hispanic, Native American, Pacific-American, newly arrived immigrants, and at-risk families. Materials are available in Spanish. Activities for families to do with their children are in easy to read format, take 15–20 minutes to do, and cost little or no money. Materials are culturally sensitive and increase positive parent-child interaction in all groups. Home learning activities are provided across the grades from pre-K to secondary school.

MegaSkills have been called the *inner engines of learning*. They are the qualities, skills, and attitudes needed for success in school and beyond. The 11 MegaSkills—Confidence; Motivation; Effort; Responsibility; Initiative; Perseverance; Caring; Teamwork; Common Sense; Problem Solving; and Focus—have been identified by Dr. Dorothy Rich, President of The Home and School Institute (HSI), in her book *MegaSkills*. They are based on the study of report cards, personnel records, and interviews with educators and employers.

A MegaSkills school uses the MegaSkills Training Programs to increase academic achievement and build school performance. The school identifies specific goals in areas such as reduced discipline incidents, fewer tardies, increased parent involvement, and increased student performance on a number of academic achievement indicators. Becoming a MegaSkills school is a two-year process, with increasing levels of excellence. To date, there are MegaSkills schools in California, Kentucky, Ohio, and Texas. Developing children's MegaSkills both in the classroom and the home creates a mutually reinforcing system with the potential for exponentially increased impact beyond what either component can accomplish independently. It ensures that every child experiences MegaSkills.

Becoming a MegaSkills school involves four synergistic components:

- The classroom component—MegaSkills Essentials for the Classroom Program.

- The parent component—the MegaSkills Parent Workshop Program.

- The adult to adult partnership component—the New MegaSkills Bond Program.

- The MegaSkills Environment—a schoolwide system including *achievement goals* based upon the individual school's needs, strengths, and challenges.

Over 10,000 registrants have completed MegaSkills training. Programs are now being conducted in 3,000 schools in 48 states. They are reaching families from diverse cultural, economic, and social backgrounds. The numbers grow daily.

Data from the field show that participation in the MegaSkills Program results in higher student interest in school, higher attendance, higher academic achievement, increased parent involvement, and a significant extension of learning time beyond the school day.

Program Benefits

- Students like school more, spend more time on learning, spend more time on homework, are more motivated to learn, receive better *effort* or *citizenship* grades, enjoy more quality time with their parents, and experience more success in academics.

- Parents develop better parenting skills, gain a deeper understanding of their children's educational strengths and needs, enjoy a better relationship with their children, and feel empowered to be more active in their children's education.

- Teachers have fewer classroom discipline problems, are able to spend more time on tasks, find more children prepared and ready to learn, and experience more positive communication with students and parents.

- Principals report fewer individual discipline incidents, better attendance, increased parent involvement, better school/parent/community relations, higher effort or citizenship grades, and academic gains over base-line performance on a number of academic achievement indicators.

MegaSkills Leader Training Program

MegaSkills Leader Training is a comprehensive, one- or two-day training for teachers, administrators, community leaders, and parents.

- Training includes discussion related to parent involvement research, content for all workshops, presentation skills development, management of the program, how-to's for recruiting families and maintaining the program, and home learning activities for family use. Participants work in small study groups and demonstrate content and presentation techniques. Action plans are discussed and developed. Only persons receiving training may conduct workshops. The two-day MegaSkills Leader Training for Parent Involvement provides full demonstrations and extended modeling of the workshops for working with adults.

- Materials provided to each participant include:
  - *MegaSkills* book by Dr. Dorothy Rich, and
  - *Leader Training Handbook* (192 pages): contents include presentation materials for 11 workshops; program management information; suggestions for working with the media; reproducible, grade-coded, Home Learning Activities for families; evaluation forms; leader skills development materials; and on-loan videos. All materials are available in Spanish.

- Technical Assistance from HSI is provided through forms, phone calls, and e-mail. With a special Personal Identification Number (PIN), clients may visit the Web site (www.MegaSkillsHSI.org) for continuing communication among workshop leaders at different sites.

A major advantage of the MegaSkills program is that workshop leaders, after receiving the training, have a complete program to present throughout their local communities, in schools, community centers, churches, and businesses. Field experience demonstrates that individuals, including teachers, administrators, and parents, with varying backgrounds and levels of experience, are effective workshop leaders using this program. The leaders, by providing a quality parent involvement program, initiate positive change for families, and build personal growth for themselves.

MegaSkills Essentials

MegaSkills Essentials provides a full curriculum and one-day training program designed directly for classroom use. It grows from the needs expressed by teachers across the country and is keyed to a unique combination of academic and character building learning objectives. Those objectives are:

- To introduce students to a new approach designed to develop strong study skills and good work habits.

- To stimulate student creative thinking for the classroom and the home.

- To extend children's reading and writing interests inside and outside the classroom.

- To build student self-discipline in coping with pressures, making individual choices, and building a strong value system—key determinants in preventing at-risk situations for children.

Data reveals that teachers recognize a positive change in the atmosphere of the classroom; the increased ability of children to be self-disciplined; and an inclination on behalf of the children to use MegaSkills for managing their own behavior. Principals report increased student achievement and decreased discipline problems.

MegaSkills Essentials Training

- Training

  Topics include presentations on MegaSkills, demonstrations of classroom sessions, integration of the academic/multiple intelligence MegaSkills activities into the classroom curriculum, instruction in the teaching and management of the program, evaluation, connections with the family, and problem-solving strategies. Participants work in small study groups to discuss and develop curriculum adaptations and integrations. Action plans are developed. Only persons receiving this training conduct this program.

- Materials provided to each participant include

  - *MegaSkills* book by Dr. Dorothy Rich, and

  - *MegaSkills Curriculum Handbook* (160 pages): contents include the MegaSkills curriculum for lower and upper grades; reproducible handouts for classroom use; program management information; activities for families; evaluation forms; curriculum adaptations and integrations; additional resources for class and home use; supplementary materials; and on-loan videos. All materials are available in Spanish.

- Technical Assistance from HSI is provided through feedback forms, phone calls, and e-mail. Clients may visit the Web site (www.MegaSkillsHSI.org) for problem-solving and ongoing communication among teachers at different sites.

The MegaSkills curriculum can be used in a variety of ways: as discrete sessions for teaching individual MegaSkills and/or as a curriculum segment to be integrated into the total instructional program. The MegaSkills classroom program has been specifically designed to provide activities in different subject areas so that teachers can simultaneously teach MegaSkills and reading, language arts, science, math, and critical thinking.

MegaSkills Bond Training

This one-day training from HSI translates national education goals and mandates into practical action for educators and parent leaders working together.

- Training provides background on issues, legislative mandates, focus on Goals 2000 strategies for designing family school/home involvement compacts, annual plan policies, exploring and coordinating community resources for new partnerships, small study sessions to design action plans and create parent/community involvement components. Participants attend these training sessions in school teams and are permitted to use the course materials with other teachers at their own schools upon completion of the training.

- Materials provided include
  - *The New MegaSkills Bond* book by Dr. Dorothy Rich, and
  - *MegaSkills Connections Training Handbook* (120 pages): contents include information about group communication strategies and decision making; school improvement plans; compacts; annual plans; and suggestions regarding the coordination of community resources.

- Technical Assistance from HSI is provided through feedback forms, phone calls, and e-mail. Clients may visit the Web site (www.Mega SkillsHSI.org). for ongoing communication among participants from the same and different sites.

MegaSkills Parent and Classroom Programs

The New MegaSkills Bond can be provided as a separate training or in conjunction with other programs. The new training, which incorporates the requirements of new legislation, outlines and activates the new partnerships that must be developed in education today. The MegaSkills Bond Program is ideal for site-based management and school improvement programs.

Research Findings

Parent Involvement Program

Schools using the MegaSkills Workshop consistently report that students benefit from having their parents become more involved in their education. Memphis State University (1990) research found:

- Homework time: number of children spending six hours a week on homework doubled, while those spending less than one hour decreased.

- Television time: average time children spent watching television during the school week decreased. Time not spent watching television was spent on homework.

- Parent/child time: average time parents spent with children each day increased.

The Austin, Texas Independent School District (1991-92) found that PreK-6 students whose parents attended MegaSkills Workshops received higher scores on statewide achievement tests, posed fewer discipline problems, and had higher attendance rates.

Data from a 1996 study conducted by the University of Louisville, Kentucky revealed that the first MegaSkills School (Maupin Elementary School) funded under a grant from the U.S. Department of Education Learning Choice Magnet Program showed these positive results:

- Strong agreement among school staff (90 percent of the staff and 100 percent of the parents workshop leaders) that the program has improved school climate and work environment
- Raised the expectations of students the school over the two-year pilot period.
- Increased the involvement of parents in activities and attendance at parent-teacher conferences.
- Teachers and parents indicated that students had developed more positive work behaviors and attitudes.

Classroom Program

The previously cited study which was conducted in 1996 at Maupin Elementary School also found that after the program had been in effect for two years, a high percentage of teachers identified:

- Student behavior and attitude gains, including more responsibility in doing school work;
- Fewer discipline problems; and
- Students were more able to work cooperatively.

Similar results were obtained at the A. N. Rico School in Waco, Texas, and the Emerson-Bandini School in San Diego, California (1996-ongoing), where the program has been in effect for one and two years, respectively. Both these schools serve predominantly Hispanic-American students, including many with limited English proficiency.

Test scores on the Texas Assessment Skills (TAAS) increased considerably at the Rico School in grades three and four after the program had been in operation for only one year (1998). Dramatic gains were made at the third-grade level, which the school staff had chosen for special program emphasis. The number of children passing the reading test in 1997-98 rose to 91 percent from 69 percent in 1996-97. The number passing the math test rose to 95 percent in 1997-98 from 75 percent in 1996-97.

A large-scale study of the implementation and impact of the MegaSkills parent involvement program in 25 schools in Broward County, Florida, and in 14 schools in San Diego, California, is underway. This study will analyze achievement data of students whose parents substantially participated in the parent involvement workshop program.

Funding Support for MegaSkills Programs

Compensatory Education Funds including Title I, Title II, Drug and Dropout Prevention, Vocational Education, Head Start, Even Start, Special Education, Bilingual Education, Migrant Education, and Staff Development are among funds used to pay for these MegaSkills training programs. Members of the business community are increasingly interested in supporting these programs.

Contact

Harriet Stonehill
The MegaSkills Education Center of the Home and School Institute
1500 Massachusetts Avenue, NW
Washington, DC 20005
Voice: (202) 466-3633
Fax: (202) 833-1400
HSIDRA@erols.com
www.MegaSkillsHSI.org

Parent Expectations Support Achievement (PESA)

Philosophy

Parent Expectations Support Achievement (PESA) is a family-oriented program that recognizes the parent as the leader in the home. Within the role as primary educator, the parent establishes expectations for their children. Parents' expectations help form their children's behavior. Expectations for achievement and high standards support children's success at home and at school. Parent Expectations Support Achievement interactions strengthen the bond between parent and child by creating an emotionally safe, mutually respectful, and caring home environment.

Parent Expectations Support Achievement is built on the belief that all children are highly valued members of society. Children model behaviors they learn from watching those around them. Children's behavior changes when parents' behavior changes. Parent Expectations Support Achievement is family-oriented, but it is the parents' behaviors that are transformed. Children, in turn, reflect those positive changes.

Background

Parent Expectations Support Achievement is the companion program to the nationally recognized, teacher staff development, program known as Teacher Expectations and Student Achievement (TESA). TESA has influenced a generation of teachers to hold high expectations for all their students. Research indicates that teachers who have been trained in TESA skills reflect classrooms of academic achievement, safety, care, and equity.

Parent Expectations Support Achievement provides a link between home and an effective transition to school by creating a consistent environment which supports children's achievements. The interactions taught in the PESA program reinforce the successful classroom practices taught to teachers in the TESA program.

Parent Expectations Support Achievement (PESA) is a powerful parent education program designed to offer opportunities for parents to meet and share family experiences while learning parenting communication skills. These skills, called interactions, build on parents' strengths to help them become even more effective care givers. The PESA program is available in English, Spanish, Mandarin, and Korean.

Program Description

Parent Expectations Support Achievement is a parent education program based on the belief that parent's expectations are the greatest predictor of their children's achievement, relationships, and ultimate success. Parent Expectations Support Achievement helps parents become actively involved with their children's achievement by establishing high expectations and building strong family bonds.

Parent Expectations Support Achievement creates a link between home and school through the development of a consistent environment which leads to achievement. Parent Expectations Support Achievement reflects the same interactions used in successful classrooms around the nation and provides the all-important connection between home and effective transition to school.

PESA Parent Workshops

The PESA program teaches parents and caregivers 15 interactions to improve communication with their children. These interactions help parents develop and support their children's academic achievement, social skills, and self-esteem.

Parents with children of all ages meet in groups of 10 to 12 for six sessions. Each session lasts about two hours. Anyone who has the responsibility for caring for children may be a part of the group—parents, grandparents, extended family, and caregivers.

At the first session, an overview of the program is presented. At each of the following five sessions, three interactions are discussed. During the time between the sessions, parents are expected to practice the interactions at home with each of their children. A handbook is provided to record significant experiences while using the interactions. Parents choose a partner from the group to provide practice, feedback, and support throughout the training. PESA workshops are offered through schools, community agencies, and businesses.

PESA Facilitators

Parent Expectations Support Achievement parent workshops are cofacilitated by a professional educator and a parent or other school district designee. The professional may be anyone with a background in education, counseling, health, human services, or other appropriate fields. The parent-facilitator may be anyone who enthusiastically embraces the PESA philosophy. Facilitator trainings are offered in English and Spanish by the Los Angeles County Office of Education.

Program Costs

The Los Angeles County Office of Education provides two-day facilitator trainings to prepare individuals to conduct Parent Expectations Support Achievement parent workshops. A registration fee of $275 per person, or $250 for teams of two or more, covers the cost of the training, the Facilitator Handbook, and instructional video. Trainings and materials are available in English, Spanish, Korean, and Mandarin. Trainings are held monthly at the Los Angeles County Office of Education. A training may be scheduled at a local site with 20 or more participants.

Parent Expectations Support Achievement Parent Handbooks are needed for each parent in the workshops and must be purchased from the Los Angeles County Office of Education. Handbooks are available in English, Spanish, Mandarin, and Korean. Parent Expectations Support Achievement kits are available for $299.95 and include 12 parent handbooks, pens, PESA lapel pins, PESA magnets, and graduation certificates. A kit includes all instructional materials for 12 parents. Handbooks may be purchased individually for $25.00. Discounts are given for orders of five or more kits. Materials may not be duplicated and are protected by copyright.

Contact

Anita Miller, Ph.D., Project Director
TESA/PESA Programs
Los Angeles County Office of Education
9300 Imperial Highway, Room 246
Downey, CA 90242-2890
Voice: (800) 566-6651 or (562) 922-6665
Fax: (562) 922-6699
Miller_Anita@lacoe.edu
www.lacoe.edu/pesa_home.html

Project Zero

Mission

Project Zero's mission is to understand and enhance learning, thinking, and creativity in the arts and other disciplines for individuals and institutions.

Background

Harvard Project Zero, a research group at the Harvard Graduate School of Education, has investigated the development of learning processes in children, adults, and organizations for over 32 years. Today, Project Zero is building on this research to help create communities of reflective, independent learners, to enhance deep understanding within disciplines, and to promote critical and creative thinking.

The research programs are based on a detailed understanding of human cognitive development and of the process of learning in the arts and other disciplines. They place the learner at the center of the educational process, respecting the different ways in which an individual learns at various stages of life, as well as differences among individuals in the ways they perceive the world and express their ideas.

Project Zero was founded at the Harvard Graduate School of Education in 1967 by the philosopher Nelson Goodman to study and improve education in the arts. Goodman believed that arts learning should be studied as a serious cognitive activity, but that "zero" had been firmly established about the field; hence, the project was given its name.

David Perkins and Howard Gardner became the codirectors of Project Zero in 1972. Over the years, Project Zero has maintained a strong research commitment in the arts while gradually expanding its concerns to include education across all disciplines; not just the individual, but whole classroom, schools, and other educational and cultural organizations as well. Much of its work takes place in American public schools, particularly those that serve disadvantaged populations. An increasing amount of work takes place in schools and other educational and cultural organizations overseas. Project Zero's work is documented extensively in a variety of publications and materials by Principal Investigators and other Project Zero researchers. In addition, Project Zero offers symposia and workshops, most notably the annual summer institute.

Current Directions

Project Zero's research programs span a wide variety of ages, academic disciplines, and sites, but share a common goal: the development of new approaches to help individuals, groups, and institutions learn to the best of their capacities. While Project Zero's past and current research has focused on school and museum communities, Project Zero is beginning to explore how its research ideas are being used as tools in the business world. Its current investigations include, but are not limited, to:

- Exploring how to teach for understanding—in other words, to help students learn to use knowledge to solve unexpected problems, rather than simply recite back facts;

- Designing strategies for creating a "culture of thinking" in the classroom that encourages students to think critically and creatively;

- Making assessment an ongoing and integral part of the curriculum, so that it reinforces instruction and guides students in reflecting upon their work;

- Developing and implementing in-school assessment criteria and procedures that can document the full range of student abilities;

- Marshaling the power of new technologies, especially computers, to advance learning and provide access to new realms of knowledge;

- relating classroom instruction to the tasks and experiences students will encounter outside of school and particularly in the world of work;

- Evaluating various efforts by cultural institutions to enrich education in the arts by bringing artists into schools as mentors, performers, or teacher trainers;

- Devising games, interactive exhibits, and other activities that appeal to a variety of learning styles and will invite new audiences into museums

- Designing learning structures and strategies in organizations to facilitate personal and organizational inquiry;

- Designing and facilitating reflective communities around personal and generative actions for the individuals in the group and their communities;

- Examining the understanding, teaching, and assessment of thinking dispositions.

Project Zero's research contributions, from Principal Investigators and other Project Zero researchers, are documented in more than 500 published articles and books, and include:

- A portrait of the steps by which children learn to use symbols and symbolic notation in music, visual arts, mathematics, and other cognitive areas;

- Discovery of the process by which students gradually relinquish their initial misconceptions or stereotypical ways of thinking about the world (e.g., the earth is flat, all doctors are male) and embrace more complex and constructive forms of understanding;

- The "Theory of Multiple Intelligences," suggesting that individuals perceive the world in at least eight different and equally important ways—linguistic, logical-mathematical, musical, spatial, bodily-kinesthetic, naturalist, interpersonal, and intrapersonal—and that educational programs should foster the development of all these forms of thinking;

- Innovative methods of assessment that evaluate different forms of learner thinking, not just linguistic and mathematical skills—methods, including projects, portfolios, video portfolios, that look at students' abilities to use information flexibly and appropriately in real-life situations;

- The "Smart Schools" model, a set of seven guidelines for good education that is based on two guiding principles:
  - Learning is a consequence of thinking—and good thinking is learnable by all students;
  - Learning should include deep understanding, which involves the flexible, active use of knowledge;

- The investigation of thinking dispositions—passions, attitudes, values, and habits of mind that play key roles in thinking—and the development of disposition-centered assessment techniques that look at aspects of high-level thinking, such as students' inclination and sensitivity to appropriate occasions to think critically and creatively;

- Strategies and models to teach thinking, designed for use across the curriculum, to develop students' critical and creative thinking competencies and to encourage intellectual empowerment.

Current Research Projects

- Adult Multiple Intelligences is a project, based on Howard Gardner's Theory of Multiple Intelligences, that supports teachers in developing innovative instructional strategies, curriculum, and assessment for adult learners.

- ALPS (Active Learning Practices for Schools) is a newly developed Web site designed to make Project Zero's "Teaching for Understanding" and "Thinking" resources readily available to schools. It was formerly called the Learning for Understanding Network.

- Art Works for Schools is a collaborative project with arts organizations and schools that focuses on teaching high-level thinking in and through the arts.

- ARTS SURVIVE is a three-year national study investigating why some arts education partnerships between schools and professional artists and/or cultural institutions survive and others do not. It works to provide a greater understanding of what survival means to arts education partnerships, as well as determining what is essential to build and sustain them.

- Assessing Historical Understanding Project is a collaboration between Project Zero and Facing History and Ourselves to develop tools, criteria, and frameworks for deep understanding of the rise of Nazi Germany and other periods in history.

- Concordia Project is a collaborative research program undertaken for the purpose of documenting, evaluating, and refining a community-driven school design process.

- Creativity and Leadership is a large-scale study of the beliefs and practices characterizing the lives of professional people. Researchers are examining both the relation between children and adolescents' beliefs and practices and their commitment to an area of work; and adults' beliefs and practices and their ability to perform cutting-edge work.

- The Evidence Project is a three-year effort, working in a small number of Massachusetts schools serving youth from low-income communities, to develop effective methods of assessing instructional practices in K-8 classrooms.

- The Galef Institute/Project Zero Web Collaboration has researchers at Project Zero and The Galef Institute joined together in creating materials and supporting discussion forums for the collaborative school projects on DWoKnet, part of The Galef Institute's Web site.

- Making Learning Visible: Children as Individual and Group Learners is a two-year collaboration between Project Zero and the municipal preschools and infant-toddler centers of Reggio Emilia, Italy. Researchers are examining how to document and assess individual and group learning in young children.

- Parent Partners is a project to develop a Web site to help parents understand and support their children's development in seven areas from prenatal through age eight.

- Project SUMIT (Schools Using Multiple Intelligences Theory) is a research project that identifies, documents, and promotes effective applications of multiple intelligences in schools.

- Project Zero/International Schools Consortium Partnership focuses on Project Zero's Framework, Teaching for Understanding, with secondary attention given to issues about assessment and thinking dispositions, multiple intelligences, and the arts in education.

- REAP (Reviewing Education and the Arts Project) is reviewing what can be learned from the massive number of studies about the effects of arts instruction (multiarts, visual arts, music, drama, and dance) on cognition and learning in nonarts domains.

- ROUNDS at Project Zero provides opportunities for educators to regularly gather together to share their work and discuss professional issues.

- Student Self-Assessment Project is aimed at improving middle school students' writing skills by engaging them in regular self-assessment using scoring rubrics.

- Understanding for Organizations is an action research endeavor that works in collaboration with the Universidad Jorge Tadeo Lozano in Bogota, Colombia, to develop a framework that foregrounds personal and organizational inquiry in the workplace and communi-

Program, Instructional, and Curricular Initiatives

ties. Project Zero researchers are working with a group of administrators at the university to cultivate personal investment and action projects that advance various aspects of university life.

- Understandings of Consequence Project explores how causal expectations, mismatches between students' and scientific causal models, and misconceptions about causality impact learning of biology and physics concepts.

Recent Research Projects

- APPLE Project (Assessing Projects and Portfolios for LEarning) was a research and development effort focused on studying effective ways of assessing student performances, fair documentation and assessment of children's work on series projects, and determining how best to implement portfolio assessment in schools.

- Arts PROPEL: Integrating Teaching and Assessment was a five-year collaborative project focused on developing model programs that combine instruction and assessment in music, visual arts, and imaginative writing.

- ATLAS Communities (Communities for Authentic Teaching, Learning, and Assessment for all Students) was a project dedicated to designing "break-the-mold schools" for the twenty-first century.

- ATLAS Seminar was a series of seminars, convened by Principal Investigators of the ATLAS Communities Project, for the purpose of examining central issues in school reform.

- Isabella Stewart Gardner Museum/Harvard Project Zero Educational Collaboration was established for the purpose of developing educational activities and curricula to help make the Museum's unique collections more accessible to schools and other populations.

- Lincoln Center Institute Project: Curricular Frameworks in Aesthetic Education was an artist-in-residence program designed to expose students to the arts, and to immerse students and teachers in an intensive aesthetic education program.

- Mather Afterschool Program: A Project-Centered Approach to Literacy Instruction was a collaborative undertaking that resulted in the development of a project-based after-school program designed to build students' literacy and thinking skills.

- Multiple Intelligences Schools was a research study examining the many ways multiple intelligences theory has been applied in schools, as well as the types of impact it has made.

- Patterns of Thinking was a multiyear investigation into the nature of critical and creative thinking. The project's focus was the understanding, teaching, and assessment of thinking dispositions.

- Practical Intelligence for School was a research project exploring the question "What do students need to know in order to succeed in school?"

- Project Co-Arts was a national study of community arts centers in economically disadvantaged communities that focused on education. The project developed a framework to help administrators and teacher/artists make thoughtful decisions regarding the provision of quality education. The project also worked to enable art centers and other educational institutions to document and assess their educational effectiveness.

- Project MUSE (Museums Uniting with Schools in Education) was a collaboration of researchers, museum educators, and classroom teachers focused on exploring the potential of art museums to serve as integral elements of education.

- Project Spectrum, based on the belief that every child exhibits a distinctive spectrum of abilities, offered an alternative approach to assessment and curriculum development during preschool and early primary years.

- Project Zero/Massachusetts Schools Network was a three-year collaboration between Project Zero, the Massachusetts Department of Education, and 11 Massachusetts elementary schools that brought together practitioners, policymakers, and researchers for the purpose of exploring how portfolios can be implemented to provide effective assessment of students and programs.

- Shakespeare & Company Research Study was a project that closely examined two components of a professional theater company's school-based educational programs.

- Smart Schools provided a structure for schools by envisioning a learning community that was steeped in thinking and deep understanding; that engendered respect for all its members; and that produced students who were ready to face the world as responsible, thinking members of a diverse society.

- Teaching for Understanding: Enhancing Disciplinary Understanding in Teachers and Students was a collaborative effort of researchers and practitioners targeting middle and high school for the purpose of developing and testing a pedagogy of understanding.

Selected Previous Research Projects

Catalyst: Developing Technology for Education was a project that investigated how computers could best be used as teaching machines.

Early Symbolization and the Transition to Literacy was a group of closely related studies centered on representation capacities in younger children.

Figurative Language was an investigation of the development of figurative language skills in children.

Contact

Patricia Varrasso
Project Zero
Harvard Graduate School of Education
321 Longfellow Hall
13 Appian Way
Cambridge, MA 02138
Voice: (617) 495-4342
Fax: (617) 495-9709
info@pz.harvard.edu
http://pzweb.harvard.edu

Copyright 1998. Harvard Project Zero and the President and Fellows of Harvard College. This material has been reprinted by permission from Harvard Project Zero.

SCORE

SCORE is a comprehensive cocurricular support program that brings together administrators, counselors, teachers, parents, and students to increase student academic performance and college/career eligibility, especially for high-risk students. SCORE places students in a rich common core curriculum that leads to university eligibility by the time they graduate from high school. SCORE supports these students in their academic endeavors by equipping them with powerful study skills, assisting them in getting in touch with their personal values and goals, and networking them with appropriate support personnel. SCORE increases academic curricular offerings and decreases remedial course offering on a school campus. SCORE enlists an entire school community in the pursuit of powerful learning. SCORE schools regularly receive commendations on their accreditation reports. Score is a U.S. Department of Education exemplary program, validated for its effectiveness by the Program Effectiveness Panel.

SCORE trainers work with school teams to design a custom program for accelerating the achievement of high-risk youth, train staff, and provide follow-through support with technical assistance and a complete set of materials, workbooks, and videotapes.

Students are heterogeneously grouped in a rich college core curriculum that leads to university eligibility by the time they graduate. Students receive support through placement in a SCORE class, learning powerful study skills, participating in tutorials, and setting personal goals aligned with their individual values.

SCORE helps schools to implement after-school programs that really work, set up mentoring programs, design tutorial and motivational programs that really work, network with college and community agencies. and work with parents of high-risk students. SCORE is used in Title I, Migrant, Independent Study, and Language Minority programs. SCORE's effectiveness has been validated with several key populations. For example:

- Title I students participating in SCORE maintain a B average in college preparatory courses.

- SCORE Migrant students enroll in 4-year colleges at a rate of 60 percent. Nationwide, the Migrant 4-year college-going rate is 5 percent.

- Students involved in SCORE test out of limited English proficient (LEP) programs at a rate of 95 percent in 4 years.

For a more detailed description of SCORE, refer to Chapter 3 of this text.

Contact

Sharon Johnson
Educational Innovations/SCORE
23706 Whale Cove
Laguna Niguel, CA 92677
Voice: (949) 363-6764
Fax: (949) 363-6764
sharonmarjo@earthlink.net
www.score-ed.com

Success for All (SFA)

Background

Success for All (SFA) is a comprehensive approach to restructuring elementary schools to ensure the success of every child. The program emphasizes prevention and early intervention to anticipate and solve any learning problems. Success for All provides schools with research-based curriculum materials; extensive professional development in proven strategies of instruction, assessment, and classroom management; one-to-one tutoring for primary grade children who need it; and active family support approaches.

Curriculum, Instruction, and Assessment

The Success for All curriculum is based on current research on the ways children learn to read and write. At the heart of the program is 90 minutes of uninterrupted daily reading instruction. Beginning in first grade, children are grouped across classes and grades by reading level, giving most teachers the opportunity to work intensively with students at one reading level. Assessments are administered every eight weeks to ensure adequate progress is being made and to determine if tutoring or family support services are needed. Cooperative learning, embedded throughout the program, focuses on individual accountability, common goals, and recognition of group success.

The Early Learning Program (pre-kindergarten and kindergarten) emphasizes oral language development using thematic units, children's literature, oral and written expression, and learning centers. Prereading activities promote the development of concepts about, alphabet familiarity, and phonemic awareness. Peabody Language Development Kits provide additional experience in language. The program is adaptable to full- or half-day schedules.

Reading Roots is the beginning reading program used in Success for All. It emphasizes a balance between phonics and meaning, using both children's literature and a series of interesting, enjoyable stories in which phonetically regular student text is enriched by teacher-read text. Students engage in partner reading and writing activities. Fast-paced, motivating lessons use puppets, sounds, chants, whole-class responses, and metacognitive skills training to build comprehensive, fluency, and confidence in reading. *Lee Conmigo* provides the same program for students learning to read in Spanish.

Reading Wings, for students reading at the second through sixth grade levels, is built around a school's existing novels, anthologies, or basals. It emphasizes cooperative learning activities in which students work in teams to improve strategic reading and comprehension skills and investigate literature. *Alas para Leer* provides the same strategies for Spanish readers.

Writing is emphasized throughout the program as a method for creative expression and for responding to literature. Students plan, draft, revise, edit, and publish compositions with feedback from teachers and peers.

One-to-One Tutoring

One-to-one tutoring is the most effective educational intervention known. In Success for All schools, children experiencing difficulties learning to read—especially first graders—receive daily one-to-one tutoring from certified teachers or well-qualified instructional assistants designed to reinforce classroom instruction. The tutor diagnoses student needs and tailors instruction to meet those needs.

Family Support and Integrated Services

Since a child's readiness to learn is often based on needs extending beyond the classroom, each Success for All school creates a Family Support Team to work closely with students, parents, and the community. This team typically includes the principal or assistant principal and program facilitator, as well as social workers, counselors, attendance monitors, teachers, and volunteers.

The Family Support Team plans activities to involve parents in their children's education, such as workshops on reading with children at home. The team also develops plans to meet needs of individual students having difficulty, closely monitors attendance, and integrates community and school resources.

Facilitator

Every Success for All school has a full-time facilitator, a certified teacher who helps faculty and staff implement the program. The facilitator provides teachers with counsel, support, and information through classroom visits, coaching, and frequent meetings. The facilitator organizes and monitors data from eight-week assessments and acts as liaison between teachers, administrators, tutors, family support staff, and parents to ensure that each child becomes a successful reader.

Professional Development

Professional development for Success for All requires three consecutive days of training for all teachers before the program begins. Success for All trainers return to the school for three two-day visits during the first year to work with the principal, facilitators, and teachers to build a strong implementation. Four additional days focus on the development of the Family Support and Tutoring programs. Success for All trainers are available for telephone consultation during the year. Facilitators follow up on initial training with classroom visits, coaching, and team meetings.

Research on Success for All: Strong, Positive Effects

Ten years of research on Success for All shows that the program significantly improves student reading performance in schools large and small, urban and rural. The research has been conducted by researchers at Johns Hopkins University, the University of Memphis, and California-based WestEd at 23 schools in 9 districts. Among the findings:

- By the end of the first grade, students in Success for All schools have average reading scores almost three months ahead of those in matching control schools;

- By the end of the fifth grade, students read more than one year ahead of control peers;

- Success for All reduces the need for special education placements by more the 50 percent, and virtually eliminates retention;

- Middle school students who come from Success for All schools continue to read more than one year ahead of those in matching schools;

- The Spanish versions of Success for All now used in bilingual classes, *Lee Conmigo* and *Alas para Leer,* show strong positive effects on student achievement; and

- Achievement effects are especially strong for students who score in the lowest quartile.

There is no magic in Success for All. Research shows that the quality and completeness of implementation are strongly related to students' achievement gains. The program provides a powerful tool for educators to increase the success of all children, but the school staff must work to make this potential a reality.

The program was launched in 1987 at a Baltimore elementary school and gradually expanded. Word of Success for All's results spread among educators, and in 1997-98 it was used in 1,100 schools in 44 states, serving over 600,000 students from Alaska to Florida.

Adoption and Cost

District and school staff should review program materials, view videotapes, and visit nearby Success for All sites before deciding whether to implement Success for All. Schools must receive an awareness presentation and then apply to become a Success for All school. The application process ensures that the school staff members are aware of the elements of the program, have the resources to implement the program successfully, and agree as a staff to make the commitment to implement the program. A vote by secret ballot of at least 80 percent of the teaching staff is required.

Costs for training and materials depend on the size and location of individual schools and the number of schools collaborating in training. Sample costs for a school of 500 students in pre-kindergarten through fifth grade range from $65,000 to $75,000 for Year 1; $25,000 to $35,000 for Year 2; and $20,000 to $30,000 for Year 3. (Add or subtract approximately $65 for each student over or under 500.) These estimates include training, materials, and followup visits. Actual costs will depend in part on the distance to training centers and specific school needs (such as bilingual or ESL training), and are calculated for individual schools.

Many schools can afford Success for All. Typically, the program is funded by reallocating a school's current Title I monies and/or other state and federal funds. Some schools receive special district or foundation grants during the first year of implementation. Success for All schools use existing personnel to staff the program, replacing existing roles with roles of facilitator and tutors. Considering the number of children served and the cost per child, Success for All is probably the most cost-effective reading program available today. Reportedly, it reduces special education placements and retentions, saving schools and districts significant expenditures in the long run.

Contact

Vernell Harris
Success for All Foundation, Inc.
200 W. Towsontown Blvd.
Baltimore, MD 21204-5200
Voice: (800) 548-4998
Fax: (410) 324-4444
sfa@successforall.net
www.successforall.net

3
Comprehensive School-Improvement Initiatives

Accelerated Schools Project

No single feature makes a school accelerated. Rather, each school community uses the accelerated school philosophy and process to determine its own vision and to collaboratively work to achieve its goals. The philosophy is based on three democratic principles and a commitment to providing powerful learning to all students. The systematic transformation process is a vehicle for getting from the here and now, to the school's vision of success for all students.

In accelerated schools, the best of what we know about education—that which is usually reserved for gifted and talented students—is shared with all students. Members of the school community work together to transform every classroom into a powerful learning environment, where students and teachers are encouraged to think creatively and explore their interests, and where they are given the capacity and the encouragement to achieve at high levels. Accelerated schools seek out, acknowledge, and build upon every child's natural curiosity, encouraging students to construct knowledge through exploration and discovery, and to see connections between school activities and their lives outside the classroom. All of these learning experiences require imaginative thinking, complex reasoning, and problem-solving.

Accelerated schools adhere to three interrelated principles that are largely absent from traditional schools:

- Unity of Purpose

    In accelerated schools, all members of the school community share a dream for the school and work together toward a common set of goals that will benefit all students.

- Empowerment Coupled with Responsibility

    Every member of the school community is empowered to participate in a shared decision making process, to share in the responsibility for implementing these decisions, and to be held accountable for the outcomes of these decisions.

- Building on Strengths

    In creating their dream school, accelerated school communities recognize and utilize the knowledge, talents, and resources of every member of the school community.

Accelerated school communities share a set of values, beliefs and behaviors which create an environment that nurtures innovation and collaboration. An accelerated school develops qualities such as equity, trust, participation, collaboration, reflection, and risk-taking; and these help guide the action and interactions of all members of the school community.

The Accelerated Schools Project does not prescribe a checklist of features for creating powerful learning experiences, because checklists lead to isolated and fragmented changes in curriculum and instruction. Rather, the entire accelerated school community makes learning relevant by building on children's strengths in a systematic way. Each accelerated school creates its own evolving set of powerful learning experiences based on its own unique needs, strengths, and vision.

Rather than focusing on a particular grade, curriculum, or approach to teaching, accelerated school communities use a systematic process, encompassing collaborative and informed decision-making, to transform their entire school. The transformation begins with the entire school community taking a deep look into its present situation through a process called *taking stock*. The entire school community then forges a shared vision of what it wants the school to be—the kind of dream school that everyone would want for their own child. By comparing the vision to its present situation, the school community identifies priority challenge areas. The school community itself then sets about to address those priority challenge areas, working through an accelerated schools governance structure and analyzing their challenge areas using the *inquiry process*. The inquiry process is a systematic method that helps school communities clearly understand problems, find and implement solutions, and assess their results.

Contact

Henry Levin
Accelerated Schools Project
Ceras Building
School of Education
Stanford University
Stanford, CA 94305-3084
Voice: (650) 725-1676
Fax: (650) 725-6140
www.stanford.edu/group/ASP

The Coalition of Essential Schools (CES)

The Coalition of Essential Schools (CES) is a national network of schools and centers engaged in restructuring and redesigning schools to promote better student learning and achievement. The schools share a common set of ideas known as the *Common Principles,* which guide their whole-school reform efforts. CES's power as a school reform movement derives from its focus on classroom practice, the simple authenticity of its principles, and its determination to measure the long-term impact of school reform on the lives of students. While the Coalition began as a secondary school reform effort, it has broadened its scope to include elementary and middle schools.

Background

The Coalition of Essential Schools was born out of *A Study of High Schools,* an inquiry into American secondary education, conducted from 1979 to 1984 under the sponsorship of the National Association of Secondary School Principals and the National Association of Independent Schools. Theodore R. Sizer distilled the findings of the study in his book *Horace's Compromise: The Dilemma of the American High School* (Houghton Mifflin, 1984). In 1984, the Coalition was established at Brown University in Providence, Rhode Island, and 12 schools took up the challenge of putting Sizer's 9 *Common Principles* into practice to become the first Essential Schools. Initially, Sizer and a small staff worked closely and directly in a mentoring relationship with Coalition member schools to help them navigate the redesign process. As interest in CES ideas spread and more schools joined the effort, CES restructured and decentralized its support for schools.

In 1988, the Coalition formed a strategic partnership with the Education Commission of the States (ECS), a Denver-based educational policy advisory and research organization. Through a joint initiative dubbed *Re: Learning* the two organizations enlisted the support of governors and chief state school officers for Essential School networks in their states and provided a vehicle for school-based professionals to influence district and state policy reform.

In November 1994, at the end of its first decade, CES chair Theodore R. Sizer convened a national committee of practitioners to assess the work of CES and help chart its future. The Futures Committee recommended that the next phase of the Coalition's work should be characterized as a Decade of Demonstration and that CES must sharpen the obligations of membership. It highlighted the need to pay more attention to the total context of schooling. Other insights suggested that collaboration and critical friendship should be central to all levels of CES work, and that CES should model democratic practices. The Committee recognized that the Coalition could no longer rely exclusively on a single charismatic leader or a national center to guide and support its work. Rather, the focus must be on the development of widely distributed, visionary leadership and the creation of strong centers of collaboration around the country, linked by a national office and governance structure.

Personnel, Programs, and Principles

Today, the Coalition of Essential Schools is a federation of more than 1,000 schools K-12, public and private, supported by approximately 40 centers and networks spanning 37 states and extending abroad.

Theodore R. Sizer is founder and chairman of the Coalition. He is University Professor Emeritus at Brown University where he served as chair of the Education Department from 1984 to 1989. Before coming to Brown, Sizer was professor and dean at the Harvard Graduate School of Education (1964-72) and headmaster of Phillips (Andover) Academy (1972-81). Sizer earned a B.A. at Yale and an M.A.T. and Ph.D. in History at Harvard. Three of his books, *Horace's Compromise* (1985), *Horace's School* (1992), and *Horace's Hope* (1996), all published by Houghton Mifflin, explore the motivation and the ideas of the Essential School reform effort.

Amy Gerstein assumed the position of Executive Director for the Coalition in June 1997. Gerstein previously served as associate director of the Bay Area School Reform Collaborative in San Francisco (1995-97) and the Bay Area Coalition of Essential Schools (1992-95). She also worked for several years at the CES national office as associate director for schools (1988-90). Gerstein holds a Ph.D. in Education from Stanford University where she codirected the Stanford Teacher Education Program, and a B.A. in Geology-Biology from Brown University.

CES National staff consists of approximately a dozen education professionals and support staff. The national office moved to the San Francisco Bay Area in June 1998 after more than 10 years at Brown University in Providence, Rhode Island. The national staff provides technical assistance to centers, convenes gatherings of CES leaders in the United States and abroad to ensure thoughtful networking.

CES National works through a variety of forums to bring the lessons learned at CES centers and schools across the country to the rest of the network. It publishes *Horace,* a substantive newsletter, each issue of which investigates a topic in curriculum, pedagogy, and assessment, school design, public policy, or community involvement in schools. The Fall Forum, CES's annual conference, brings together nearly 3,000 educators for an exciting array of practical workshops, study sessions, and discussions. CES's newly designed site on the World Wide Web, along with general information about the coalition and work in particular centers, includes an interactive area for ongoing discussions of the work on reform. In the interactive area, one can follow strands of interest in each discussion, and, of course, join in. CES National also convenes quarterly meetings of directors of the regional centers, so the centers can learn from each other's work. And it convenes twice-yearly the CES National Congress, delegates to which are practitioners from schools and centers around the country, who meet to guide policy for the Coalition, establishing priorities and inquiring together into substantive questions of educational policy. All of these forums also serve to disseminate learning from the research and professional development projects sponsored by CES National.

The Common Principles that guide the work of the Coalition and its member schools call broadly for schools to set clear and simple goals about the intellectual skills and knowledge to be mastered by all the school's students; to lower teacher/student loads, personalize teaching and curriculum, and make student work the center of classroom activity; to award diplomas based on students' Exhibition of their mastery of the school's program; to create an atmosphere of trust and respect for the school, faculty, students, and parents; and to accomplish such changes with no more than a 10 percent increase in the school's budget. In November 1997, the CES National Congress adopted a 10th Principle calling for democratic and equitable practices at all levels of the work. The 10 Common Principles of the Coalition of Essential Schools are:

- The school should focus on helping adolescents learn to use their minds well. Schools should not attempt to be *comprehensive* if such a claim is made at the expense of the school's central intellectual purpose.

- The school's goals should be simple: that each student master a limited number of essential skills and areas of knowledge. While these skills and areas will, to varying degrees, reflect the traditional academic disciplines, the program's design should be shaped by the intellectual and imaginative powers and competencies that students need, rather than necessarily by subjects, as conventionally defined. The aphorism *less is more* should dominate: curricular decisions should be guided by the aim of thorough student mastery and achievement rather than by an effort to merely cover content.

- The school's goals should apply to all students, while the means to these goals should vary as those students themselves vary. School practice should be tailor-made to meet the needs of every group or class of adolescents.

- Teaching and learning should be personalized to the maximum feasible extent. Efforts should be directed toward a goal that no teacher have direct responsibility for more than 80 students. To capitalize on this personalization, decisions about the details of the course of study, the use of students' and teachers' time, and the choice of teaching materials and specific pedagogues must be unreservedly placed in the hands of the principal and staff.

- The governing practical metaphor of the school should be *student as worker* rather than the more familiar one of *teacher as deliverer of instructional services*. Accordingly, a prominent pedagogy will be coaching to provoke students to learn how to learn and thus to teach themselves.

- Students entering secondary school studies are those who can show competence in language and elementary mathematics. Students of traditional high school age but not yet at appropriate levels of competence to enter secondary school studies will be provided intensive remedial work to assist them to quickly meet these standards. The diploma should be awarded upon a successful final demonstration of mastery for graduation—an *Exhibition*. This Exhibition by the student of his or her grasp of the central skills and knowledge of the school's program may be jointly administered by the faculty and by higher authorities. As the diploma is awarded when earned, the school's program proceeds with no strict age grading and with no system of credits earned by time spent in class. The emphasis is on the students' demonstration that they can do important things.

- The tone of the school should explicitly and self-consciously stress values of un- anxious expectation ("I won't threaten you but I expect much of you"), of trust (until abused) and of decency (the values of fairness, generosity, and tolerance). Incentives appropriate to the school's particular students and teachers should be emphasized, and parents should be treated as essential collaborators.

- The principal and teachers should perceive themselves as generalists first (teachers and scholars in general education) and specialists second (experts in but one particular discipline). Staff should expect multiple obligations (teacher-counselor-manager) and exhibit a sense of commitment to the entire school.

- Ultimate administrative and budget targets should include, in addition to total student loads per teacher of 80 or fewer pupils, substantial time for collective planning by teachers, competitive salaries for staff, and an ultimate per pupil cost not to exceed that at traditional schools by more than 10 percent. To accomplish this, administrative plans may have to drop services now provided students in many traditional comprehensive secondary schools.

- The school should demonstrate nondiscriminatory and inclusive policies, practices, and pedagogues. It should model democratic practices that involve all who are directly affected by the school. The school should honor diversity and build on the strengths of its communities, deliberately and explicitly challenging all forms of inequity.

Eight organizational principles serve as tenets of organizational practice to help deepen the work of schools. First and foremost is the notion that CES should be a learning community, modeling the practices it expects of schools. The work at all levels should be of a size and scale to allow for personalization. The principles stress the importance of valuing the local wisdom of the schools and centers and recognize the whole school as the fundamental unit of change. The current priorities of the national organization are reflected in the principles—a commitment to demonstration and documentation, an emphasis on collaboration and critical friendship at all levels of the work, and attention to issues of equity and democracy. The principles also assert that CES should maintain a voice in the national discourse about educational reform and seek alliances with like-minded organizations. The eight organizational principles are:

- CES should be a learning community, modeling the practices it expects of schools. Inquiry should inform the practices of the organization as well as of the schools and of adults and young people within them.

- CES and its member schools should commit themselves to documentation of change efforts, demonstration of student achievement, using the most effective combination of objective, subjective and performance based data, and public sharing of all that has been learned.

- Just as students differ one from another, so do teachers, schools, and communities. Therefore, CES and its member schools should value local wisdom and have the flexibility to respond to their local contexts.

- The whole school, including parents, should be the fundamental unit of change.

- Collaboration and critical friendship should be central to all levels of CES work, whether in classrooms or among colleagues and community members, to fully explore and thoughtfully utilize the enormous potential of a wide range of technologies to advance this goal.

- CES should maintain a voice in the national discourse about educational reform and should seek alliances with like-minded organizations. Decisions about the nature and extent of such alliances should be made as close as possible to the school and community.

- CES and its member schools should model democratic practices and should deliberately and explicitly address challenges of equity in relation to race, class and gender.

- Because it has direct bearing on intellectual, interpersonal, and organizational processes, CES work at all levels should be of a size and scale to allow for personalization.

Member schools in the Coalition are diverse in size, population, program, and geographic location, and represent both the public and private sector. The Coalition offers no specific model or program for schools to adopt. What Essential Schools share is the 10 Common Principles, which focus each school's effort to rethink its own programs, suited to its particular structures and practices. Each school develops its own programs, suited to its particular students, faculty, and community—hence, no two Essential Schools are alike. Members enjoy the commitments and benefits of a network which provides access to tools and resources, thereby helping schools make progress on whole-school change. These schools demonstrate evidence of schoolwide commitment to the Common Principles and agree to share their learning with other schools and communities. In addition to member or Essential Schools, the Coalition recognizes schools in the *learning/networking* stage and the *exploring* stage.

Schools applying to the Coalition must present a plan for change consistent with the Common Principles and must demonstrate faculty and governing board support for extending the plan to the entire school. While membership has traditionally been handled through the national office, schools now affiliate through a center. There is no fee to join the Coalition; however, most schools require at least $50,000 a year for 3 to 5 years during the initial study and redesign phases for release time, travel, and professional development activities. Schools are responsible for securing their own funds.

CES centers are not regional outposts of CES/National but, rather, are gatherings of schools that work in concert, supporting each other and presenting a shared set of common principles to their adjoining communities. Centers are responsible for carrying out the substantive programmatic work of the Coalition while also building support for reform among broader constituencies to strengthen their own bases of operation.

Governance

To achieve its mission, CES has chosen to evolve from an informal, centrally run organization to an intentionally decentralized association relying on the local wisdom and guidance of those closest to school change work. Coalition of Essential Schools promotes ownership, commitment, and leadership through its Congress and Executive Board, which provide direction, establish priorities, and give a national voice to member schools and centers. The Executive Director and national staff are responsible for leading CES in the directions established by the Congress and Executive Board, and for the efficient and democratic operation of CES.

The CES Congress, formed in November 1996, is the main governing body of the Coalition. It is comprised of delegates from Coalition schools and centers, the Executive Board, and the CES Chair or a designee. The Congress meets twice a year, once at the fall Forum and again in the spring. It serves as a vehicle for developing leadership and sharing learnings and ideas within CES by bringing the collective experience, perspective, judgment and wisdom of its members to bear on those issues which face CES and school reform generally in the United States. Primary responsibility for determining matters of policy, long-term directions, and key national strategies for CES is vested in the Congress, which is also responsible for reviewing the appropriateness of the CES organizational structure and making changes (as needed) in its own structure and operations.

The CES Executive Board supports the work of the Congress and national staff, provides counsel and leadership to CES, and appoints and works closely with the Executive Director. The Board also takes primary responsibility for identifying and addressing long-term organizational and financial needs and provides direction in assuring CES a strong and confident national voice. The Board consists of 12 members, 9 of whom are nominated by centers and schools. The other three members are CES allies, neither directly affiliated with a member school or center, nor part of the national staff. In addition, the Executive Director, CES Chair, and Vice Chair serve as ex officio members of the Board.

Contact

Helen Ortiz
Coalition of Essential Schools
1814 Franklin Street, Suite 700
Oakland, CA 94614
Voice: (510) 433-1451
Fax: (510) 433-1455
www.essentialschools.org

The Developmental Studies Center Child Development Project

The Child Development Project is a comprehensive school change program of the Developmental Studies Center (DSC). For more than 15 years, DSC has been working with schools across the United States, helping and learning from teachers who have found ways to build caring classroom learning communities.

The Developmental Studies Center is a nonprofit educational organization, founded in 1980 and dedicated to the integration of children's social, ethical, and intellectual development. The DSC mission is to deepen children's commitment to values such as kindness, helpfulness, personal responsibility, and respect for others, while helping children develop their capacities to think deeply and critically.

Developmental Studies Center offers K-8 teacher support materials in community building, parent involvement, collaborative learning, mathematics, and literature to support student character and competence. The materials have been piloted and field-tested in public schools nationwide.

The DSC Difference

Many educational improvement programs focus on nurturing students' intellectual, ethical, or social growth. The elementary schools that the Developmental Studies Center (DSC) works with consciously and explicitly focus on all three aspects of children's development. And they do so all the time—through the lessons their teachers teach, the materials their students use, their school wide activities and policies, and through the ways their staff members interact with children, parents, and each other.

At a time when the nation seems narrowly focused on boosting children's scores on standardized tests, DSC staff advocate a more balanced view of education's purpose—one that recognizes the need to develop children's hearts as well as their minds. In an era when certain sectors of the American electorate have tried to appropriate *family values* for their own ends, DSC staff deliberately speak out for the common values that unite all of us—fairness, respect, responsibility, kindness—for the benefit of all children, not just a select few. When so many suggest simplistic solutions or expect quick fixes, DSC staff are not apologetic when asking for the time and resources that schools need to transform themselves into institutions that effectively educate every child who crosses their thresholds—and that help all children fulfill their promise and potential.

The Belief

A school community is a set of relationships: among children, among school staff members, between staff members and children's families. In a caring school community, these relationships are valued, supported, and nurtured. Every day they are in school, children interact with others and absorb lessons about what to value and about how to get along with others. So it is important that they be in an environment where they are absorbing *good* lessons.

Developmental Studies Center staff want elementary school students to master the academic skills of reading, writing, arithmetic, and science. They also want them to be able to punctuate, spell, speak, add, subtract, multiply, and divide; as well as to get lots of practice using their minds to analyze, to judge, to reason, to solve problems, and to figure out things.

Just as important, DSC staff want students to use their hearts. They believe that students should be learning important values, such as fairness, respect, helpfulness, and responsibility. They should be learning about putting those values into action, about accepting each other's differences, about playing by the rules. Additionally, they want them to leave their classrooms with a love of learning for its own sake, not for the good grades or free pizzas they might earn.

Students in DSC schools are learning in many different ways. They are reading real books, doing hands-on lessons, and venturing outside the classroom into their communities. Additionally, they are also learning well because they are with adults who are modeling good values, adults who practice what they preach, who treat children with gentleness and respect, who reach out to families as full partners in their children's learning, who have the courage to learn from each other and continuously grow, who consciously integrate the intellectual, ethical, and social growth of their students, and who are passionately committed to the well-being of children—all children.

Background

The Developmental Studies Center is a nonprofit organization formed in 1980 to conduct research and develop school based programs that foster children's intellectual, ethical, and social development. The organization's mission is to deepen children's commitment to being kind, helpful, responsible, and respectful of others—qualities they believe are essential to leading humane and productive lives in a democratic society. They also strive to help children think skillfully and analytically, so they can make the most of their schooling and continue learning throughout their lives.

Developmental Studies Center staff engage in these activities: providing professional development services that are strengthening the skills of teachers, principals, and other educators; disseminating materials—books, curriculum resources, and videos; developing programs, including the Child Development Project, a comprehensive elementary school program aimed at creating caring communities of learners in classrooms and in whole schools; developing curricula in mathematics, reading and language arts; and conducting research into how children learn and develop, in order to ascertain what makes for an environment that helps children succeed.

Professional Development

Projects are designed and conducted by a staff of educators, researchers, curriculum developers, and media specialists of diverse backgrounds and interests. Consulting services are specifically designed to support DSC's programs and educational philosophy to build a learning environment that fosters children's intellectual, social, and ethical development. Developmental Studies Center staff seek to help schools address the following goals: integrated development of the whole child; development of humane values; creation of a warm supportive school environment; promotion of learning for understanding; development of meaningful school-community relations; and provision of strategic support for school change.

Three Options for DSC's In-Depth Approach

Currently, DSC is focusing its consulting on creating partnerships with schools that recognize that implementing a coherent philosophy is a long-term process of change. At present it offers at least three entry points or *strands* to initiate the DSC approach:

- A language arts strand in the context of a caring community, using *Reading, Thinking and Caring* (K-3) and *Reading for Real* (4-8);

- A cooperative approach to mathematics and social development, using *Number Power* (K-6);

- Building a sense of classroom community—creating classroom practices and a school environment that emphasizes kindness and caring, personal responsibility, social competence, collaborative learning, and family involvement (K-6).

A program to support each of these entry points can be designed to include a series of workshops (for example, two days in the summer and two followup workshops during the year) and a number of onsite days with DSC staff developers, including work with teachers in classrooms and meetings.

Focused Support

The Developmental Studies Center also contracts for short-term support for concepts such as *Buddies, At Home in Our Schools,* and *Homeside Activities.* An introductory workshop can jump start a school's implementation of these ideas. A followup meeting can be useful for idea sharing, problem solving, or deepening understanding and expanding to the next steps. The DSC training process can supplement a school's collegial study work or provide an introduction to the DSC philosophy for a meeting of various school staffs in a district.

Cost

Grant support for DSC's work has come from more than 30 national and regional foundations and federal agencies. The cost of workshops provided at school sites starts at $750 for 1 day (plus materials and travel expenses), with prices scaled to favor long-term contracts.

Contact

Denise Wood
Developmental Studies Center's—Child Development Project
2000 Embarcadero, Suite 305
Oakland, CA 94606-5300
Voice: (800) 666-7270 or (510) 533-0213 ext. 239
Fax: (510) 464-3670
info@devstu.org
www.devstu.org

The Edison Project

Founded in 1992, the Edison Project is the country's leading private manager of public schools. After engaging in three years of intensive research and development to design innovative schools that could operate at public school spending levels, Edison opened its first four schools in August, 1995. Edison has now implemented its school design in 51 public schools, including many charter schools, which it operates under management contracts with local school districts and charter school boards. Approximately 24,000 students currently attend Edison partnership schools.

The Edison Project establishes partnership schools in contract with public school districts or charter school authorities within the local community. In either case, the Edison Project takes responsibility for implementing the educational program, technology plans, and management systems, and is accountable to a local authority for the performance of the school. Edison schools remain public schools, open to all students and funded with tax dollars.

The Edison Project offers a comprehensive school design that features an ambitious and wide-ranging curriculum; pervasive use of technology, including a computer on every teacher's desk and technology in the home of every student in grade three and above; an extended school day and year; and an innovative organization that allows teams of teachers to work with the same students over several years.

In 1995, Edison entered into contracts with its first four partners—three local school districts: Mount Clemens, Michigan; Wichita, Kansas; and Sherman, Texas; and one state-chartered board overseeing the Boston Renaissance Charter School in Boston, Massachusetts. Each of these contracts called for the opening of Primary and Elementary Academies (Edison's organizational units for grades K-2 and 3-5).

In 1996, all four of the initial sites expanded to include programs for middle school students, and Edison opened additional K-5 schools in Colorado Springs, Colorado; Lansing, Michigan; Miami, Florida; and Worcester, Massachusetts.

In 1997, Edison increased its total number of schools to 25—more than double the number it operated the previous year—and student enrollment rose from 7,100 to 13,000 nationwide. In 1998, 26 new schools joined the Edison national network, bringing the total number of Edison schools to 51 and their combined student enrollment to approximately 24,000. Edison now operates public schools in 11 states—California, Colorado, Connecticut, Florida, Kansas, Massachusetts, Michigan, Minnesota, New Jersey, North Carolina, Texas—and Washington, DC.

Under contract to public authorities, Edison Project staff bring education programs and management systems into one or more schools in a district or community. The schools remain public schools, open to all students at no cost and funded with tax dollars. The Edison Project is a private company that provides a service to a public authority—thus, it is accountable to the public. Communities have had many ideas for ways to forge such partnerships. For example, districts looking to create new schools or to revitalize existing ones are turning to The Edison Project. In states that have passed *charter legislation* to allow for innovative, publicly funded schools freed from bureaucratic and regulatory constraints, Edison may enter a system as a charter school. In all communities, partnerships with The Edison Project have several features in common.

- Edison works to tailor its comprehensive school design to the needs of the local community.

- Edison invests substantial private capital in every partnership.

- Edison takes responsibility for the day-to-day operation of the partnership school.

- Edison is accountable to the local community for the performance of the school—for higher student achievement, greater family involvement, and enhanced teacher satisfaction, among other things. The local community may terminate Edison's contract if school performance does not meet the terms stated in the contract. Families can withdraw from the school if it does not meet their expectations.

- Edison is compensated with what the community generally receives —from federal, state, and local sources—for each student's education.

Guiding Principles

The Edison Project school design is the product of the thought, discussion, observations, and ideas of educators from all walks of school life. It is supported by volumes of research documenting successful educational practices from this country and around the world.

Edison partnership schools base their principles on deep rooted and well tested philosophies about the central role of learning in what it means to be human. Edison Project staff believe that every person has an innate desire to know and to understand, and that learning is the most important journey in every person's life. The Edison Project is committed to these principles, which reflect America's best ideals:

- Liberty—the conviction that learning is the surest path to individual freedom;

- Equality—the belief that every child should be given exciting educational opportunities and that every child has a tremendous capacity for learning;

- The individual—the principle that each person's character and individuality are to be not only respected, but also celebrated;

- Community—the idea that a school can and should be a center for people of all ages who seek kindred spirits, enlightenment, and recreation;

- Diversity—the notion that respecting, affirming, and learning from our differences is central to what ties us together;

- Joy—the truth that a great school is a place that nurtures the creative spirit, prizes the beautiful as much as the useful, and inculcates a love of learning.

Ten Fundamentals

With a thoughtful philosophy to guide it, the Edison school design is founded on 10 fundamentals. Radical improvement in any of these areas would bring major improvement to a school, but it is by putting all of them together into a coherent strategy that Edison and its partners achieve dramatic results.

- Schools organized for every student's success

  Edison Project staff commit to invest the organization's resources in people and materials that directly nurture the growth of students. Each one is a special citizen—part scholar, part artist, part athlete—who deserves an educational community that cares. To achieve that, staff have organized small, flexible academies, where teachers work with the same students for several years, getting to know each student well and forming strong, mutually supportive relationships with families. The program features a Readiness Academy for three- and four-year-olds; a Primary Academy for grades K-2; an Elementary Academy for grades 3-5; a Junior Academy for grades 6-8; a Senior Academy for grades 9-10; and a Collegiate Academy for grades 11 and 12.

- A better use of time

  Edison partnership schools follow a schedule that makes sense for families today, adds the equivalent of several years to what is now a typical K-12 academic career, and builds in more fun for students, too.

- A rich and challenging curriculum

    Edison Project staff have designed an absorbing curriculum that provides schools and every teacher and student in them with a program of variety and possibility. The curriculum is carefully integrated to help students see the connections between knowledge and ideas and to encourage practical applications of learning. The curriculum is built around five domains: humanities and the arts, mathematics and science, character and ethics, practical arts and skills, and health and physical fitness.

- Teaching methods that motivate

    Edison Project staff are committed to vital and diverse instructional strategies that encourage innovation and excitement in teaching and learning. Partnership schools are full of the sounds of discussion, debate, discovery, and delight.

- Assessment that provides accountability

    Edison monitors student progress in many ways to help ensure that standards are met. Students participate in Edison's own performance assessment system as well as state and local testing programs. Edison is accountable for student performance on all of these measures; and believes in regular, clear, understandable reporting to families and to the public.

- Educators who are true professionals

    Teachers are at the heart of Edison partnership schools. They receive the career development, resources, responsibilities, and opportunities that talented professionals deserve. They also find the best possible working conditions in an atmosphere that encourages the highest respect.

- Technology for an information age

    Edison's plan for technology puts everyone—students, educators, and families—to work with the powerful information, communication, and construction tools available today. It prepares students for the workplaces of tomorrow. And the technology connects the members of the partnership community. Edison Project staff provide home technology for every family of a student in grade three or higher. Every student, teacher, and administrator—everyone on the education team—has personal access to technology and is linked to Edison's national online network. Innovative software puts everyone in touch with a world of ideas and information.

- A partnership with families

    Edison makes a commitment to families to keep them engaged in their children's progress. Student portfolios and quarterly meetings with teachers give family members an accurate and vivid picture of their children's accomplishments and needs. Edison Project staff also see to it that every student in a partnership school has a caring adult whose responsibility is to oversee school achievement. As well, technology links schools and students' homes, teachers and families, ensuring communication—and plenty of it.

- Schools tailored to the community

    Edison designs the core curriculum for all of its schools, then works with individual schools to tailor the core program to the interests of each community. In addition, partnership schools are open early in the morning and late in the afternoon. They are hubs of activity, bringing together adults and children. Edison also opens its schools' doors to the social services a community can offer, linking service providers with the needs of students and their families.

- The advantages of system and scale

    Every school automatically becomes a part of a national network of partnership schools, linked by a common purpose and plan—and linked literally through the technology system. Every school contributes to, and benefits from, the extensive curriculum and professional development efforts. Each has access to an array of specially conceived print and electronic materials to enhance all aspects of the learning program. And every school is served by a business services department that advises on matters related to the upkeep, cleanliness, and general management of the building. Thus, when a school forms a partnership with The Edison Project, it joins a family of schools across the country and expands its resources, both human and material.

Special features of the Edison Project

- School organization
  - Small schools-within-schools through academy structure
  - Houses of 100–180 students
  - Reading and math groups of 15–20 students
- Use of time
  - 200–205-day school year
  - 7-hour day for primary students
  - 8-hour day for older students
- Curriculum
  - Reading/language arts for 150 minutes daily
  - Mathematics for 60 minutes daily
  - Science or social science for a minimum of 75 minutes daily
  - Art or music for a minimum of 45 minutes 2 or 3 times weekly
  - World language for a minimum or 45 minutes 2 or 3 times weekly
  - Character and ethics taught daily through humanities curriculum and morning meeting
  - Physical fitness and health for a minimum of 45 minutes 2 or 3 times weekly
  - Practical arts and skills integrated daily
- Technology
  - 1 laptop computer for every teacher
  - Home technology for the family of every student in grade 3 or higher
  - 3 computers per classroom
  - 1 multimedia machine per house, including scanner and video camera
- Teachers
  - 1½–2 hours planning time for teachers daily

- 4–6-teacher teams supported by specialists in world language, art and music, and physical fitness and health
- 4-week summer institute for all staff before each new partnership school opens

Contact

Saundra Brown
The Edison Project
521 Fifth Avenue, 15th Floor
New York, NY 10175
Voice: (212) 419-1600
Fax: (212) 419-1604
sabrown@newyork.edisonproject.com
www.edisonproject.com

The Efficacy Institute

Our Vision

Our Vision is a nation dedicated to producing successive generations of citizens prepared to constructively participate in the society of their time.

Our Mission

Our Mission, therefore, is development. We work to release the inherent intellectual capacity of all children, and to affirm their right to learn.

We commit ourselves to break the cycle of underdevelopment that afflicts far too many children, especially children of color and the economically disadvantaged. We will eradicate the myth that they are incapable of learning at high levels by demonstrating the truth of their capacities to rapidly build knowledge and skills.

We appeal to the most positive and powerful human instinct: *develop the children*. We, all adults, are responsible for managing their development, and we can learn how to do it.

Our ultimate objective is freedom. Developed people are free to find meaning, to build quality lives and to leave a legacy of wisdom and humanity.

Background

The Efficacy Institute begins with the assumption that America's problems with education are not local, and that they are not peculiar to a particular school, school system, or region of the country. America's problems are systemic and national, and are embedded in the way Americans think about children and their learning capacities. Further, educators and parents use a core set of fundamentally ineffective methods to teach America's children. The Efficacy Institute's intention is to deploy its framework to address these problems in a national movement of education reform and transformation.

The Efficacy initiative is built on a new paradigm about the learning capacities of children. This is a constructive belief system supported by an operational framework that can be quickly and effectively adopted by families, institutions and communities to help achieve twenty-first century educational outcomes for their children.

The Paradigm

> Efficacy is founded on a simple, powerful belief: Smart is not something you just are; Smart is something you can *get*.

Intelligence is constructed, built up through the action of effective effort. It is a dynamic set of capabilities that grow and develop as children commit sustained effort to challenging tasks. Children get smart—they become more intelligent in the normal course of engaging their effort in everyday activities ranging from sports, to conversation with their peers, to complex computer games. They can get smart in school, too, in critically important ways. High-level education will happen for all children if responsible adults know what to do. The necessary transformation of adult practices to maximize intelligence in children begins with belief. The Efficacy Institute teaches American adults that typical American children have all the intellectual capacity they need to learn at high levels—a belief that, in too many cases, is absent today. The first crucial element of Efficacy's mission is a campaign to build a stronger belief, in all Americans, about the capacity of children to learn and the capacity of parents and teachers to teach them.

The Operational Framework

The Efficacy Institute has developed uncomplicated teacher and parent training frameworks. The training frameworks are based on the idea that the great majority of children can achieve at high levels if adults are effective at mobilizing their effort toward clearly defined educational outcomes.

Efficacy Operating Principle

> It is the capacity of adults to mobilize the Effective Effort of children that determines which children do well and which do not. Practices make the difference—teachers and parents get results who understand what to do to actively engage children's efforts at learning tasks.

The Operational Framework has three key elements:

- *Identification of targets*—Adults, and children, must be explicitly aware of the targeted outcomes. Both need to know what the child is expected to know, and able to do, by the end of the 12th grade? By the end of the academic year?

- *Effective instructional practices*—The Efficacy Institute provides specific, concrete practices adults can use to mobilize the effective effort of children toward achieving targeted outcomes.

- *Frequent use of data and feedback*—The Efficacy Institute focuses adults on effective use of achievement data to guide more effective instructional strategies. Instead of using achievement data in the standard way, as a basis for judgments about the intelligence of children, the Institute uses it as feedback to guide strategic changes in practices used by adults, aimed at improvements in performance.

The Efficacy Institute strongly emphasizes there is only one measure of the effectiveness of adult practices—the learning outcomes of children. The Institute expects strong improvements each year, and hold adults responsible for using the tools provided to achieve those improvements. The Institute will transfer the Operational Framework to adults in communitywide initiatives to achieve targeted learning outcomes with their children.

EI Inside

Efficacy has worked hard to develop ways to make the Paradigm, and the Operational Framework readily available to all who wish to use them. The Efficacy Institute has dubbed this approach *EI (Efficacy Institute) Inside*. EI Inside represents The Efficacy Institute's capability to package its own approach and efficiently transfer it as an "operating system." The ultimate goal is to empower willing people and organizations with beliefs, and language to communicate them, and an easy-to-use framework of practices to get results.

Efficacy Operating Principle

Reshape the way children think about intelligence. Teach them that they can "get smart." Tell them you believe in them.

Make sure they all understand that effective effort is the basis of development.

Teach them to be confident that if they work, they *will* learn!

Efficacy Training, Services, and Publications

The following illustrates the various training opportunities available to introduce and learn how to use the Operational Framework effectively in the classroom, in the home and in one's community.

- Presentation

    A three-hour overview of the Efficacy approach to development, during which Efficacy staff explain a step-by-step process of accelerating the development of teachers and students to meet increasing challenges. Staff examine assumptions about learning capacity, focusing on the Efficacy Model of Development as the behavioral approach to how people learn and develop. Participants critically examine the prevailing belief, "some have it and some don't," and how it results in behaviors, which defeat the best efforts to develop all children. This is an effective way to give large groups an initial exposure to core Efficacy concepts.

    A particular focus on the role of parents and families in accelerating their children's development and encouraging a collaboration of teacher/parent efforts is used for community meetings. Parent groups and key members of the community focus on how they can use the Efficacy process to coordinate their efforts to change outcomes for children in their homes and school/community.

- Extended Presentation

    An interactive one-day workshop comprised of the previously described standard presentation followed by focused group discussions and action planning. These group discussions are structured to examine the implications of the Efficacy Model of Development for their school systems. This format is appropriate for administrators, staff developers, and other members of the school community.

- Executive Seminar

    An intensive, two-day seminar offering an introduction to Efficacy and a framework for assessing the policies and practices of school organizations. This seminar is held to introduce senior administrators, board members, corporate leaders and community stakeholders to the Efficacy approach, and represents the first stage in the process of bringing Efficacy into a community.

- Efficacy Seminar for Educators

    This four-day seminar is a highly experiential process that provides educators with tools to implement effective classroom practices that mobilize their students' effort toward high standards. Educators acquire tools to align their classroom curricula to year-end benchmarks; to develop effective lessons that educate students at higher cognitive levels (analysis, synthesis, evaluation) required by new standards and assessments; and to use student performance data to continuously revise their teaching strategies. Educators also receive instructional tools to teach their students how to apply the belief that "smart is not something you just are; smart is something you can *get*;" how to use their data (scores and grades) to continuously build new learning strategies; and how to sustain their effort in the face of academic/social challenge and difficulty. Conducted in two sessions of two consecutive days each, separated by approximately four weeks, this seminar is a prerequisite for further Efficacy training. Each participant will receive one classroom set (30) of student tools for use with their students.

- Efficacy for Administrators

    This six-day workshop focuses sharply on using data to identify where students stand in relationship to clearly identified academic targets. Administrators learn a new method for providing accurate information about the effectiveness of instruction so that teachers can decide based on feedback, not assumptions, what each student needs to hit the target. Administrators also learn a strategy for conducting a coaching session to discover the nature of the problem and how to offer support for improved teacher performance. Principals and senior level, on-site staff learn how to integrate Efficacy management and team building strategies into their day-to-day operations to ensure that they provide the instructional leadership and cultural change needed for measurable improvement in "hard" classroom outcomes.

- Efficacy Community Services Seminar

    This is a three-day seminar for policy makers, staff, and volunteers of community-based organizations. The seminar is a content-rich and highly interactive process that is a powerful vehicle for making structural, cultural, and institutional changes in programs and services consistent with the belief that all people can develop at high levels. It focuses on teaching and infusing practices that transfer the concepts and operational approaches of Efficacy. The goal is to build and sustain a culture of high standards and high expectations.

- Efficacy Workshop for Parents and Families

    This one-day workshop introduces parents and families to the Efficacy approach as an effective tool for developing their children. Participants, through a series of exercises, build confidence in their own parenting capabilities and develop concrete strategies for supporting their children's learning processes; that is, they learn how to build their children's confidence, to shape their children's Effective Effort, and help their children overcome obstacles that get in the way of their development. The workshop is facilitated in English and Spanish.

- Efficacy for Job Training Programs

    This workshop serves unemployed and under-employed individuals in a job training venue. It defines the core elements of a "quality life," and establishes that development is the foundation. Through stories and activities, individuals learn *how* to become developed so that they can build a quality of life for themselves. They begin by exploring two fundamental beliefs about intelligence that answer the question "what leads to development?" Individuals learn that effective effort is the key to development, and experience a step-by-step process for applying focused, committed effort to accomplish challenging goals, and ultimately to obtain and maintain suitable employment.

Sustaining the Efficacy Approach

- Efficacy for the Instructional Support Team Leaders (IST)

    The Instructional Support Team is "Efficacy certified" to provide onsite support to teachers and administrators as they implement Efficacy at their schools. It is an important component of institutionalizing the Efficacy approach—building in-house capacity to sustain the use of Efficacy tools after formal training has ended. Team members learn how to coach teachers as they implement effective practices, congruent with the Efficacy paradigm. The IST facilitates biweekly teacher-team meetings to coach teachers as they transform student performance data into feedback, and support them in devising strategies to improve student achievement based on the feedback. Members of this team also guide teachers' development of an instructional repertoire and serves as an advocate for the resource needs of teacher. The IST process involves seven days of training, and seven consultation days to provide members with ongoing practice and support in using the Efficacy approach to achieve measurable improvements in student achievement. The process also includes ongoing telephone consultation with the Efficacy Institute trainers for one year.

♦ Efficacy Tech-Transfer (Train-the-Practitioner)

A process designed to certify practitioners to deliver the following Efficacy workshops: The Efficacy Mission Orientation; The Use of Efficacy Tools; The Efficacy Presentation; The Efficacy Workshop for Parents and Families; and Efficacy for Job Training Programs. It is customized to meet the needs of each district. The certification process includes prework; a two to five-day working session onsite or at the Efficacy Institute with certified trainers; and a cotraining/observation schedule that is managed by an Efficacy-certified trainer.

Additional Services

♦ Building Collaborative Relationships

A two-day workshop that provides a concrete, step-by-step approach to establish and maintain relationships with school/community leadership and its members. Participants explore techniques for identifying and getting buy-in to common objectives, learn how to build trust, and explore the barriers to communication that often block the formation of effective teams.

♦ Efficacy for Students

During this session, students gain an understanding that development—the process of getting better, stronger and smarter—is a function of the effectiveness of one's effort. They explore how variables such as self-confidence, the expectations of others, and the fear of failure impact an individual's capacity to learn and develop. Students discuss a model for learning that teaches them how development takes place, and learn a Process of Development. The session builds students' belief in their own capabilities to learn at the highest levels and increases their commitment to their development. It can be a one- or two-day workshop and is designed to address the needs of undergraduate and graduate students; however, it may be customized to meet the needs of elementary and secondary students as well.

- Consulting/Onsite Coaching

Efficacy trainers/consultants are available to assist those who are implementing Efficacy in their classrooms and their programs by providing onsite coaching, either individually or in small groups. This includes teachers, parent and family groups, and organizations, as well as community volunteers and agency staff. Institute staff are also available to consult with managers at all levels of school organizations to assist them in evaluating school and/or districtwide practices, policies, and operating principles in order to make these congruent with an institutional mission that acknowledges the educability of all students to high levels of achievement. Consulting days are "customized" to meet the expressed needs of individual schools, districts and communities.

Publications

- *Your Tools for Getting Smart*

These Efficacy student tools are included in the participant materials of Efficacy Seminar for Educators. Individuals who have completed the Efficacy Seminar for Educators may purchase additional copies of the elementary (grades 1–3) and the middle (grades 4–8) student tools for their students. Schools with certified Efficacy practitioners may purchase copies for use in training.

- *The Efficacy Parent Guide*

This magazine provides a step-by-step approach to development —getting better, stronger, and smarter at anything that builds a quality of life. Parents are introduced to the Efficacy concept of Effective Effort as a tool for managing the development of children. Through articles, stories, Q&As, and activities, parents learn "at home" strategies for increasing their children's use of Effective Effort, communicating high expectations, building confidence, and managing obstacles to their children's development. It is intended for use by parents, other adults in the home, or in organized parent-based workshops and meetings sponsored by schools, parent organizations, and community-based agencies. Both English and Spanish editions are available.

Videos

- *Efficacy in Action: Working to Get Smart*

    It is a coproduction of Phi Delta Kappa International, Agency for Instructional Technology, and the Efficacy Institute. This 25-minute video shows how the Efficacy approach works in classrooms and schools. The viewer learns how Efficacy concepts are taught and used and observes its effects on students, teachers, and administrators. A companion guide facilitates the use of the video. The intended audience for this video is administrators, teachers, parents, and other members of the community.

- *Positive Insights in Education: Jeff Howard Redefining Intelligence*

    This is a coproduction of Phi Delta Kappa International and Agency for Instructional Technology. In this 30-minute video, Jeff Howard presents a view which contrasts the traditional view of intelligence, describes the implications of both views for school policy and practice, and outlines a plan for future action in developing children at high levels.

Contact

Karen Spiller
Client Services
The Efficacy Institute, Inc.
128 Spring Street
Lexington, MA 02421
Voice: (781) 862-4390
Fax: (781) 862-2580
efficacy@tiac.net

Effective Schools

Mission and Goals

Effective Schools Products, Ltd. is a consulting, training, and publishing firm dedicated to advancing the vision of successful learning for all children. Organizational efforts are based on the effective schools research and practices that have been identified and described over the past 25 years. Experiences with school reform include programs at the state, local district, and individual school levels which are located in rural, suburban, and urban settings.

Because Effective Schools Products, Ltd. is dedicated to advancing school improvement based on effective schools research, staff strive to be faithful to the underlying philosophy and beliefs that characterize the effective schools movement. Key among those beliefs are:

- All children can learn and come to school motivated to do so;
- Schools have sufficient control over enough of the variables to assure that all students do learn; and
- Schools should be held accountable for measured student results, and should disaggregate their measured student achievement to be certain that all students, regardless of gender, race, ethnicity, social class, or family background, are successfully learning the intended curriculum.

Effective Schools Products, Ltd. has developed a variety of video programs, books, and other written training materials, as well as computer software programs—all aimed at empowering individual schools and districts with the tools and the conceptual framework they need to engage in long term, systemic changes necessary to assure that all students learn. The programs offered emphasize critical components such as site-based management and collaborative planning with teachers, administrators, and parents. The *effective schools research model* attempts to help local teachers develop systems of instruction that are mission driven, results oriented, and research based. This model has been implemented in thousands of school districts and has good evidence to support that, when implemented with fidelity, all students will learn.

The Effective Schools Process

The Effective Schools process is based on proven research and case studies. The process is unique in that it is collaborative in form, ongoing, self-renewing, based on quality, equity, and high student achievement, and grounded in the belief that *all* children can learn. The process includes knowledge-based, high-yield improvement strategies. The Effective Schools process has been used throughout the United States at all levels of schooling, and serves as the basis for several federal and state reform efforts.

Any school seeking to improve their practices based on research findings will find the Effective Schools process sensible and straightforward. Schools will use research findings as a guide to planned program change and implementation. Research findings provided by Effective Schools are focused on those variables that have been found to add value in student learning and student performance. The Effective Schools Improvement Process approaches school change from three interdependent vantage points. First, since school change is regarded as people change, schools must examine the research on effective staff development. Second, because school change can take place in organizational change, schools must look at effective organizational development. Third, whether school change is to be thought of as people or systems change, a school must approach it as planned change.

In using the research findings, an Effective Schools approach follows four guiding principles on school change:

- Preserve the single school as the strategic unit for the planned change.

- Principals, though essential as leaders of change, cannot do it alone, and thus, teachers and others must be integral parts of the school improvement process.

- School improvement, like any change, is best approached as a process, not an event. Such a process approach is more likely to create a permanent change in the operating culture of the school that will accommodate this new function called continuous school improvement.

- Finally, like the original Effective Schools, these improving schools must feel as if they have a choice in the matter, and equally important, they must feel as if they have control over the process of change.

As a school starts its journey of effective change, it relies on some underlying assumptions.

- First, the effective school has an orderly, purposeful, businesslike atmosphere that is free from the threat of physical harm. This environment must have certain desirable behaviors where students are actually helping each other. In this environment, there is an interaction of students and teachers in a collaborative/cooperative approach.

- Second, there is an expectation that all students can attain mastery of the essential school skills. This will also include teachers having high expectations for themselves. To meet these high expectations, a school is restructured to assure that teachers have access to more *tools* to help them achieve successful learning for all. And these schools must be transformed from institutions designed for *instruction* to institutions designed to assure *learning*.

- Third, in the effective school, the principal and all adults must take an active role in instructional leadership. The principal will become a *leader of leaders* rather than a leader of followers. Specifically, the principal will become a coach, partner, and cheerleader.

- Fourth, in the effective school, there is a clearly articulated school mission through which the staff shares an understanding of and commitment to the instructional goals, priorities, assessment procedures, and accountability expectations. This school mission will promote learning for all students and will acknowledge the school's responsibility for achieving this.

- Fifth, the effective school's teachers allocate a significant amount of classroom time to instruction in the essential skills. This instruction must take place in an interdisciplinary curriculum. A school, in order to be effective in its instruction time, must focus on areas that are valued the most, with abandonment of some less important content.

- Sixth, in the effective school, student academic progress is measured frequently through a variety of assessment procedures. The results of these assessments are used to improve individual student performance and also to improve the instructional program. These results will show the alignment that must exist between the intended, taught, and tested curriculum. Also, assessment tools must emphasize more *authentic* assessment of curriculum mastery.

- Finally, an effective school must form a partnership with the parents. Schools must build trust and communicate to parents that they all share the same goal. The goal is an effective school and home for all children.

Contact

Becky Hulburt
Effective Schools Products, Ltd.
2199 Jolly Road, Suite #160
Okemos, MI 48864
Voice: (800) 827-8041 or (517) 349-8841
Fax: (517) 349-8852
staff@effectiveschools.com
www.effectiveschools.com

Foxfire

Mission Statement

The Foxfire mission is to teach, model, and refine an active, learner-centered approach to education that is academically sound and that promotes continuous interaction between students and their communities, so that students will find fulfillment as creative, productive, critical citizens.

To accomplish its mission, Foxfire has developed the following set of interrelated and complementary strategies:

- To encourage and support change in schooling by working with educators, primarily through teacher training and support programs, to redefine the relationship among teachers, learners, and the curriculum;

- To model the redefined relationship among teachers, learners, and the curriculum by working directly with students; and

- To model the significance of the relationship between the community and learning environments through the Foxfire Center, which preserves elements of the local Appalachian culture and facilitates Foxfire programs.

Foxfire's primary purpose is to train teachers to be active, learner-centered facilitators of student learning. Teachers using the Foxfire Approach implement strategies that are academically sound, and they work to promote continuous interaction between learners and their communities so that learners will find fulfillment as creative, productive, thoughtful citizens.

- Learners

  Learning environments are characterized by student involvement and action, by thoughtful reflection and rigorous assessment, by imagination and problem solving, by applications beyond the classroom for what is learned, and by meaningful connections to the community. In these classrooms, students build the ability to work collaboratively and assume responsibility for their own learning processes.

- Teachers

  In small, isolated schools and massive urban campuses across the nation, teachers use the Foxfire Approach to Teaching and Learning to bring new excitement and meaning to the work they and their students do together. Guided by the 11 Core Practices and supported through formal and informal connections to Foxfire, these teachers create classrooms with strong community where learning grows out of student interest and where high standards for student achievement are set.

- Community

In 1996, Foxfire grew out of interaction between a teacher and a group of high school students and their community. The richness of this educational experience resulted in the publication of *The Foxfire Magazine* and *The Foxfire Book* series and formed a core component of the Foxfire Approach to Teaching and Learning. Through the implementation of the Approach, learners' connections with the classroom, the surrounding community, and the world beyond the classroom are clear; and curricular content is connected to the world in which students live. For many students, the process engages them, for the first time, in identifying with and characterizing their community.

The Foxfire Core Practices

- The work teachers and learners do together is infused from the beginning with learner choice, design, and revision. The central focus of the work grows out of learners' interests and concerns. Most problems that arise during classroom activity are solved in collaboration with learners, and learners are supported in the development of their ability to solve problems and accept responsibility.

- The role of the teacher is that of facilitator and collaborator. Teachers are responsible for assessing and attending to learners' developmental needs, providing guidance, identifying academic givens, monitoring each learner's academic and social growth, and leading each into new areas of understanding and competence.

- The academic integrity of the work teachers and learners do together is clear. Mandated skills and learning expectations are identified to the class. Through collaborative planning and implementation, students engage and accomplish the mandates. In addition, activities assist learners in discovering the value and potential of the curricula and its connections to other disciplines.

Different Ways of Knowing— The Galef Institute

Founded in 1989, the Galef Institute is a nonprofit educational organization whose primary goal is to work with educators in public schools, schools of education, and other reform agencies to improve student achievement by strengthening the teaching profession.

To achieve this goal, the Institute assembled a leading team of educators and researchers, under the direction of senior author Linda Adelman Johannesen, to develop the comprehensive school reform initiative Different Ways of Knowing. Extensively field tested in more than 500 primary and elementary classrooms over four years, Different Ways of Knowing (DWoK) collaborative multiyear school reform partnerships are now underway in California, Florida, Kentucky, Michigan, Mississippi, and Pennsylvania.

Different Ways of Knowing helps teachers facilitate standards driven interdisciplinary learning in their classrooms. It offers a three-year course of study blended with powerful curriculum tools for kindergarten through 8th grade. The curriculum integrates the study of history and social studies with literature and writing, math and science, and the performing, visual, and media arts. The arts focus of Different Ways of Knowing is an important pathway to children's understanding and expression of deep knowledge in all disciplines. Different Ways of Knowing stresses positive expectations for the academic and social achievement of all children, thematically integrated instruction across disciplines, active student participation, early intervention, and parent participation in the classroom and at home.

Curriculum

- A rigorous curriculum with powerful teacher and student learning resources;
- Content-rich, developmentally appropriate, teacher planning guides as powerful tools to accelerate teachers' understanding of interdisciplinary instruction;
- Strategies for reaching at-risk populations;
- A large library of thematically organized, culturally diverse, children's literature and reference books for every classroom;

- Historical documents, maps, videos, and related media;
- A professional library series of best practices from the field, connecting theory to practice in all subject areas.

Different Ways of Knowing also offers a three-year course of study for professional growth and community building, which includes:

- Developmental schoolwide, districtwide, capacity-building support for teachers, administrators, and parents;
- Annual summer orientations and renewal institutes;
- Seminars and workshops throughout the school year;
- Instructional coaching and technical assistance;
- Facilitated support and study;
- Summer school practicum sessions;
- Leadership training and national fellowships;
- Leadership teams of school and district personnel to facilitate change; and
- Teacher-to-teacher communications and other professional connections through newsletters and DWoKnet—the interactive professional development Web site for educators who are implementing high standards at the classroom level.

Different Ways of Knowing has been studied by research teams in two large-scale implementation trials: A national longitudinal study was published in 1995 by Dr. James Catterall at the UCLA Graduate School of Education and Information Studies. A second study, published in 1997, was led by researchers Drs. Ric Hovda, Diane Kyle, and Joseph M. Petrosko of the University of Louisville, and Cecilia Wang and David Sogin of the University of Kentucky.

The two studies identify continuously rising academic and social achievement of Different Ways of Knowing students. Their success is tied not only to the content of the Different Ways of Knowing curriculum, but also to a supportive interdisciplinary infrastructure and an integrated vision at both the school and district level; ongoing professional growth opportunities for teachers and administrators including regularly scheduled workshops and support group meetings; shared learning and collaboration among artists, coaches, and teachers; and integrated teacher and student materials.

Collaboration to Improve and Support Teaching and Learning

Different Ways of Knowing collaborative projects are now underway throughout the nation—thousands of students are participating along with their teachers, administrators, and families. The Galef Institute has active and effective partnerships with teachers, principals, artists, and other educators in schools, school districts, and state departments of education; college and university researchers and faculties; private foundations, corporations, and businesses dedicated to school improvement; visual and performing arts organizations working to link arts and learning; professional education associations; and parents and other individuals who commit time and resources to improving education.

Offering both professional development and a student-centered, interdisciplinary curriculum, Different Ways of Knowing helps teachers improve the learning climate in their schools. From kindergarten through sixth grade, it integrates the study of history and social studies with literature, writing, math, science, and the performing, visual, and media arts. The interdisciplinary and hands-on approach to learning helps children develop their multiple intelligences—their artistic and social skills, their verbal and math skills, as well as their intuitive and logical thinking skills.

The arts focus of Different Ways of Knowing is an important pathway to children's understanding and expression of deep knowledge in all disciplines. It builds students' self-confidence and interest in their own learning—supporting research studies that show the more students play an active role in their own learning and achievement, the more likely they are to stay in school and value learning.

Different Ways of Knowing is not a one-size-fits-all approach to school improvement that can be instituted overnight. School change is a local process. The initiative, when fully integrated into the culture of a school and school district, becomes a part of the overall plan for improvement. Because Different Ways of Knowing promotes changes in teaching, ongoing support and assistance are crucial parts of the program. Teachers form collegial support study groups and coach each other in new ways to reach their students.

Assumptions Underlying Different Ways of Knowing

Different Ways of Knowing draws upon an extensive research base of related educational theories and their perspectives on learning and teaching—all designed to help teachers tap the full potential of every child.

The assumptions underlying the development of Different Ways of Knowing are powerful:

- Positive expectations

    All children can succeed in school academically and socially—when we build on their strengths and talents and provide appropriate learning opportunities and a positive learning environment.

- Active thematic learning

    Children learn best when they are active participants in learning and when instruction is organized around compelling themes and problem solving inquiry.

- Early success

Children who develop confidence as learners are more likely to stay in school and value learning.

- Powerful curriculum

    A rigorous, content-rich curriculum and child-centered instruction help children develop their multiple intelligences so that they can express what they know in many different ways.

- Professional collaboration

    Teacher's have ongoing opportunities to learn with and from each other.

- Ongoing assessment and evaluation

    Both students and teachers have regular opportunities to reflect upon their learning.

- Home-community partnerships

    Parents and community members are links to learning about the past, and partners in children's pursuit of knowledge and success in learning.

Contact

Sue Beauregard
Galef Institute
11050 Santa Monica Boulevard, Third Floor
Los Angeles, CA 90025
Voice: (310) 479-8883
Fax: (310) 473-9720
sue@galef.org
www.dwoknet.galef.org

The League of Professional Schools

Mission

- To promote the school as a democratic learning community that is student oriented and focused on improving teaching and learning for all.

Philosophy

Given information and time to collaborate, teachers and administrators can create effective school improvement plans. When teachers are given decision-making power in the planning of an initiative, they implement that initiative with a vigor and determination lacking in top-down decisions.

As one of the most outstanding educational collaborations in the United States, The League is a three-time recipient of the Certificate of Merit awarded by the National Business-Higher Education Forum.

The League of Professional Schools is foremost about the democratization of education—through changes in schoolwide roles, relationships, governance, study, and, most importantly, teaching and learning practices (across classrooms, grades, and departments)—to challenge all students to learn in intellectually and experientially demanding ways. A major premise of the League is that it is the people in the school who best know and care about their students, their programs, and the future possibilities for improvements.

The League's Framework

League schools initiate, implement, and assess schoolwide instructional improvement using a three-part school-renewal framework.

- Part one is a democratically derived covenant of teaching and learning that captures a school's beliefs about the characteristics and expected results of exemplary teaching and learning. The covenant serves as the guiding vision of a school's effort to provide the best possible educational experiences to students.

- Part two is a democratic shared-governance process that all agree to follow in bringing the covenant to life. This includes agreements about how decisions are made and about the roles to be assumed by administrators, teachers, parents, and community members.

- Part three is an action research process that provides the school with information about how it is doing in bringing the covenant to life. This process helps schools investigate issues, take actions, and study the results so that new actions can be taken.

Implementation of this framework can help transform a school into a learning community where everyone learns and grows.

The League of Professional Schools is:

- A school-based improvement program in which the staff sets its own goals;

- A voluntary program supported by at least 80 percent of the school staff;

- A program where the school community establishes a covenant of teaching and learning that is enacted through a shared governance and action research; and

- A program that helps a school study itself and evaluate its instructional goals.

The League currently consists of over 100 schools in Georgia and collaborates with networks in Nevada, and eastern Washington. The Georgia League serves schools in urban, suburban, and rural settings across all grade levels. Georgia League schools receive:

- A two-day planning and orientation workshop for a school team;

- Quarterly meetings;

- A bi-annual newsletter, *In Sites,* about the work occurring in League schools written by League practitioners;

- An annual League conference highlighting the work of the schools, the latest in research-based innovations and trends, sharing sessions, and presentations from nationally known educators;

- An onsite facilitation visit to each school by a League practitioner, staff member or associate;

- Special summer institutes related to issues the schools wish to pursue in greater depth;

- ♦ An information retrieval system to honor school requests for information and research related to educational issues, policies, and practices;

- ♦ Other publications of interest, including a comprehensive directory of schools and occasional monographs on the experiences of schools as they implement the premises of the League; and

- ♦ Funding provided by the College of Education, The University of Georgia, membership fees, the Annenberg Rural Challenge, and the Lettie Pate Evans, BellSouth, UPS, and Pittulloch Foundations.

A successful League school is foremost one which defines good education for itself, through its goals and desired practices, and then engages in the moral equivalent of war in achieving that vision.

Contact

The League of Professional Schools
124 Aderhold Hall
The University of Georgia
Athens, GA 30602
Voice: (706) 542-2516
Fax: (706) 542-2502
lps@coe.uga.edu
www.coe.uga.edu/lps

The Paideia Program

Background

Paideia is an approach to restructuring schools to foster more active learning and a better use of teacher and student time. Paideia educators focus on a significant curriculum and three types of teaching and learning for all students. The goals of Paideia are to prepare students to:

- Earn a living;
- Be citizens; and
- Be lifelong learners.

The curriculum stresses key ideas and basic skills with primary sources used for seminars and text books for references. The stress is on active learning for both students and teachers. The three types of teaching and learning are:

- Socratic teaching for understanding;
- Coaching for the development of skills (e.g., reading, writing, listening, analyzing, computing, and problem-solving); and
- Didactic instruction for recall of important facts.

Results have indicated improvements in school climate, attendance, communication skills and student behavior. In addition, students are reading and writing more with discussions linked to improvement in comprehension.

The Paideia Group was a group of educators chaired by Mortimer Adler that met over a period of several years to discuss education reform. The Paideia Group members published three books: *The Paideia Proposal* (1982), *Paideia Problems and Possibilities* (1983), and *The Paideia Program* (1984). In response to many requests for training, Dr. Adler formed Paideia Associates to design and conduct the training programs in 1985.

The Paideia Group, Inc. (PGI) is a national nonprofit organization with national and international members. Mortimer Adler is the Honorary Chairman. Its purpose is to monitor and guide development, foster networking, and share information. In 1992, PGI instituted the stages of development for a Paideia school. In 1993, the board issued the certification process for trainers. Paideia Group, Inc. conducts regional workshops, an annual national conference, and onsite Paideia training programs.

A true Paideia school is more than regular Socratic seminars, less lecturing and more student-centered learning. It is an ever-growing community of learners—adults as well as students—who are dedicated to their own learning and that of others.

The National Paideia Center promotes the efforts of educators who are implementing the long-term reform of public education known as the Paideia Program (paideia is from the Greek *paidos*: the upbringing of a child).

The goal of the Paideia Program is to provide a rigorous, liberal arts education in grades K-12, which will allow all graduates to have the skills necessary to earn a living, to think and act critically as responsible citizens, and to continue educating themselves as lifelong learners. The program promotes these teaching techniques to ensure both educational quality and equality:

- The didactic mode is the acquisition of organized knowledge through means such as textbooks, lectures, and videos. John Goodlad has estimated that roughly 85 percent of our classroom instruction time in the U.S. is currently spent this way. While necessary, this portion of learning should be more interactive and should monopolize much less of the school day.

- The coaching aspect of the program is the way students actively gain the intellectual skills which are necessary for further learning. Coaching is the core of the Paideia Program and requires practice, mastery, and learning by doing. The amount of time given to this activity should be greatly expanded, and a wide array of methods and approaches should be used in the classroom (e.g., labs, cooperative learning techniques, project-centered learning).

- The seminar component is a way for students to deepen their understanding of the ideas they have been studying, and apply them to their own lives and values. Seminars should be used as a regular instructional method in all grades, K-12. The seminar process, with the teacher facilitating an open exploration of the ideas in a work, has the greatest capacity to transform the nature of school for students and teachers because a bond of mutual respect is created, both peer to peer and teacher to student. Additionally, each student must think critically to understand ideas, solve problems, make decisions, resolve conflicts, and apply knowledge and skills to new situations; and articulation, listening, and critical thinking skills are improved. For these reasons, the seminar is usually the method first introduced to schools. Students and teachers find that skills in seminar transfer to their other subjects, improving attitudes and motivation.

Since *The Paideia Proposal* was first published, hundreds of schools have adopted aspects of the program. Schools that implement the plan often report positive results with better attendance rates, increased college acceptance rates, and lower incidence of dropping out.

The National Paideia Center was established at the University of North Carolina at Chapel Hill in 1988, primarily through the partnership of Adler and then University President William Friday. Paideia staff collect and disseminate information; plan, coordinate, and report on research; and work closely with schools and school systems to train teachers and administrators.

Mission

- Act as an information clearinghouse for schools nationwide that are establishing Paideia programs;

- Provide training in Paideia methods and technical assistance to interested schools and educators, focusing on whole-school Paideia reform;

- Create a group of Paideia schools to serve as national demonstration sites for implementation;

- Continue research on and evaluation of the results of Paideia methods.

Paideia Principles

The principles of the Paideia Program are:

- That all children can learn;

- That, therefore, they all deserve the same quality of schooling, not just the same quantity;

- That the quality of schooling to which they are entitled is what the wisest parents would wish for their own children, the best education for the best being the best education for all;

- That schooling at its best is preparation for becoming generally educated in the course of a whole lifetime, and that schools should be judged on how well they provide such preparation;

- That the three callings for which schooling should prepare all Americans are (a) to earn a decent livelihood, (b) to be a good citizen of the nation and the world, and (c) to make a good life for one's self;

- That the primary cause of genuine learning is the activity of the learner's own mind, sometimes with the help of a teacher functioning as a secondary and cooperative cause;

- That the three types of teaching that should occur in our schools are didactic teaching of subject matter, coaching that produces the skills of learning, and Socratic questioning in seminar discussion;

- That the results of these three types of teaching should be (a) the acquisition of organized knowledge, (b) the formation of habits of skill in the use of language and mathematics, and (c) the growth of the mind's understanding of basic ideas and issues;

- That each student's achievement of these results would be evaluated in terms of that student's competencies and not solely related to the achievements of other students;

- That the principal of the school should never be a mere administrator, but always a leading teacher who should be cooperatively engaged with the school's teaching staff in planning, reforming, and reorganizing the school as an educational community;

- That the principal and faculty of a school should themselves be actively engaged in learning;

- That the desire to continue their own learning should be the prime motivation of those who dedicate their lives to the profession of teaching.

The Essential Elements of a Paideia School

These elements are offered by The National Paideia Center as a set of working guidelines, not as a prescription. They are 14 statements that educators can use to measure the progress of their own local initiative.

- General characteristics
  - A Paideia school is a student-centered school.
  - Students in a Paideia school learn to become self-governing, both as individuals and as a group. As much as possible, discipline should be administered through conflict resolution and student governance. Students participate in the democratic process.

- All teachers and administrators in a Paideia school are lifelong learners.
- The Paideia school is the center of a larger learning community.
- A Paideia school is dedicated to the intellectual development of both children and adults.
- A Paideia school is dedicated to the learning of *all* students; all students succeed.

♦ Teaching Strategies and Techniques

- All teachers in a Paideia school use Socratic seminars as a central teaching learning device, both school-wide and integrated into the curriculum.
- All teachers in a Paideia school use coaching techniques for the majority of their instructional program.
- All of the teachers in a Paideia school use relatively little didactic teaching and that which they do use is of very high quality.

♦ Curriculum

- A Paideia school stresses the same integrated core curriculum for all students and teaches all students in heterogeneous groups.
- The Paideia school allows curriculum needs to shape scheduling, and scheduling flexibility is the rule rather than the exception.
- A Paideia School should educate all students across a wide range of intelligences, nurturing them in fine arts, movement, music, and the manual arts and giving them the opportunity to explore these areas as they relate to core academic subjects.

♦ Evaluation

- In a Paideia school assessment of students and teachers is individualized rather than standardized—emphasizing portfolio and narrative assessments rather than traditional grading and appraisal. Individual growth is always stressed.
- Since the goal of schooling is to foster lifelong learning in all those involved, a Paideia school is full of adults and children who view themselves as constantly growing and learning, whose self-assessment is both demanding and fluid.

Results

A recent program evaluation by the Department of Research and Evaluation at the University of North Carolina at Greensboro suggests that the whole-school implementation facilitated by the National Paideia Center has a powerful impact on all students:

> Paideia has similar effects on majority and minority students, and in one case where there were effects relating to race, fully implementing Paideia reduced the negative effects of social comparison for minority students.
>
> —1998 Program Evaluation
> University of North Carolina at Greensboro

Contact

Dr. Terry Roberts
The National Paideia Center
School of Education
PO Box 26171
University of North Carolina at Greensboro
Greensboro, NC 27402-6171
Voice: (336) 334-3729
Fax: (336) 334-3739
troberts@email.unc.edu
www.unc.edu/depts/ed/cel-paideia.html

The School Development Program

Mobilizing the "Village"

The School Development Program was started in 1968 by Yale University's Dr. James P. Comer, a physician, educator, and writer. Dr. Comer is also the Maurice Falk Professor of Child Psychiatry and Associate Dean of the Yale University School of Medicine. Dr. Comer recognized that children need schools that nurture them through a collaboration of teachers, administrators, support staff, families and others in the community. Children are the center of the school.

Inspired by the universal wisdom of the African proverb "it takes a whole village to raise a child," and backed by extensive child development research, the School Development Program brings caring adults together to work for the children of each school or *village*. In 1968, Dr. Comer and his colleagues at the Yale Child Study Center introduced the program to two New Haven, Connecticut public schools. Since then, the School Development Program has been adopted by 600 schools in 20 states, the District of Columbia, Trinidad-Tobago, and England.

The School Planning and Management Team

The team includes parents, teachers, administrators, support staff, and in middle schools and high schools, students. The team coordinates all school activities and is responsible for:

- The Comprehensive School Plan, which sets academic, social and public relations goals;
- Staff Development that meets the needs identified in the Comprehensive School Plan; and
- Assessment and Modification, which identifies opportunities and areas needing adjustment, based on school data and patterns.

The Student and Staff Support Team

This team includes the school principal and staff members with specific child development expertise, such as a school social worker, psychologist, counselor, or a nurse. The team connects all of the school's student services, promotes sharing of information and advice, addresses individual student needs, accesses resources outside the school, and develops prevention programs.

The Parent Team

This team develops activities for parents to support the school's social and academic programs and selects representatives to serve on the School Planning and Management Team. Parents contribute to the development of all of the children in the school as well as to that of their own children.

All three teams are guided by these principles:

- Collaboration

    Everyone participates and helps create a climate of cooperation, trust and support. The teams do not paralyze the principal, and the principal does not use the teams as a *rubber stamp*.

- No-fault

    The premise is that many mistakes result from misunderstandings, misinterpretations or miscommunications. No-fault focuses on solving problems rather than on placing blame, which helps create a safe environment and fosters productivity.

- Consensus

    Everyone has the opportunity to comment on the issues. Decisions are made by consensus rather than by vote. *Winner/loser* situations are avoided. Everyone supports the group's decisions.

Expanding the "Village"

Experience shows that the success of the School Development Program depends on a full-time program facilitator designated by the district superintendent. Assigned to four or five participating schools, the facilitator provides information, training, support and coaching. The facilitator also accesses resources for the program and monitors progress.

In addition, a central office steering committee is necessary to enhance understanding and encourage support of the School Development Program in the district office. With representatives from the participating schools, parent organizations, the central office and unions, the steering committee enables the superintendent to monitor the program and assess the support provided by the central office staff.

The School Development Program helps bring change to one school at a time. Over the years, however, the program has worked best when the *village* is expanded to include the central office and the school board. A number of districts have undertaken systemwide school reform using the School Development Program. Valuable lessons about how best to reorganize a central office to support school reform are emerging.

The program is dynamic at the national level as well. In much the same way that it asks school people to look at data to help them improve, the School Development Program continuously uses insights and information from its work with schools and districts to refine the program and to inform the field and the policymaking community.

The program promotes districtwide school reform in the following two ways: providing a mechanism to coordinate all reforms and programs within each school and facilitating the coordination of districtwide activities through parallel mechanisms at all the schools and in the central office.

New Directions

The School Development Program has evolved and expanded. The program originally addressed the needs of urban students and schools, but experience has shown that it can benefit all children. The program is now being implemented in a broad array of diverse communities. Leaders of the School Development Program are increasingly called upon by those who fund programs, by schools of education and by state and federal agencies, for information about the program and about school reform in general.

The program uses the talents and strengths of the school's administrators, teachers, support staff, parents, and, when appropriate, students to plan the school's program. The model works well with other school improvement programs.

The School Development Program began more than 25 years ago as a public school/university partnership. Several universities and social service agencies across the country have taken the program's lead in providing training and technical assistance to school districts implementing the program in their communities.

The School Development Program uses four research strategies to assess its achievements in academics, school climate, self-concept, and behavior: longitudinal and cross-sectional quantitative research using survey instruments and archival data; qualitative research, such as ethnographic studies; theory development; and a national database of information, including demographics.

Results include improved school climate, enhanced self-esteem and improved behavior on the part of students, better collaboration among staff members, improved relationships among adults, and greater focus on children.

When compared with their districts as a whole, School Development Program schools showed greater declines in absenteeism and suspension rates and higher gains in academic achievement, as measured by standardized and state mastery test scores. When compared to non-Comer schools, Comer school students showed significantly higher self-concepts and academic gains. For example, West Mecklenburg High School, in Charlotte, North Carolina, has enjoyed impressive results with the help of the School Development Program. Besides a renewed sense of community, the School Development Program has provided the platform that enabled educators to make good decisions which led to greater student learning. The number of students on the honor roll jumped 75 percent; the number of students enrolled in advanced-level courses increased by 25 percent; and attendance rates rose from 89 percent to almost 94 percent. In addition, the school's American history curriculum has received national recognition for its teaching of civic and social responsibility. Another example is District 13 in Brooklyn, New York, which adopted the School Development Program as the umbrella mechanism for implementing state-mandated, site-based school management. Many District 13 schools are showing academic achievement gains. In addition, parents and other community members are involved in greater numbers and in more meaningful ways than in the past. Interviews with parents, students, teachers and administrators in schools throughout the nation reveal that the School Development Program:

- Increases parental and community involvement;
- Creates a positive school environment;
- Promotes teamwork; and
- Puts children's needs at the center of school planning and management.

Contact

Joanne Corbin
Yale Child Study Center
School Development Program, Department A
53 College Street
New Haven, CT 06510
Voice: (203) 737-1020
Fax: (203) 737-1023
info@clsr.win.net
info.med.yale.edu/comer

SCORE

SCORE is a comprehensive cocurricular support program that brings together administrators, counselors, teachers, parents, and students to increase student academic performance and college/career eligibility, especially for high-risk students. SCORE places students in a rich common core curriculum that leads to university eligibility by the time they graduate from high school. SCORE supports these students in their academic endeavors by equipping them with powerful study skills, assisting them in getting in touch with their personal values and goals, and networking them with appropriate support personnel. SCORE increases academic curricular offerings and decreases remedial course offering on a school campus. SCORE enlists an entire school community in the pursuit of powerful learning. SCORE schools regularly receive commendations on their accreditation reports. Score is a United States Department of Education exemplary program, validated for its effectiveness by the Program Effectiveness Panel.

SCORE trainers work with school teams to design a custom program for accelerating the achievement of high-risk youth, train staff, and provide follow-through support with technical assistance and a complete set of materials, workbooks, and videotapes.

Students are heterogeneously grouped in a rich, college core curriculum that leads to university eligibility by the time they graduate. Students receive support through placement in SCORE class, learning powerful study skills, participating in tutorials, and setting personal goals aligned with their individual values.

SCORE helps schools to implement after-school programs that really work, set up mentoring programs, design tutorial and motivational programs that really work, network with college and community agencies, and work with parents of high-risk students. SCORE is used in Title I, Migrant, Independent Study, and Language Minority programs. SCORE's effectiveness has been validated with several key populations. For example:

- Title I students participating in SCORE maintain a B average in college preparatory courses.

- SCORE Migrant students enroll in 4-year colleges at a rate of 60 percent. Nationwide, the Migrant 4-year college-going rate is 5 percent.

- Students involved in SCORE test out of limited English proficient (LEP) programs at a rate of 95 percent in 4 years.

There are five major components in an effective SCORE program:

- Guidance

    The guidance program includes career counseling, self-esteem development, placement in a rich, academic course of study, reinforcement of progress, intervention, prevention counseling, and college entrance support.

    Each student receives individual guidance counseling at least twice a year. During these sessions, student transcripts are evaluated relative to college preparation, career counseling is provided, and information about positive activities for student involvement is made available. A full training curriculum is provided, enabling the guidance load to be shared by peers, cross-age counselors, community agencies, or parents.

- Tutoring and study skills

    Students receive academic support from a variety of sources to help them succeed in college preparatory courses. Teachers, tutors, and aides receive study skills training. Students learn study skills and practice applying them across the curriculum. A complete tutor training package and study skills curriculum are provided.

- Parents

    School planning teams receive training in strategies to help parents become active and informed supporters of their children's education and partners in pursuing their educational goals. Parents are involved in workshops and meetings to gain the skills necessary to encourage and support their children's educational goals and to reinforce learning in the classroom.

- Motivation

    A motivational program supports students' academic and career goals, promotes their voluntary participation in tutoring, provides them with leadership experiences, and involves them in school/community service. A SCORE club develops leadership skills and provides group motivation and support. A motivational curriculum empowers students to make healthy life choices and to assume personal responsibility for their learning,

- Summer acceleration

    Students are involved in a variety of activities during summer sessions, ranging from a study skills or content acceleration course, to college classes, to residential programs at nearby colleges or universities. Summer programs improve student attitudes toward schoolwork, provide them information about college, motivate them to pursue higher education, accelerate their academic achievement, and acclimate them to a college environment.

SCORE is committed to the ideal that all students are capable of achieving in academic coursework at a level we consider to be college preparatory. SCORE has successfully up-placed students into a rigorous common core curriculum, provided them with academic support, and watched them succeed in numbers greater than the norm.

SCORE's success is based on:

- High expectations

    Students are treated as gifted. When they struggle to learn, strategies are sought to resolve the problem. Lack of ability is never even considered.

- Support groups

    Students are involved in numerous group activities that identify them with academic success.

- Honors focus

    Students' strengths are developed (rather than their weaknesses being remedied). Students are urged to strive for content mastery rather than just a passing grade.

- Flexibility

    SCORE provides a framework and keys to success around which individual schools design their own program. This allows local ownership, and program institutionalization can occur, helping to insure that it will last beyond the original implementers.

- Staff development

    SCORE provides schools with an extensive staff development curriculum that allows them to extend the program through a variety of cost-effective means.

- Focus

    SCORE programs are both curricular and cocurricular. Study skills are infused into the curriculum and academic support is provided through a variety of innovative strategies: group study sessions, after-school tutorials, homework centers, and community tutorial partnerships.

- Student responsibility

  SCORE empowers schools with techniques to assist their students in assuming personal responsibility for their educational success.

- Holistic approach

  SCORE schools approach student success from multiple perspectives, getting at root issues rather than patching symptoms to problems.

- Student-centered approach

  SCORE seeks to personally develop each student in an appropriate manner rather than to fit them into predeveloped molds of learning.

- Active learning

  SCORE develops students into active, lifelong, thinking learners.

- Multidimensional teaching

  SCORE provides teachers with whole-brain, active teaching strategies that utilize multiple intelligences and modalities.

- Leadership

  SCORE develops students into tomorrow's leaders, providing them with many opportunities to explore authentic tasks in the world they will inherit.

- Partnerships

  SCORE enlists multiple partners in designing a school program that graduates productive citizens and students, eligible to enter the college or career of their choice. In SCORE, the entire community plays on the same team and works toward the same goal.

The SCORE Implementation Process:

- Step 1: School planning teams attend a 3-day SCORE Adoption Training workshop that results in a school-wide action plan for change.
- Step 2: School planning teams begin the implementation of their plan. This includes identifying study skills teachers.

- Step 3: All teachers who will be involved in the study skills program participate in a 2-day study skills workshop.
- Step 4: SCORE is launched. Process evaluations are conducted. The program is adapted based on the results of that evaluation.
- Step 5: SCORE schools conduct a formal end-of-the-year evaluation and make programmatic changes based on that evaluation. The evaluation is submitted to SCORE central.
- Step 6: SCORE sites indicate their readiness to host visitors to view the program and select key staff members to complete a trainer of trainers program.
- Step 7: Local trainers are certified. These trainers can maintain the program on their site, providing in-service to new staff members as necessary.

Training and Assistance

- Staff development

    School teams may participate in centralized training or may host onsite personalized staff development. SCORE can operate within existing school facilities using current curriculum and equipment. A director, teacher, tutors, counselors, and parent workers are required to fully implement SCORE.

- Adoption training

    During Adoption Training, school planning teams design the strategy that will be the most workable on their site, given the dynamics of change and faculty readiness. Adoption sites plan a personalized program. Additional staff is trained 4 to 12 weeks later during the study skills in-service. This approach to staff development allows planning teams to rethink the way they run their school, adapt the program to their individual setting, and personalize the program to their site. It also promotes local ownership of the ideals and keys to success. It allows the school's staff to build on their school's strengths.

    SCORE Adoption Training sessions are three-day intensive workshops. Training will prepare participants to adapt the SCORE model to meet their unique needs. The training program is a participatory experience covering management strategies; local need assessment; designing academic support programs; utilizing project-developed materials; program development techniques; parent partnerships; counseling strategies; and effective program evaluation.

Adoption Training Costs

Training is required before purchasing SCORE training manuals. Participants may attend a centralized workshop for $350 per person plus $600 per site for materials or sponsor a local training for $3,750 plus travel, expenses, and materials.

Study Skills Training

Four to 12 weeks after the planning team has designed a personalized SCORE program, all teachers, tutors, and aides participate in a Study Skills In-service. Teachers learn to:

- Teach to all four personality and learning styles;
- Build student strengths;
- Design lessons around whole brain teaching strategies;
- Infuse study skills into their existing curriculum using a theoretical basis;
- Teach students effective listening, communication, note-taking, memory, and test-taking strategies;
- Train students to reduce test anxiety;
- Plan the school curriculum to include teaching study skills in one content area (SCORE classes, study skills, freshman orientation classes, English, or social sciences are common); and
- Design a strategy to communicate with SCORE counselors and tutors, thus extending their effectiveness beyond the classroom.

The two-day Study Skills Training will provide staff developers, teachers, tutors, and aides with strategies and techniques to identify learning preferences; prepare students to take tests; insure student retention; teach; memory techniques; enhance student interest level; utilize peer study groups; teach note taking strategies; and create a support network.

Study Skills Training Costs

Participants may attend a centralized training for $275 per person or sponsor a local training for $2,500 plus travel and expenses, plus $60 per person for materials which includes the booklet entitled *Smarter Not Harder!* (See the Web site [www.score-ed.com] for more detailed information regarding costs, etc.)

Teacher Assistance

Site visits by SCORE trainers provide personalized assistance with implementation. The staff of SCORE is available to consult with individual districts and educational agencies in these areas: technical assistance; teaching student learning styles; program evaluation; cooperative learning; development of a summer; residential program; and effective use of homework.

Teacher-Assistance Costs

After Adoption Training, the consultation fee is $1,000 per day plus travel and expenses within the continental United States, and $1,250 per day, 5-day minimum, plus travel and expenses outside the continental United States.

Local Trainers

Once the program has been in operation for one year, has outcome data available, and is ready for site visits, local staff have the opportunity to become SCORE trainers. Trainees shadow a trainer through both the Adoption Training and Study Skills In-service, following an extensive staff development guide. They copresent with the SCORE director, then with another trainer. Once that sequence is completed, trainers are certified, can maintain their local staff development, and may be hired as consultants/trainers.

Contact

Sharon Johnson
Educational Innovations/SCORE
23706 Whale Cove
Laguna Niguel, CA 92677
Voice: (949) 363-6764
Fax: (949) 363-6764
sharonmarjo@earthlink.net
www.score-ed.com

4

Teacher Training and Professional Development Initiatives

The Center for the Study and Teaching of At-Risk Students (C-STARS)

The Teacher Education Component

Background

The Center for the Study and Teaching of At-Risk Students (C-STARS) was founded in 1987 and is a division of the Institute for the Study of Educational Policy located at the University of Washington (UW) and housed in the College of Education. A sister center is also located at Washington State University.

Mission Statement

The mission of C-STARS is to join with and help facilitate efforts by K-14 schools and early childhood education programs to link with community based health and social service organizations, in order to better coordinate and integrate their respective services to common client populations of children at risk of school failure and to their families. The focus of these efforts ultimately addresses dropout prevention and academic achievement, particularly among student populations that disproportionately experience difficulty with school success.

This mission is accomplished through an array of training, program development, evaluation research and outreach activities. A majority of these activities are associated with a school-based or school-linked case management approach that C-STARS has been demonstrating in school communities throughout the country for the past 12 years. A new Center component addresses contextual teaching strategies and learning activities targeting at-risk student populations. To learn more about other activities in which this Center is involved, refer to Chapter 5 of this text.

C-STARS currently implements two federally funded teacher training/staff development programs that address the needs of students at risk in Washington state: the Pre-service Teacher Education Consortium for Contextual Teaching and Learning and the Schoolwide Enrichment Model in Eight Rural-Isolated Elementary School–Communities of Washington State. Following is a brief description of the two programs.

The Washington State Pre-service Teacher Education Consortium for Contextual Teaching and Learning

The Center has been awarded a contract from the United States Department of Education (USDOE), which positions C-STARS, seven other Washington state universities and colleges, and several school districts located throughout the state, to form a statewide partnership intended to enhance attention to contextual teaching and learning in the state's pre-service teacher preparation programs. Particular attention will be given to the new Washington State Learning Goals.

Contextual teaching is teaching that enables K-12 students to reinforce, expand, and apply their academic knowledge and skills in a variety of in-school and out-of-school settings to solve simulated or real world problems either alone or in a variety of group arrangements. Contextual learning occurs when students apply and experience what is being taught referencing real problems and needs associated with their roles and responsibilities as family members, citizens, students, and workers. Contextual teaching and learning emphasizes higher-level thinking, knowledge transfer across academic disciplines, and collecting, analyzing, and synthesizing information and data from multiple sources and viewpoints. The award is for 18 months (ending March 2000) and is designed to accomplish and/or produce:

- Summaries of Relevant Literature, which is a series of *talking papers* that address the need for attention to contextual teaching and learning by teacher preparation programs;

- Teaching Strategies and Learning Activities, which is a compendium of effective contextual teaching and learning strategies, activities, and curriculum materials for use with K-12 students;

- Pre-service Teacher Education Models, which is a compendium of effective pre-service teacher preparation models addressing K-12 contextual teaching and learning;

- An Academy of Education Professors, which is an ongoing Contextual Learning Academy of K-12 Professors of Education that represents teacher preparation programs operating throughout Washington State.

♦ A K-12 Academy, which is an ongoing Contextual Learning Academy of K-12 Practitioners that represents school-community-business partnerships located throughout Washington State.

The authority for this contract is the School-to-Work Opportunities Act of 1994 (Public Law 103-239). This project is one of seven funded nationally as a joint initiative of the Office of Vocational and Adult Education and the National School-to-Work Office.

The Schoolwide Enrichment Model in Eight Rural-Isolated Elementary School-Communities of Washington State

Over the three-year duration of this project (1999-2002), eight rural school districts serving large numbers of Hispanic and Native American children will partner with C-STARS, the Washington State Migrant Council, and Heritage College to develop and demonstrate an enhanced version of the Schoolwide Enrichment Model targeting elementary students often underrepresented in traditional programs for the gifted and talented, as well as other students frequently identified as being *at-risk*. The project will closely reference new essential academic learning requirements (i.e., state content and performance standards) in developing challenging contextual and culturally relevant teaching strategies, learning activities, and curriculum materials in core subject areas of mathematics, reading, writing, and communications. Results and/or products evaluated as effective with targeted students will be adapted for use with all children of the participating elementary schools.

Elementary teachers of the partner school districts will work closely with university curriculum and instruction specialists, experts in gifted and talented education, content and performance standards consultants, and the Washington State Migrant Council to develop a series of challenging enrichment activities using the Schoolwide Enrichment Model as a framework for addressing new state content and performance standards with a strong focus on producing activities that are both contextually and culturally relevant. As these challenging learning activities are field tested with highly able and other K-4 students, those evaluated as effective will be annually shared with K-4 teachers of all eight partner school districts through university-sponsored summer Staff Development Institutes. These teaching strategies, learning activities, and curriculum materials will also be shared with the 22 teacher preparation programs operating in Washington State for their reference in pre-service training of teachers. Project results will also be disseminated statewide and nationally through professional conferences, published journal articles, publications, and so on.

The community partnership component of the project will focus on parent involvement, family support, and parent education activities designed to involve parents and community representatives in supporting K-4 children as they participate in these new enrichment activities which address real world problems, issues, concerns, and so forth. Two school district communities, Sunnyside and Grandview, designated as Enterprise Communities by USDOE will serve as *hub school communities* in demonstrating the schoolwide enrichment activities developed through this project. A cadre of eight K-4 elementary teachers from the *hub districts* will team with parents, university faculty, community representatives, and national and local consultants on standards-based school reform and gifted education to develop and demonstrate the efficacy of the project's enhanced Schoolwide Enrichment Model.

Formative evaluation of the project will be conducted on an ongoing basis by evaluators from the University of Washington. Each quarter, the project's steering committee will collaborate with university evaluators to assess progress toward objectives, adjust objectives and related tasks, and to cumulatively document progress made, program revisions, rationale for changes, and lessons learned.

Summative evaluation of the project will be conducted by a third-party external evaluator in close collaboration with all project partner organizations. Use of quasi-experimental methodologies will be encouraged along with appropriate qualitative approaches. Statewide testing in the fourth grade addressing new state content and performance standards in the core subjects targeted by this project will be a major focus of this summative evaluation component. Other outcomes examined will include impacts on all K-4 children of the partner schools, pre-service teacher training, in-service staff development activities, and parent/family involvement with schooling.

Contact

Dr. Albert J. Smith, Director
Center for the Study and Teaching of At-Risk Students (C-STARS)
4725 30th Avenue NE
Seattle, WA 98105-4021
Voice: (206) 543-3815
Fax: (206) 685-4722
alsmith@u.washington.edu

The National Writing Project

Background

The National Writing Project (NWP) is a nationwide program that works to improve student writing abilities by improving the teaching and learning of writing in the nation's schools, to provide professional development programs for classroom teachers, and to expand the professional roles of teachers.

The NWP funds 158 writing project sites in 45 states, Washington, DC, and Puerto Rico. The NWP trained 104,255 teachers and administrators in 1995-96 and 1,699,730 teachers and administrators from 1973 to 1996. The NWP operates in a teachers-teaching-teachers mode. Selected writing teachers attend Invitational Summer Institutes at their local universities. During the school year, these teachers provide workshops for other teachers in the schools. Literacy is at the foundation of school and workplace success, of citizenship in a democracy, and of learning in all disciplines. In addition, modern technology has increased the need for students to write and think clearly and coherently. The National Writing Project focuses on the teaching of writing for practicing teachers while providing a model for ongoing professional development that builds independent local programs.

The National Writing Project's 24 years of success is due to a handful of simple but crucial principles:

- Excellent professional development is an ongoing process.
- Universities and schools accomplish more in partnership.
- Teachers are key to educational reform.
- Teachers are the best teachers of other teachers.
- Effective literacy programs are inclusive—reaching all teachers in order to reach all students.
- Writing deserves constant attention from kindergarten through university.
- Exemplary teachers of writing are themselves writers.

Program Components

- Summer institutes

    In the spring, every writing project site identifies exemplary teachers of writing who represent all grade levels from kindergarten through university, and all subject areas from English to mathematics. These teachers attend summer institutes at the local writing project's university campus. During the institutes, teachers demonstrate their successful classroom practices, study research, pose their own research questions, and write extensively. In the process, teachers rethink their own teaching approaches to benefit their students. They also prepare to teach their fellow teachers during the academic year.

- School year programs extend learning

    During the school year, institute graduates provide extended writing and reading program in-service workshops in their local schools and districts. At the same time, they continue their own professional growth as researchers, publishing writers, and expert practitioners whose combined and ongoing scholarship helps them to create more and more effective learning experiences for their students.

- Year-round service reaches the community

    Writing project teacher-leaders serve as crucial resources in the community, not only working with their own students and colleagues, but also with parents, administrators and policymakers. Teacher-leaders develop standards, frameworks, and assessments. They conduct conferences, school programs, and forums for young authors. They design community newsletters. In short, NWP teacher-leaders initiate reform at all levels—national, state, and local—and in doing so open new doors for students.

- Technical Assistance Program

    The Technical Assistance Program draws on the talents, experience, and particular strengths that exist within the network. Directors serve as mentors for each other, visiting sites across the country, sharing materials and working together on all aspects of leading a site.

Teacher Training and Professional Development Initiatives 195

♦ Teacher exchange

During the summer institutes, teachers participating in the NWP Teacher Exchange Program spend two weeks visiting another writing project site. Traveling teachers bring new perspectives and approaches to their host sites and gather ideas to take back to their home sites.

♦ Director's retreat

Thirteen site directors gathered in Flagstaff, Arizona in the spring of 1996 to inaugurate the first NWP directors' retreat. The five-day program began with a team-building adventure on the Colorado River, followed by three days in residence at the Northern Arizona University campus. Directors took this time to discuss site responsibilities and issues as well as to write and conduct strategic planning.

♦ Project Outreach

Project Outreach is a long-term effort to extend the quality and quantity of NWP services to teachers who work with low-income youth. Sponsored by a four-year, $2,000,000 grant from DeWitt Wallace-Reader's Digest Fund, Project Outreach sites are working with local teachers to study the needs and strengths in their service areas. Project Outreach sites will then serve as research and development sites for the full NWP network, exploring ways to improve access, diversify leadership, and improve the impact of their professional development work.

♦ Annenberg Rural Challenge

In 1996, the National Writing Project joined 14 other national organizations as founding partners the Annenberg Rural Challenge. The Rural Challenge is a long-term national effort to strengthen rural education and to bring the lessons learned from effective rural schools into the mainstream of national school reform. Along with organizations such as Foxfire, the Breadloaf Rural Teachers Network, Schools at the Center, PACERS, and the League for Professional Schools, the NWP will receive support to strengthen its own programs in rural American and to establish strong ties to other partners in the Annenberg Rural Challenge.

Contact

Maggie Madrigal
National Writing Project Corporation
University of California
5511 Tolman Hall, #1670
Berkeley, CA 94720-1670
Voice: (510) 642-0963
Fax: (510) 642-4545
nwp@socrates.berkeley.edu
www-gse.berkeley.edu.nwp

Reading Recovery

Background

Reading Recovery is an early intervention program for young readers who are experiencing difficulty in their first year of reading instruction. Such children often go through a cycle of confusion, frustration, and anxiety. This pattern of thinking quickly leads to feelings of failure for at-risk children. They often fall behind their classmates and require expensive, long-term remedial help, and some never learn to read.

By intervening early on, Reading Recovery can halt the debilitating cycle of failure for at-risk children and can enable them to read at the average level of first-grade students in their schools or classrooms. The Reading Recovery program is designed to serve the lowest achieving readers in a first-grade class. In the Reading Recovery program, children receive individual daily lessons from a specially trained teacher.

Accelerated learning for at-risk children is impossible without experienced, highly skilled teachers who are expert at observing children and making the moment-to-moment decisions necessary to teach for and support independent learning. Developing expertise at this level requires substantially more than traditional professional development models can deliver. Rather than hearing about and then performing a set of teaching activities, Reading Recovery educators develop analytical skills and use them to adjust and frame instruction for children. They do so through a combination of academic course work, intensive interaction with colleagues, and ongoing work with children.

Program History

Reading Recovery was developed by New Zealand educator and psychologist Dr. Marie M. Clay, who conducted observational research in the mid-1960s that enabled her to design techniques for detecting early reading difficulties of children. In the mid-1970s, she developed Reading Recovery procedures with teachers, and tested the program in New Zealand. The success of this pilot program led to the nationwide adoption of Reading Recovery in New Zealand in the early 1980s.

The New Zealand program was monitored closely by a group of researchers at the Ohio State University who were looking for alternatives to traditional remedial reading programs. In 1984-85, funding was made available to implement Reading Recovery as a collaborative effort by the Ohio Department of Education, Columbus Public Schools, and Ohio State University. Reading Recovery was implemented throughout Ohio beginning in 1985-86.

Program Components— Program for Children

Children are selected for the program based on authentic measures of assessment and teacher judgment. Their regular classroom instruction is then supplemented with daily one-to-one 30-minute lessons for 12–20 weeks with a specially trained teacher. The lessons consist of a variety of reading and writing experiences designed to help children develop effective strategies for reading and writing. Instruction continues until the child can read at or above the class average and has demonstrated the use of independent reading and writing strategies. The student is then "discontinued" from the program, providing the opportunity for another child to enter the program.

Approximately 560,000 children have benefited from Reading Recovery since its introduction to North America in 1985. Over 83 percent of the children who have completed a Reading Recovery program have become independent readers. Longitudinal studies conducted in New Zealand and the United States show that Reading Recovery helps a large majority of low-progress readers achieve continued reading success.

The Observation Survey

At the beginning of each academic year, children at-risk of failing reading are selected for Reading Recovery using classroom teacher judgment and results from *An Observation Survey of Early Literacy Achievement* (Clay, M. M. (1993). Portsmouth, NH: Heinemann). Looking across measures, teachers select first the children who are the lowest achieving. The *Observation Survey* is also used to determine the progress made by children who receive the intervention. The following six measures comprise the *Observation Survey*, which is administered individually:

- Letter identification

    The child is asked to identify 54 different characters, including upper- and lowercase letters and conventional print for "a" and "g."

- Word test

    The child is asked to read list of 20 words drawn from the words used most frequently in early reading material.

- Concepts about print

  The child is asked to perform a variety of tasks during a book reading. These tasks, presented in a standard situation, check on significant concepts about printed language, such as directionality and concept of word.

- Writing vocabulary

  Within a 10-minute period, the child is asked to write all the words the child knows. The score on this measure is the number of words written accurately.

- Hearing and recording sounds

  The child is asked to record word by word the sounds heard in a sentence that has been read. This measure indicates the child's ability to both hear and record sounds in words.

- Text reading level

  Measures of text reading level are obtained by constructing a gradient of text difficulty, then testing for the highest level read with accuracy of 90 percent or better. Levels are drawn from a basal reading system that is not part of Reading Recovery instruction.

Program Overview— Program for Educators

The remarkable progress that children make in Reading Recovery demonstrates that reading failure is not a foregone conclusion for at-risk students. The key to success for such children is specialized teaching that enables them to improve quickly (before they are labeled as failures) without disrupting their regular classroom curriculum.

In Reading Recovery, teacher training begins with a year-long curriculum that integrates theory and practice and is characterized by intensive interaction with colleagues. Following the training year, teachers continue to develop professionally through ongoing interaction with their colleagues and instructors. Teachers in training teach a child while colleagues observe and analyze practice. Thus, they reflect on their professional tasks in the light of literacy theory and peer critique over an extended period of time. Reading Recovery teachers in training become literacy experts with keen observational skills and a repertoire of interventions that can be tailored to meet the individual needs of at-risk students.

The program is adopted by entire school districts or groups of school districts that have made a long-term commitment to early literacy intervention, These Reading Recovery "sites" send an experienced teacher to one of 23 university "regional training centers" in North America for a year of full-time training, Following the training year, these trained "teacher leaders" return to their home districts and work full time teaching children, training teachers in Reading Recovery, and performing other duties related to the maintenance of a site.

The benefits of adopting Reading Recovery extend well beyond the success of individual at-risk students who complete the program. The results achieved by the teachers and children involved in Reading Recovery demonstrate for the entire district the impact that powerful teaching can have on low-progress children. Through interaction with Reading Recovery teachers, classroom teachers often begin to construct new theories about how children learn—theories that tend to carry over into classroom instruction.

Many districts that have adopted Reading Recovery have enjoyed the additional benefit of lower costs for special services. Reading Recovery has been shown to reduce the rate of retention, special education placements, and remediation beyond first grade. In addition, no time is lost delivering the services that will affect these changes. At most sites, teachers undergo training outside of regular school hours, and they actually begin working with students as the training begins.

The Network of Educators and Institutions

Educators and institutions that have adopted Reading Recovery form an extensive network to support early literacy. In 1997-98, the Reading Recovery network included 10,612 schools, 3,596 district level sites, and 23 universities. The staffs of these institutions include over 19,000 educators, including 18,831 Reading Recovery teachers, 739 teacher-leaders, and 35 university faculty.

These individuals and institutions work together to preserve the integrity of Reading Recovery and improve its effectiveness as an early intervention program in North America.

Reading Recovery Council of North America

The Reading Recovery Council of North American (RRCNA) is a professional organization dedicated to successful literacy for all children. The membership of RRCNA consists of Reading Recovery (RR) teachers, teacher leaders, university-based trainers, site coordinators and partners (other educators and private citizens interested in supporting the work of RR).

The purpose of RRCNA is to support the wide dissemination of the RR program, making this successful early intervention program available to every child who needs it. The Reading Recovery Council of North American is also dedicated to forming wide-ranging partnerships that will enhance collaborative research and development of literacy education. Reading Recovery Council of North American members receive a professional journal, several newsletters, access to an online network and opportunities for participation in Council related events and activities.

The Reading Recovery Lesson

In schools where Reading Recovery has been implemented, trained teachers use their judgment and a battery of six measures called the Observation Survey to select the most at-risk children from the lowest-achieving children in first-grade classrooms. In addition to regular classroom reading instruction, these children receive one-to-one Reading Recovery lessons for 30 minutes each day.

The first two weeks of each child's program are designed to develop the student's strengths. This period, referred to as "roaming around the known," is comprised of a variety of activities based on what the child can do. The child's confidence is built and a rapport between teacher and child is established. The teacher uses this time to learn more about the child's abilities, build a foundation, and get the passive learner active.

After the "roaming around the known" sessions, lessons begin. Each lesson includes:

- Reading familiar stories.
- Reading a story that was read for the first time the day before.
- Working with letters and/or words using magnetic letters.
- Writing a story.
- Assembling a cut-up story.
- Reading a new book that is read independently the next day.

During these holistic reading and writing activities, the teacher demonstrates and teaches for problem-solving strategies and then provides just enough support to help the child develop these effective strategies. The child learns to use both reading and writing strategies flexibly and independently.

Characteristics of Reading Recovery

- Lessons are individualized instruction

    Many early literacy programs try to move at-risk children along an artificial literacy continuum by teaching skills that somehow "add up" to good reading and writing. In contrast, Reading Recovery teachers carefully observe each student as a reader and writer, with particular attention to what the child can do within the processes of reading and writing. By working from the unique knowledge base of at-risk students in a one-to-one lesson format, Reading Recovery teachers move well beyond the traditional "skills and drills" approach associated with remedial reading programs.

- Working with books and stories

    Reading Recovery students work in the context of an entire book or a complete story, rather than with unconnected sentences or word lists. By reading and writing continuous texts, children learn to use many different aspects of printed text, including letters, words, sentences, and pictures, to understand complete stories, just as successful readers do. Each lesson is organized so that students, no matter how inexperienced they are with print, will be able to act like readers and writers.

- Accelerated learning

    The goal of Reading Recovery is accelerated learning. Each child is expected to make better-than-average progress so that the child can catch up with other children in the class. The majority of Reading Recovery children typically reach an average reading level after 12–20 weeks of daily instruction. During this period, they continue to work in the regular classroom for all but 30 minutes each day.

- Independent learning

    The goal of Reading Recovery is not just to improve the reading and writing ability of at-risk children, but to help them learn how to continue improving on their own, so that later remediation is unnecessary. With the assistance of their Reading Recovery teacher, children learn the strategies that good readers use to solve their reading problems "on the run" while reading real books. Reading Recovery instruction continues until the child has a self-extending system for literacy learning. Only then is the student "discontinued" or successfully released from the program, providing an opportunity for another child.

- Implementing Reading Recovery at the district level

  Reading Recovery is a system intervention that operates within entire school districts. Districts that have adopted the program according to established guidelines are designated as Reading Recovery sites. Each approved site is staffed by Reading Recovery teachers, one or more teacher leaders, and a site administrator. Reading Recovery teachers spend approximately one-half of each day working one-to-one with four or more children selected for the program and the rest of the day teaching, usually as a classroom or small-group teacher. Teacher leaders work with students, train teachers, provide continuing staff development for previously trained teachers, and participate in the Reading Recovery network. It generally takes a school district or consortium of districts two years to implement a Reading Recovery site—one year to have a qualified member of its staff trained as a teacher leader at a university training center, and a second year to establish a training site.

- The application process

  To become an approved training site, a school district or consortium begins by applying to a university training center to have a qualified member of its teaching staff trained as a teacher-leader. As part of the application process, prospective sites must secure financial support within the district, obtain the approval of the district superintendent, and reach an agreement with a local university or college to award graduate credit to the teachers who will be trained at the site.

  The applying district or consortium also selects an administrator in the district to assume administrative responsibilities for Reading Recovery. This "site coordinator" oversees the preparation of the facility, manages the budget, negotiates contracts, and acts as administrative liaison with the Reading Recovery network.

The Training Year for Teacher Leaders

Applicants are selected for the program in the spring, and the year-long residency program begins the following autumn. The program for teacher leaders includes five components:

- A graduate-level curriculum consisting of a clinical practicum, a seminar in theory, and a leadership practicum.

- The daily teaching of four Reading Recovery students.

- Field requirements including observing experienced teacher leaders at work, participating in some aspects of training teachers, and conducting colleague visits to observe other class members teaching a Reading Recovery lesson.

- Preparation for implementing Reading Recovery at their home sites.

- Attendance at professional development conferences, institutes, and meetings.

During the training year, teacher leaders work with their site coordinators to prepare the site for its first year of operation. They inform appropriate groups about the program, prepare the space where the teacher training classes will be held, order materials for teacher training, secure secretarial support for the program, and assist in the selection of appropriate teachers for the training class.

Levels of Training

Training for Reading Recovery educators consists of one year of instruction, followed by extensive continuing contact, and is offered on three levels:

- Teacher training is master's level instruction, provided by Reading Recovery teacher leaders at approved district-level training sites, and prepares experienced teachers to provide Reading Recovery for children in their schools. During the training year, teachers attend weekly classes, work with at least four children daily, and participate in school visits with their instructor and colleagues.

- Teacher leader training is post-master's instruction, provided by trainers of teacher leaders at approved university regional training centers, and prepares qualified educators to teach children, train teachers, and operate a Reading Recovery training site. Teacher leaders in training spend one year in residency at a university training center. They complete a graduate-level curriculum, teach four Reading Recovery students daily, meet numerous field requirements, attend professional development events, and prepare to implement the program in their home districts.

- Instruction for trainers of teacher leaders is provided at the postgraduate level in North America by The Ohio State University and Texas Woman's University. The one-year residency program prepares university faculty to teach children, provide instruction to teacher leaders in training, and operate a university training center.

After the Training Year

Following the training year, Reading Recovery educators at all levels hone their expertise through a variety of professional development activities, including regional meetings, site visits from instructors, conferences and workshops, and information updates. They also participate in the Reading Recovery network through data collection, committee work, participation in research projects, and other activities.

The Implementation Year

Following their training year, teacher leaders and site coordinators work together to maintain the site. Teacher leaders train new teachers and visit previously trained teachers, conduct continuing contact sessions, collect data on children served, and prepare an annual site report. They also participate in a variety of continuing contact events and activities, including national conferences and training seminars, to further their own professional development.

Teacher Training at Reading Recovery Sites

To implement Reading Recovery in districts where the program has been adopted, qualified teachers enroll in a year-long academic course taught by a certified teacher leader. Through interactive clinical experiences and theoretical study guided by a teacher leader, teachers learn how to implement all components of a Reading Recovery lesson and to select teaching procedures appropriate for individual students.

Teachers in training continue to work full-time in their school district as they receive instruction in Reading Recovery procedures. The most common arrangement during the training year and subsequent years is for the teachers to spend a half a day teaching Reading Recovery students and the other half performing other assigned duties. Teachers work with a minimum of four Reading Recovery students daily. Many teachers teach in the classroom the other half day or work with small groups of students in Title I programs.

Contact

Jean Bussell, Executive Director
Julie Reeves, Program Coordinator
Reading Recovery Council of North America
1929 Kenny Road, Suite 100
Columbus, OH 43210
Voice: (614) 292-7111
Fax: (614) 292 4404
bussell.4@osu.edu
www.readingrecovery.org

(Source: Executive Summary of the Reading Recovery Council of North America. Reprinted with the permission of the Reading Recovery Council of North America.)

Teach For America (TFA)

Program Goals

Teach For America (TFA) is a national corps of outstanding, diverse, recent college graduates, of all academic majors, who commit two years to teach in urban and rural public schools. Teach For America's central purpose is to expand the educational opportunities available to students in underresourced areas. Teach For America does this through providing students with excellent teachers who are dedicated to ensuring that their students fulfill their true potential, and through simultaneously influencing the consciousness of the corps members themselves, who will continue to work throughout their lives, from inside and outside the education system, to expand educational opportunity and improve the quality of life in underresourced areas.

Background

Teach For America's annual programmatic activities involve recruiting and electing a corps of 500 members, preparing them for teaching through a national pre-service institute and local orientations to their schools and communities, working with schools to ensure that they are hired as regular beginning teachers, and coordinating an ongoing support network among the corps members. Teach For America is also building an alumni association to foster alumni's ongoing connection with the organization and each other.

In 1989, a senior at Princeton University, troubled by the inequities in the American education system and convinced that her peers were searching for the chance to make a difference, thought: "Why doesn't this country have a national teacher corps that calls upon its most talented, recent college graduates to commit two years to teach students in urban and rural public schools?" Wendy Kopp, who was 22 at the time, thought that a national teacher corps would not only change the lives of some of the nation's most underserved students, but would also help shape the priorities of a generation of future leaders.

After developing the idea in her undergraduate senior thesis, Wendy wrote to dozens of corporate CEOs to ask for their support. The day after she graduated, she received her first seed grant, and began pulling together a team of recent college graduates to help bring her plan to life. Within a few months, this team had inspired more than 150 student leaders, representing colleges from all parts of the country, to organize a nationwide grassroots recruitment campaign. In January 1990, these *campus representatives* began spreading the word—Teach For America.

The response on college campuses was tremendous. At Yale University, 170 seniors left phone messages with their campus representative in the span of one weekend after receiving flyers that had been slipped under their doors. Over half of these seniors ultimately applied. By the end of April, 2,500 men and women from more than 100 colleges across the country had submitted applications to Teach For America, and five pairs of staff members began driving from campus to campus in donated rental cars to interview them. The pragmatic idealism demonstrated by these college seniors was matched by the philanthropic community, which provided $2,500,000 to fund the selection, training, placement, and support of the charter corps. That fall, Teach For America's first set of 500 recruits set out for New York City, Los Angeles, New Orleans, Baton Rouge, rural North Carolina, and rural Georgia to begin their teaching assignments.

Each year since then, 500 new corps members have joined Teach For America to have a considerable impact in the lives of thousands of students. And each year, 500 additional corps members have completed their two-year commitments to join a growing force of Teach For America alumni who have been fundamentally influenced by their experiences teaching in some of the nation's most under-funded public schools. Already, alumni have started their own schools, influenced education policy on Capitol Hill, and assumed leadership roles as teachers and administrators in their schools. Many other alumni have returned to top graduate schools to pursue advanced degrees in areas ranging from applied mathematics to public policy to business administration. Those who are working in other sectors, whether law, business, medicine, or politics, have continued to serve as advocates for educational excellence and equity.

Teach For America, started by a group of young people who wanted to act on their convictions and make a difference in the lives of children, remains essentially as it was envisioned eight years ago. It is an ever-expanding group of individuals who are brought together by their vision that one day, all children in this nation will have the opportunity to attain an excellent education—and who are committed to surpassing traditional expectations in pursuit of that vision.

Recruitment

Teach For America recruits aggressively at approximately 200 campuses chosen for their selectivity and ethnic and racial diversity. Full-time recruiters, working out of three offices nationwide, coordinate additional help from student volunteers, corps members, and alumni. Through information sessions hosted near each campus, college students hear what it's like to teach in urban and rural schools from alumni and corps members. Potential applicants are also exposed to Teach For America through posters, flyers, announcements in campus newspapers, email, career service offices and other types of advertisements.

Selection

Candidates are selected according to the degree to which they demonstrate commitment to the mission and vision of Teach For America as well as these leadership qualities: achievement in past endeavors, personal responsibility, a commitment to constant learning, an ability to maintain perspective in difficult circumstances, sensitivity, and good writing, thinking, and speaking skills. Teach For America staff have found that individuals who demonstrate these qualities are most able to rise to the challenge of teaching in urban and rural schools, and most likely to develop into lifelong leaders and effective advocates for expanding educational opportunity.

In 1997, 85 percent of the incoming corps had held leadership positions on their college campuses; they attended some of the nation's leading colleges, and had an average grade point average of 3.4; and their self-reported average score on the Scholastic Achievement Test (SAT) was 1,200. When contrasted with education majors 11 percent of education majors are people of color while 35 percent of Teach For America's nearly 1,000 corps members are of color. Also, 18 percent of the education majors are male, and 29 percent of TFA's corps members are male.

Admissions

The Teach For America Program admissions process is driven by the desire to build a corps of leaders who will have a lasting impact on children and schools during their two-year teaching commitments, and who will ultimately serve in a variety of professions as lifelong advocates for quality education. Teach For America staff seek outstanding men and women of all ethnic backgrounds and academic majors who have excelled in their past endeavors. To better meet the needs of school districts, Teach For America staff make a particular effort to recruit bilingual, Spanish speakers and math, science, and engineering majors. While all corps members must have bachelor's degrees, no previous education course work is necessary. Teach For America draws its strength from the distinct backgrounds and experiences of its corps members and strives to build a corps that is both highly qualified and diverse in every respect, particularly with regard to ethnic, racial, and cultural background. Teach For America's commitment to diversity results from the conviction that America's future leaders will emerge from the broad array of communities that comprise this nation. In addition, Teach For America staff believe that students should have teachers who share their backgrounds to serve as an important source of motivation for them, as well as teachers who are diverse in every respect to provide them with a greater understanding of people of all backgrounds.

All candidates for admission complete an intensive selection process, which begins with a written application. The selection committee reviews the applications and invites the most promising candidates to participate in an interview day, which includes a sample teaching session taught to other candidates, a group discussion, and a personal interview. Candidates who are interested in teaching in a bilingual Spanish classroom also complete a brief written language assessment. Applicants are notified by mail of their acceptance and given tentative assignment to a certain region, subject area, and grade level.

Admission to Teach For America is highly selective. Each year almost 3,000 men and women from more than 300 undergraduate institutions and almost all 50 states apply for approximately 500 places in the corps.

Math, science, or engineering majors, should ask about Teach For America's special initiative to bring more math and science teachers into schools where they are greatly needed, and to ensure that math and science corps members remain connected to the broader mathematics and scientific communities throughout their two-year commitment.

Assignment and Placement

Teach For America places corps members in K-12 positions in public school districts that have difficulty filling all of their teaching positions with qualified, certified teachers. These districts hire corps members at first-year teacher salaries. Corps members can assume teaching positions in these shortage areas without meeting conventional certification requirements, although they are usually required to work toward certification by enrolling in local university programs or in programs run by their school districts or states. In addition, corps members assigned to teach in Houston, the Rio Grande Valley, or Washington, DC, must obtain certain academic credits in education through coursework completed at Teach For America's summer institute.

Teach For America staff assign teaching positions based on the needs and requirements of school districts, the college course work of corps members, and the geographic, grade level, and subject area preferences that corps members express on the interview day. While Teach For America staff aim to meet every corps member's top preferences, they face certain constraints that are beyond their control. Therefore, all corps members must be flexible.

Because of the external variables involved in placement, all assignments are tentative until the corps member has actually signed a district contract or is on a district payroll. Placement in the originally assigned location is contingent on the ultimate availability of jobs in that area and on the corps member's ability to fulfill all district and state requirements, including but not limited to, successful interviews with school district personnel, passing scores on all required standardized tests, and completion of other hiring provisions such as security checks and medical examinations. While districts commit a certain number of placements to Teach For America, in rare instances last-minute budget cuts or changes in district needs or requirements can prevent them from honoring these commitments. A corps member who meets all the requirements but who is displaced due to changes in district needs or requirements is reassigned to another Teach For America site after specifying a geographical preferences. A tentative assignment becomes an official two-year placement once a school district formally offers a corps member a position.

Corps members are currently placed in urban sites in Baltimore, the Bay Area, Greater New Orleans, Houston, Los Angeles, New Jersey, New York City, Phoenix, and Washington, DC, and in rural sites in Arkansas, Mississippi, North Carolina, the Rio Grande Valley, and Southern Louisiana.

Pre-Service Training

Once accepted, corps members complete independent work which includes observing experienced teachers for 12 hours and completing written reflections on what they see. They then travel to Houston, Texas, to participate in a five-week national training institute. Upon completion of the institute, they attend a one- to two-week induction to the schools, school district, and communities in which they will teach.

During the institute, corp members assume teaching positions in the morning and receive training in the afternoons from a faculty of experienced teachers and corps members. Teach For America staff work to ensure that corps members leave the institute able to establish clear, measurable goals for their students; build investment in the goals among students and students' parents; use effective teaching and assessment strategies to ensure student understanding; establish a positive classroom environment; approach schools and communities with respect and an understanding of political and cultural dynamics; and maximize their ongoing professional development.

Regional Induction

After completing the summer institute, corps members travel to their assigned regions for a one- to two-week induction, which provides an opportunity for corps members to become oriented to the schools, school districts, and communities where they will be teaching and living. Meetings with community leaders, school and district personnel, and other corps members placed in their sites help prepare new corps members for teaching in their particular assignments. In addition, corps members attend professional development activities organized by the local school district or Teach For America, which are designed to help them acquire resources and materials to begin the school year successfully. During induction, corps members also have time to take care of transitional needs and settle into their new regions.

Corps Support and Professional Development

Teach For America staff strive to place at least two corps members in each school so that they can collaborate on school-based projects and better support one another's professional growth. Throughout their two-year commitment, corps members work to strengthen their teaching by regularly reflecting on how they can better help students learn. Meanwhile, they seek critical feedback on their teaching, observe other teachers, and access additional resources on the theories and practices of teaching.

To support corps members' individual professional development efforts, local Teach For America offices publish a monthly newsletter, sponsor guest speakers, and maintain a resource room. They also organize retreats, social events, and discussion groups on topics related to urban and rural education. Local staff also work with area school districts, schools of education, professional associations, and other organizations to ensure that corps members have access to the best professional development and teaching resources available. Nationally, interregional conferences, the Teach For America Web site, and the magazine of Teach For America help corps members stay in touch with their colleagues across the country. Additionally, national corps member organizations allow corps members to work together on common interests such as rural education, special education, bilingual education, and technology in education.

During and after their two-year commitment, corps members work to strengthen Teach For America in a variety of ways. Corps members help organize events, assist with corps member recruitment and selection, work as institute faculty, contribute to newsletters, assist in raising funds for the organization, and serve on corps member advisory committees.

Alumni Association

After completing a two-year commitment, corp members become part of the TFA Alumni Association. Alumni chapters exist in several metropolitan areas. In addition, TFA produces an alumni magazine, a national Alumni Summit, and an alumni section on the TFA Web site.

Financial Arrangements

- Salaries

    Teach For America corps members are paid directly by the school districts that hire them. Salaries, which are roughly commensurate with the local standard of living, currently range from $20,000 to $33,000 depending on the site and subject matter, with corps members making an average of approximately $26,000. Corps members earn the same salaries as other beginning teachers with equivalent qualifications in their regions.

- Health insurance

    Teach For America does not provide health insurance, although the school districts in which Teach For America places corps members generally offer health benefits and insurance that usually begin about 30 days after a teacher assumes his or her duties.

Contact

Teach For America
315 W. 36th Street
New York, NY 10018
Voice: (800) 832-1230 or (212) 279-2080
Fax: (212) 279-2081
www.teachforamerica.org

Teacher Expectations and Student Achievement (TESA)

Background

Development of Teacher Expectations and Student Achievement (TESA) began in 1970 under an Elementary and Secondary Education Act (ESEA), Title III grant to the Los Angeles County Office of Education from the California Department of Education. Teacher Expectations and Student Achievement was conceived by Mary D. Martin, who directed the project during the first two years while the teacher training program was developed and tested. Sam Kerman directed TESA during the dissemination phase, designed the facilitator training component, and spread awareness of TESA throughout the country. The Los Angeles County Office of Education publishes the TESA Coordinator Manual and Teacher Handbook.

TESA Interventions

Teacher Expectations and Student Achievement is designed to intervene both by heightening teachers' awareness of their perceptions and their understanding of how those perceptions affect their expectations. Teachers are encouraged to give all students more opportunities to perform in class, to receive more feedback, and to establish personal relationships with every student. As a result, teachers can expect to minimize the negative and maximize the positive effects of expectations.

Teacher Expectations and Student Achievement is not merely concerned with quantity of interaction, but also its quality. To move teachers toward more meaningful and equitable interaction with all students, TESA offers five units of teacher instruction. Each unit involves three interactions, one in each of the three strands: response opportunities, feedback, and personal regard. The interactions were selected because research indicated that they were ways in which teachers differentiated their behavior with perceived high- and low-achieving students. As teachers advance through the five units, the interactions become more complex and powerful.

Outcomes

Over the more than 20 years since TESA began, results have been noticeably consistent. Most evaluations of the program focused on student achievement. During the pilot and field test years, comparison of reading achievement test scores between TESA and control classrooms revealed that the TESA classrooms were consistently two months ahead of their control counterparts.

Most recently, the Los Angeles County Office of Education's interdivisional TESA team planned and conducted a followup survey of California teachers trained in TESA over the last two years. The goal of the TESA Training Followup Survey was to ascertain the effectiveness of the current training from the perspective of recent trainees. The survey included items dealing with the usefulness of TESA interactions in classroom practices, overall teacher satisfaction with the TESA training, and effectiveness of TESA strategies in today's climate of restructuring. Encouraging results were found from responses obtained from the first mailing of the survey.

Teachers attest that TESA positively affects student self-esteem and builds a collaborative climate in which both students and teachers enjoy learning. Students are stimulated by the warmth of an enhanced learning climate and report more intense feelings of encouragement and inclusion.

Teachers describe a new sense of self-awareness and growth as they discover, through partnership with and feedback from team members, how inequitable their interactions with students have been. They become more open, accepting, and creatively interactive in their teaching. As insight and skills increase, teachers report becoming more confident, more sensitive in meeting student needs, and better able to constructively handle the daily barrage of classroom challenges.

Less frequent but more dramatic are reports of TESA changing teachers' lives, of the entire TESA experience becoming a transformational turning point in their personal lives and a stimulus for renewed interest in the teaching/learning process. These reports confirm that the surest way to create change is to change ourselves.

Teacher Expectations and Student Achievement was originally called Equal Opportunity in the Classroom. When it was developed in the early 1970s, many classrooms were experiencing enforced desegregation. Teacher Expectations and Student Achievement staff saw the self-fulfilling prophecy as one factor mitigating against integration. In the 1990s, classrooms across the nation are becoming increasingly diverse ethnically, racially, and culturally. Teacher Expectations and Student Achievement offers a way of helping teachers to assess how these changes affect their expectations.

Another impetus for TESA was concern about that small group of students who continually performed poorly. Teacher Expectations and Student Achievement does not accept the rarely voiced but insidiously prevalent notion that a pool of poor academic performance will always stubbornly puddle at the bottom of the class. The *disadvantaged* students of the 1970s are the *at-risk* students of the 1990s. Perhaps TESA and other successful interventions will help educators to recognize that all people have both problems and possibilities, both limits and potential, and to interact with students in ways that reflect our belief in their (and our own) unlimited potential.

Program Costs

In implementing TESA, it is recommended that a district identify two or more members of its staff to participate in the Coordinator Training Seminar. One member should be experienced in conducting staff in-service or have demonstrated the potential for doing so. Although many districts have successfully implemented TESA with one coordinator, a team of coordinators has proven to be more successful in distributing responsibilities and conducting workshops.

Startup costs vary depending on the implementation design selected. Teacher Expectations and Student Achievement is a program for behavior change, the major components of which consist of workshop attendance followed by observing and coding. The major costs for the program are therefore determined by the degree to which substitutes are used to release teachers to attend workshops, observe, and code.

Workshops may be conducted during the following time frames: on school time; on shortened days; immediately after school; during the dinner hour; or after a Saturday morning breakfast meeting. However, those conducted on school time or as dinner workshops have proven to be significantly more successful than those conducted on shortened days or immediately after school. (Note: The observing/coding component must be conducted on school time.) School staffs are highly creative in designing ways to release teachers for observing and coding opportunities (e.g., find support staff, enlist the assistance of retired teachers, schedule special programs in classrooms, arrange for community services to provide instruction at the school site).

It is recommended that the person(s) selected as the district coordinator(s) be provided adequate time for program administration. For example, if a teacher is selected as coordinator, the teaching assignment could be reduced by one period per day in order to give the teacher time to implement TESA—without negatively impacting the instructional program.

Training Options and Support

To assist in implementing TESA training, several types of support are available. Selected examples follow:

- Coordinator Training Seminars

  The TESA program is coordinated in each school or school district by staff who have been trained at a two-day Coordinator Training Seminar on how to administer the program and conduct teacher in-service workshops.

- Ad hoc TESA Coordinator Training Seminars

  If 20 participants can be guaranteed from a district, several districts, or an identified area, a trainer will be sent to that location to conduct a two-day, ad hoc TESA Coordinator Training Seminar on the date of choice.

- Teacher in-service workshop series

  At this teacher in-service, the TESA Interaction Model is conducted by the district TESA-trained coordinator in a series of five workshops held approximately one month apart. Between workshops, participants develop their skills by observing each other in the classroom to see how often interaction occurs with target students.

Contact

Anita Miller, Ph. D.
Los Angeles County Office of Education
9300 Imperial Highway
Downey, CA 90242-2890
Voice: (800) 566-6651 or (562) 922-6665
Fax: (562) 922-6699
Miller_Anita@lacoe.edu
www.lacoe.edu/tesa

Teachers of English to Speakers of Other Languages, Inc. (TESOL)

Background

The discipline is called TESOL. The name of the organization to which people in the profession belong is Teachers of English to Speakers of Other Languages (TESOL). The members of TESOL are classroom teachers, researchers, curriculum specialists, computer and video specialists, administrators, and other professionals.

Teaching English to speakers of other languages is an activity that requires specialized training because it is a multifaceted, academic discipline requiring training in linguistics, second language acquisition, language pedagogy, methodology, materials development, testing and research, curriculum and syllabus design, program administration and cross-cultural communication, among other subjects.

Teachers of English to Speakers of Other Languages (TESOL) educators are found around the world, working in a variety of situations in both the public and private sectors. They work in countries where English is spoken only as a foreign language, such as Japan and Saudi Arabia, as well as in countries where English is the dominant language, as in the U.S., Canada, and Australia. They work with immigrants and refugees, in primary, secondary, and higher education, as well as adult education in community college and community-based programs. Professional preparation in TESOL is available throughout the world with certificate, BA, MA, and PhD programs.

Program Components

- *TESOL Matters*

    This is in-depth newspaper which is published bimonthly. It contains articles on ESL/EFL professional concerns and issues, calls for papers and other association-related information. Many articles are written by contributors in the field. Included are columns/departments that provide networking information, lists of interesting Web sites, updates on projects such as standards, accreditation efforts and ESOL Teachers in World Politics, to name a few.

- Serial publications

    Two additional quarterly publications are available on a subscription basis. These publications are refereed and governed by field editors.

    - *TESOL Journal* is a practical, hands-on magazine for language educators in diverse settings, and levels. It explores the hows and whys of successful teaching:
        - Featuring practical classroom strategies,
        - Emphasizing ESL/EFL methodology,
        - Underscoring techniques,
        - Highlighting materials, curriculum design and development, and
        - Stressing teacher education, program administration, and classroom observation and research.
    - *TESOL Quarterly* is a scholarly journal, dedicated to cross-disciplinary concerns that cover:
        - Research, analysis, and application in all aspects of second language learning and teaching;
        - Curriculum development, testing, and evaluation;
        - Professional preparation; and
        - Language planning and professional standards.

- Networking

    Sharing similar experiences, comparing notes, and learning from others in the field. Attendance at the annual convention provides maximum networking opportunities with nearly 8,000 participants from around the world.

- Placement services

    The TESOL Placement Services provides opportunities to find a job in the ESL/EFL field, whether you have a certificate, masters, or a doctorate, or are searching for a position in teaching or in administration. The service includes 10 issues of the *Placement Bulletin* per year.

The Employment Clearinghouse is held annually during the TESOL Convention. It brings recruiters and job candidates together for onsite interviews for positions around the world. These positions include long- and short-term contracts for teaching and administrative posts.

- Advocacy

    Through the services of an education consulting firm, TESOL has been successful in seeking funding for bilingual and adult education, defeating official English legislation, and preserving access to education for legal immigrants.

Contact

Director of Membership
Teachers of English to Speakers of Other Languages, Inc.
1600 Cameron Street, Suite 300
Alexandria, VA 22314-2751
Voice: (703) 836-0774
Fax: (703) 836-6447
tesol@tesol.edu
www.tesol.edu

5

District, State, and National Systemic Initiatives

The Center for Educational Renewal

The Center for Educational Renewal has created and sustained a set of powerful and effective initiatives for the simultaneous renewal of teacher education and public schools in the United States.

This initiative is powerful and effective because it has an agenda; it has a strategy for attaining this agenda; and it prepares leaders to achieve this agenda.

Directed by John I. Goodlad and Roger Soder, the Center for Educational Renewal has maintained, since its founding in 1985, a sharp focus on an agenda: *the simultaneous renewal of schools and the education of educators*. At first glance, the 10 words of this agenda are simple ones. Put together, however, they mean something complex. And even taken separately or in short phrases, the words need to be examined carefully.

- *Simultaneous* implies a relationship. Schools will not be better schools until there are better teachers, but there will not be better teachers unless there are better schools in which teachers learn, practice, and develop.

- *Renewal* suggests an ongoing process of self-examination, reflection, and change. This term captures the organization's mission better than the terms *restructure* or *improvement*.

- *Education* implies more than formal schooling in a formal teacher preparation or training program.

- *Educators* means more than just teachers. Principals, other administrators, and support staff are important actors in simultaneous renewal, as well as schools of education faculties, arts and sciences faculties, and university administrators.

- *Schools* indicates that the focus is on public schools, pre-kindergarten through grade 12, and on schools as part of an education community.

The Strategy for Simultaneous Renewal

As stated, The Center for Educational Renewal focuses on the agenda of simultaneous renewal of schools and the education of educators. Part of the agenda is based on Goodlad's, *A Place Called School* (1984).

Another part of the agenda is derived from the Center's Study of the Education of Educators. This national, comprehensive study resulted in the designation of 19 postulates, or essential conditions, for a good teacher education program, an assessment of existing programs at 29 selected institutions, and a strategy outlining the steps to get from where we are to where we ought to be. The 19 postulates, the assessment, and the strategy were reported in Goodlad's *Teachers for Our Nation's Schools* (1990).

Representing a comprehensive cross-section of teacher education programs and school districts in America, the National Network for Educational Renewal (NNER) includes small private colleges, flagship research universities, historically black colleges, and rural universities, among others. The wide variety of institutions following the simultaneous renewal agenda demonstrates its effectiveness across academic differences. In keeping with the basic agenda of simultaneous renewal, each setting consists of one or more institutions of higher education working in close collaboration with one or more school districts and one or more partner schools within each district.

Maintaining Connections

To help advance the agenda, the Center works with the Education Commission of the States in Denver, Colorado, and with the American Association of Colleges for Teacher Education (AACTE) in Washington, DC. The Center also maintains ties with other major reform efforts such as the Coalition of Essential Schools at Brown University, the National Center for Restructuring Education, Schools, and Teaching (NCREST) at Columbia University, the Accelerated Schools Project at Stanford University, the School Development Program at Yale University, and Project Zero at Harvard University.

Contact

Joan Waiss
Center for Educational Renewal
College of Education
313 Miller Hall, Box 353600
University of Washington
Seattle, WA 98195-3600
Voice: (206) 543-6230
Fax: (206) 543-8439
weber.u.washington.edu/~cedren

The Center for Leadership in School Reform (CLSR)

"The Schlechty Group"

The Center for Leadership in School Reform (CLSR) provides vision, strategies, and support for public schools and school districts connected to improving the quality of students' classroom experiences. The work of (CLSR) is based on a set of clear and powerful ideas developed by Dr. Phillip Schlechty. Students are the primary customers of schools, and the work the students perform is the school's most important product.

The uniqueness of CLSR stems from two sources:

- The staff of CLSR understands that superintendents, principals, and teachers are the real reformers, and that it is their task to support them.

- The staff of CLSR views school reform as a districtwide matter. The capacity of the district to support change is a critical factor in winning community support for education reform.

The Center for Leadership in School Reform is creating strategies for change in more than 30 school systems across the nation. Ranging in size from small schools and rural systems to large, urban school districts, the goal for each system is to create work for students that develops their ability to solve problems and think well.

The Center for Leadership in School Reform is a nonprofit corporation with headquarters in Louisville, Kentucky. The mission of CLSR is to be a dependable and responsive source of strategic consultation, technical assistance, training, and support to school district leadership and is aimed at:

- Enhancing the capacity of the district to support and sustain reform at the building and classroom levels.

- Redesigning schools so that they are more clearly focused on providing quality work for children and so that students become the true focus of all decisions made in and around schools.

- Helping teachers, parents, and others who work in schools and classrooms to better understand the characteristics of quality work for students and ensuring that teachers have the tools and support they need to design and deliver the highest-quality work for students.

The Center for Leadership in School Reform staff operate under the premise that if educators improve the quality of experiences students have in school, the quality of what students learn will improve. They also support the belief that the purpose of any school is to provide work for students that is engaging and relevant to today's society. Experience has shown that if students have satisfying classroom experiences daily, they stay engaged in school work and are more likely to acquire critical thinking and problem solving skills that are important to becoming productive members of their community.

The work of CLSR proceeds from the assumption that students are the first-line customers of the school and that the work students are provided or encouraged to undertake is the primary product of schools. It is assumed as well that teachers are viewed as leaders and inventors, principals as leaders of leaders, and superintendents as the chief executive officers of the largest knowledge/work enterprise in a community.

Center for Leadership in School Reform staff believe that it is essential that schools be restructured so that the quality of student learning, will improve; and that this improvement can only occur when school leaders improve the quality of the experiences that students have in school. In the context of the work of CLSR, this means that schools and school leaders must be prepared to alter the rules, roles, and relationships that govern the way time, people, physical space, information, and technology are deployed and used. In so doing, they can ensure that schools are organized around students and the work they are expected to do. Further, they can see to it that families, communities, and all child- and youth-serving agencies in those communities are oriented to ensure that each child has the support that the child needs to be successful in school and in the community at large.

In support of this agenda, the staff of CLSR provide consultation and technical support to client schools and school districts, conduct workshops, facilitate seminars and conferences, provide advice, prepare materials, and conduct studies for boards of education, superintendents, principals, teachers, business leaders, parents, and others committed to bringing about real changes in our system of schooling.

Contact

Center for Leadership in School Reform
950 Brekenridge Lane, Suite 200
Louisville, KY 40207
Voice: (502) 895-1942
Fax: (502) 895-7901
info@clsr.org
www.clsr.org

The Center for Research in Human Development and Education (CRHDE)

Background

The Center for Research in Human Development and Education (CRHDE) at Temple University, established in September 1986 under the leadership of Margaret C. Wang, is devoted to the study of emerging educational problems and challenges facing children and their families. With the overall goal of investigating the forces that influence human development and education, the interdisciplinary team of CRHDE researchers and collaborating field-based professionals work together to identify and shape the most effective programs and policies for educating America's children and youth and for improving their life circumstances.

Among some of the Center's more notable achievements are its groundbreaking program of research on fostering educational resilience and the development of the Community for Learning Program, a comprehensive approach to school reform that draws from over two decades of educational research. The program is grounded in research that shows students' that learning is affected by environments in addition to schools, such as the workplace, church, home, community organizations, and social service agencies. More important, it provides ways that schools can restructure, improve practices and strategies, and involve the community to support educational resilience. It is just one example of how the Center has used an interdisciplinary approach to solve problems in education.

Questions and Answers About Community for Learning

- What is Community for Learning (CFL)?

    Community for Learning is a comprehensive school reform program that draws on two decades of research on what makes schools work and what helps each student learn, even those children who are faced with some of the most challenging circumstances. Community for Learning builds on the strengths of diverse communities by redeploying existing resources and professional expertise to achieve the most positive impact on children's development and educational success. A centerpiece of the CFL program is an integrated design framework for a collaborative process of finding ways to sustain a high standard of academic achievement for each student. This is achieved by linking schools with the resources, expertise, and energies of other learning environments, including homes, churches, libraries, the workplace, higher education institutions, community organizations, and social service agencies—in short, a community for learning.

- Why should a school or district want to use this program?

Many students have difficulty achieving success in school and need more help. If all students are to complete a basic education through equal access to a common curriculum, school responses to increasingly diverse student needs must undergo a major shift. With CFL, this type of shift does not require a school to purchase fancy equipment, adopt an entirely new curriculum, or hire new teachers. Instead, CFL provides professional development and technical assistance to all individuals involved in the child's learning environment, building their capacity to sustain positive change.

- Has this program been tried or is it just a theory?

Elements of CFL have been used successfully in schools in more than 20 states over the past 25 years. The classroom instruction component of CFL is Adaptive Learning Environments Model (ALEM), which has been shown to increase student learning and achievement.

- Who developed this approach to school reform?

Margaret C. Wang, a professor of educational psychology and the founding director of the Center for Research in Human Development and Education (CRHDE) at Temple University, in collaboration with more than a dozen researchers and teachers from a variety of disciplines, spearheaded the creation of the CFL program. These researchers and practitioners, spurred by the need to increase the nation's capacity to effectively respond to an increasingly diverse student population, especially in urban schools, were committed to developing a program that was based on extensive research and practical wisdom.

- How do I know that CFL really works?

  Schools across the country that have used Community for Learning (CFL) have experienced reduced dropout rates, raised achievement scores, and boosted morale. Students have developed positive attitudes about learning and have taken more responsibility for their own learning. Teachers have adopted effective practices that are based on research and have raised their expectations for all students.

- What kinds of districts or school should use CFL?

  Community for Learning (CFL) has been implemented in a variety of schools and districts that believe schools can make a difference in promoting the learning success and educational resilience of each student. Much is known, from research and practical experience, that works in improving the teaching and learning process to better meet the needs of diverse students. By incorporating this knowledge base in a capacity-building approach to school reform, schools in inner-cities, suburban areas, and rural towns have found CFL to be flexible and effective in meeting their site-specific improvement needs. CFL is known to work with individual schools at the preschool through high school levels. However, because of CFL's emphasis on family and community connections, it works best in districts and schools with a districtwide plan or districts with a cluster of schools using CFL as a whole-school reform program.

- Who takes responsibility for initiating CFL?

  Whether you are a parent, policymaker, government official, school administrator, teacher, education specialist, or community leader, you can help ensure that the process of getting CFL into your school or district takes place.

- How long does it take to achieve a high degree of CFL implementation?

  Community for Learning aims to build the capacity of school staff to implement effective instructional and planning strategies over a three-year period. During the first year, CFL staff provide intensive training, consultation, and evaluation support to school staff and administrators. For two more years, it provides technical assistance as needed and monitors progress. This approach strengthens the capacity of participating sites to deliver support and professional development to staff. Depending on site-specific needs and resources, some schools achieve full implementation in less than three years.

Research and Development Programs

The research and development programs at CRHDE are organized in five units, with interrelated activities ranging from research to information dissemination:

- The National Center on Education in the Inner Cities (CEIC)

  CEIC, one of the national R&D centers established through initial funding from the U.S. Department of Education in 1990, focuses on transforming research into practical strategies that support student success, especially in inner-city schools. The Center is devoted to examining ways to harness the diverse resources and expertise of this nation's cities to improve the education and life circumstances of children and youth. A team of interdisciplinary researchers study how the family, school, and community support student learning and the educational resiliency of children and youth, including those who live in even the most dire situations.

- The Laboratory for Student Success (LSS)

  LSS was established in 1995 by the U.S. Department of Education as the Mid-Atlantic Regional Educational Laboratory and is designated as the lead regional laboratory with a specialty area in urban education. The Laboratory for Student Success is responsible for transforming research-based knowledge into tools that can assist the educational reform process at the national and regional levels. Building on the diverse strengths of families, schools, and communities, LSS works to provide technical assistance and to support professional development activities for educational professionals; to conduct outreach to grassroots organizations to ensure their participation in the process; and to disseminate and implement educational reform programs such as Community for Learning. LSS researchers work in conjunction with field-based professionals to identify effective educational practices, systems of service delivery, and school environments. The ultimate goal of the LSS is a regional network of schools, parents, community agencies, and institutions of higher learning that supports children's learning and that is connected to a nationwide system of information exchange.

- The Adult Development and Education Program

    This program focuses on developing effective ways to deliver education to disadvantaged adults in urban communities. The program provides training and technical assistance to literacy service and health and human services providers. Through aggressive outreach efforts and coordination with education and related social services agencies, this program affects the lives of even the most isolated adults who otherwise would not participate. Graduates of the program go on to pursue higher education and job training in a variety of fields.

- The Program on Improving Instruction and Learning in Schools

    This program aims to provide educational leaders and policymakers at the local, state, and national levels with state-of-the-art information on innovative school programs, and with technical support for instituting and evaluating these programs in their schools. It focuses on topics related to teacher effectiveness, school leadership, policy development, and program implementation. Through demonstration projects with local school systems and universities, the program offers insight into how research on these topics affects practices and policies.

- The Child Development and Early Intervention Program

    This program focuses on the study of infants and young children who are diagnosed as developmentally delayed and/or otherwise considered to have special needs. It aims to:

    - Develop policies and procedures that support and promote family involvement in early identification and use of services for children;

    - Assess the effectiveness of evaluation and intervention planning services; and

    - Foster collaboration among service providers to develop a family centered, early intervention and prevention system of service delivery.

Contact

Cynthia Smith
Temple University Center for Research in Human Development and Education
1301 Cecil B. Moore Avenue
Philadelphia, PA 19122-6091
Voice: (800)-892-5550
Fax: (215) 204-5130
lss@vm.temple.edu
www.temple.edu/LSS

The Center for the Study and Teaching of At-Risk Students (C-STARS)

The School-Community Partnership Component

Background

The Center for the Study and Teaching of At-Risk Students (C-STARS) was founded in 1987 and is a division of the Institute for the Study of Educational Policy located at the University of Washington (UW) and housed in the College of Education. The Center is colocated at the University of Washington and Washington State University.

Mission Statement

The mission of C-STARS is to join with and help facilitate efforts by K-14 schools and early childhood education programs to link with community-based health and social service organizations in order to better coordinate and integrate their respective services to common client populations of children at risk of school failure and their families. The focus of these efforts, ultimately, is on dropout prevention and the academic achievements of student populations that disproportionately experience difficulties with school success.

This mission is accomplished through an array of training, program evaluation, research, and outreach activities. A majority of these activities are associated with a school-based or school-linked case management approach that C-STARS has been developing and evaluating for the past 12 years.

C-STARS Guidelines and Standards for Interprofessional Case Management

C-STARS has been developing and testing a set of guidelines and standards for reference by local school communities in planning and evaluating school-based or school-linked interprofessional case management programs. C-STARS defines interprofessional case management as:

> A series of logical and appropriate interactions within a comprehensive service network of schools, social service agencies and health organizations responsible for the well-being of common client populations of children and families. These interactions maximize opportunities for children, at-risk of school failure and their families to receive a variety of needed services in a supportive, efficient, and coordinated manner while empowering parents and guardians.

The C-STARS guidelines outline procedures or steps to follow for local program development, implementation, and evaluation. The Center's standards for case management delineate criteria for reference in measuring or judging capacity and quality of local school/community case management models.

Computer-Assisted Risk Accountability System (CARAS) Case Management Software

CARAS is an acronym for the Computer-Assisted Risk Accountability System, a computer-based case management software package designed to help schools and their community-based partners identify risk factors, monitor different services these students and their families are receiving, and routinely provide data/information that can aid in evaluating and adjusting these efforts. At present, the CARAS process includes three distinct components: initial screening and individualized planning, school-based case management, and ongoing monitoring/followup.

Current C-STARS Research and Evaluation Projects

- Early Head Start Research Project

    This five-year research grant project entitled "An Investigation of Early Head Start and Beyond for Hispanic, Native American and Other Rural Poor Families in Communities of Washington State" was awarded to C-STARS in spring 1996. The grant is one of 16 awarded nationally by the U.S. Department of Health and Human Services under its program for Local Research Partnerships for Early

Head Start Programs. C-STARS is collaborating with the Washington State Migrant Council (WSMC) to conduct local research in five Lower Yakima Valley communities, addressing the efficacy of WSMC's Early Head Start program, which includes variations of the C-STARS case management approach. This study is part of a national research project focusing on capabilities of Early Head Start to enhance the development and well-being of infants, toddlers and their families.

- The Intimate Partner Violence Prevention Project

    This three-year grant project entitled "A Community-Based Primary Prevention Program to Prevent Intimate Partner Violence for a Safe America" is a partnership between Centro Latino SER of Tacoma, the Tacoma Urban League, and the University of Washington. C-STARS is contracted to evaluate this project, which is centered around four principal project components: a school-based component, which involves the delivery of a dating violence curriculum to middle and high school-aged students; a community-based component, which involves the delivery of a dating violence awareness curriculum to parents in the surrounding community; a school staff component, which involves presenting dating violence material to public school staff through in-service training; and a juvenile detention component, which involves the delivery of a dating violence curriculum to middle and high school-aged students incarcerated in the Pierce County Juvenile Detention facility. This project, located in Tacoma, is 1 of 10 awarded nationally by the Centers for Disease Control and Prevention.

- The Kenai Peninsula Family Support Program (Alaska)

    The Kenai Peninsula Borough School District and the Central Peninsula Mental Health Association have been collaborating for four years to coordinate delivery of school-based and school-linked education and mental health counseling services to at-risk students and their families. Mental health counselors are co-located in four schools and use a variation of a case management approach with school personnel in providing multiple services to children and their families, many of whom are eligible for Medicaid billing. C-STARS is funded through a service contract with the Association to evaluate the program and produce annual reports of findings.

District, State, and National Systemic Initiatives

- Sacramento County Healthy Start Partnership (California)

  Three Sacramento County (CA) school districts with state-funded Healthy Start grant programs have partnered with Sacramento Cities in Schools to adapt the C-STARS case-management approach, particularly its software component referred to as CARAS, to more efficiently address the California Department of Education's annual reporting requirements mandated via SB620: The State of California Healthy Start Support Services for Children Act (1991). C-STARS is currently under service contract with this partnership to provide in-service training to Healthy Start personnel serving in case manager type roles. This training is designed to orient staff to the C-STARS case management guidelines and standards and to the corresponding CARAS software for use in program monitoring and evaluation.

- The Regional Safe School Program of the West 40 Intermediate Service Center (Illinois)

  Secondary teachers, counselors, and other school personnel of eight school districts serving townships located in the greater Chicago area are currently receiving case management training and technical assistance from C-STARS. These districts are utilizing school-based case managers to assume leadership roles with Regional Safe Schools Programs operating in alternative high schools and middle schools. C-STARS is also evaluating each of the eight programs in collaboration with the Illinois State Board of Education and the West 40 Intermediate Service Center.

Contact

Dr. Albert J. Smith, Director
Center for the Study and Teaching of At-Risk Students (C-STARS)
4725 30th Avenue NE
Seattle, WA 98105-4021
Voice: (206) 543-3815
Fax: (206) 685-4722
alsmith@u.washington.edu

The Clearinghouse for Immigrant Education (CHIME)

Background

Building a society where all cultures, languages, and peoples are respected is difficult. To support this important work, the National Coalition of Advocates for Students has established the Clearinghouse for Immigrant Education (CHIME). The Clearinghouse for Immigrant Education is an interactive clearinghouse and networking service that provides literature, referrals, project models, and other supports to the education community on education issues for immigrant students. The Clearinghouse for Immigrant Education offers customized searches of its database, free periodic bibliographies on selected topics, and other resources. The Clearinghouse for Immigrant Education is available to assist schools, parents, advocates, students, and others who support the school success of immigrant students and who are working to build a multicultural U.S. society.

The Clearinghouse for Immigrant Education is a service offered by the National Center for Immigrant Students, a project of the National Coalition of Advocates for Students (NCAS). The National Coalition of Advocates is a national education advocacy organization with 22 member groups in 14 states which works to achieve equal access to a quality public education for the most vulnerable students—those who are poor, children of color, recently immigrated, and children with disabilities. Focusing on kindergarten through grade 12, NCAS informs and mobilizes parents, concerned educators, and communities to help resolve critical education issues.

In 1988, NCAS published *New Voices: Immigrant Students in U.S. Public Schools,* the first comprehensive examination of the status of young newcomers in the nation's public schools. The National Coalition of Advocates established the National Center for Immigrant Students and CHIME in 1990 to stimulate networking and information-sharing, to expand advocacy on behalf of foreign-born students, and to examine emerging federal, state, and local policies likely to impact upon their school success.

The Clearinghouse for Immigrant Education staff members will become your partners in problem solving. They will survey available resources, help you make networking connections, and provide information about how to obtain relevant documents. For documents that are available from CHIME, there is a nominal fee to cover duplication, shipping, and handling. Other services are free, including complimentary copies of the *Mobilization for Equity* newsletter and annotated bibliographies.

Finding solutions to such complex problems is a two-way process. With help from CHIME, you can benefit from the experience of others while others benefit from your experience as well.

CHIME Resources

- Literature

    CHIME continually evaluates and abstracts articles and research on a wide range of topics relevant to immigrant students.

- Resource listing

    CHIME maintains a national listing of resource centers, community-based organizations, and individuals with resources, experience, or knowledge to share.

- Publications

    CHIME develops periodic annotated bibliographies on specific topics in immigrant education. Entitled *Selected Readings from CHIME*, these resource lists are available to CHIME users free of charge. A free newsletter, *Mobilization for Equity*, is also available, along with information about all publications developed as part of other NCAS projects.

Contact

Jan Buettner, Resource Center Coordinator
Clearinghouse for Immigrant Education
The National Coalition of Advocates for Students
100 Boylston St. Suite 737
Boston, MA 02116
Voice: (800) 441-7192 or (617) 357-8507
Fax: (617) 357-9549
NCASMFE@aol.com
www.ncasl.org

Education Commission of the States

Mission

The mission of the Education Commission of the States (ECS) is to help state leaders develop and carry out policies that promote improved performance of the education system as reflected in increased learning by all citizens.

Background

The initial concept of an interstate planning commission for education was proposed by the late James Bryant Conant, president emeritus of Harvard University. His concern about the haphazard way in which states had approached education policy decisions, served as the impetus for the creation of what he personally called "...my major social invention—the Education Commission of the States." Conant's studies of American education convinced him that the country needed a way for states to become more deeply involved in shaping education policy.

Under the guidance of former North Carolina Governor Terry Sanford, Conant's proposal became reality. A unanimous vote at the 1966 National Governors' Conference called for a nationwide alliance for the improvement of education with the active leadership and personal participation of the governors.

In 1977, the ECS Steering Committee established the James Bryant Conant Award in honor of this great educator, scientist and statesman. This award is presented annually to an individual for outstanding service in education.

Membership

Today, 49 states, the District of Columbia, Puerto Rico, American Samoa, and the Virgin Islands have passed legislation to join ECS. Each member state or territory appoints, usually through the governor's office, seven ECS commissioners who represent all segments of education. These 371 commissioners include all the governors, more than 130 state legislators (usually heads of House and Senate education committees), state and local school board members, chief state school officers, state higher education executive officers, college presidents, superintendents, teachers and dozens of other prominent education leaders from all over the country. Commissioners serve one- to three-year terms as liaisons to other education leaders in their state and throughout the country. More than 4,000 policymakers and education leaders are ECS alumni.

One ECS commissioner in each state is a member of the Steering, Committee. Three times each year, these commissioners meet to discuss important education issues affecting, their states. Their discussions help guide the commission's work.

Officers and Staff

The ECS chair alternates each year between a Democratic and a Republican governor. The vice chair is traditionally a legislator from the major political party opposite that of the chair. To balance the roster of officers between political and education leaders, a treasurer is chosen from among the Steering Committee members representing the education field.

Headquartered in Denver, Colorado, the ECS staff includes educators, policy analysts, economists, testing and evaluation experts, government relations experts, information and communication strategy specialists, writers, editors, public relations and production personnel, researchers and support staff.

Networks

The Education Commission of the States sponsors five formal networks of education and political leaders and provides numerous opportunities for constituents to network informally. The formal networks are:

- ECS Advisory Commissioners, who are the executive directors of more than two dozen diverse public and private national education associations. They advise ECS on the priorities of their constituents, who represent major education audiences.

- The ECS Policy Network, which is a bipartisan forum that enables ECS commissioners and other policy leaders to explore and discuss education issues. As successor to the State Education Policy Seminars program, the Policy Network is designed to help state leaders work toward a bipartisan agenda for K-12 and postsecondary education improvement.

- The Legislative Education Committee Chairs, who, in conjunction with the National Conference of State Legislatures, organize national and regional seminars to stimulate legislative leaders' thinking on education issues.

- The Governors' Education Policy Advisors network, which links both ECS and the National Governors' Association to the governor's office in each state. Group members meet at least twice a year to study education issues and to interact with their peers in other states.

- The Legislative Education Staff Network, which is cosponsored with the National Conference of State Legislatures and which enables legislative staff to share information and talk with experts about education issues.

Funding

As a nonprofit organization, ECS obtains financial support through a mixture of state fees, state contracts, and foundation and federal grants. Funding for FY1998 is approximately $8 million. About 43 percent of this amount is derived from state fees.

Priorities

The Policy and Priorities Committee (PPC) assesses priority concerns of ECS commissioners. The PPC then makes recommendations for priorities to be addressed and ensures that the commission's budget is consistent with these priorities. This committee meets 3 times each year and consists of 15 ECS commissioners and other education leaders from across the country.

Current priorities reflect ECS' focus on promoting improvement in public education and on anticipating important developments affecting the education system. They also affirm the organization's commitment to providing high-quality, useful information and assistance to state education policymakers. Following is an array of selected, ongoing ECS priorities:

- Promote needed and positive transformation in public postsecondary education systems, with emphasis on state policy and strategies.
  - Under the leadership of 1998-99 ECS Chairman Paul E. Patton, governor of Kentucky, launch a new initiative focused on the transformation of post-secondary education; carefully examine needed changes in the functions, services and priorities of public postsecondary education, and consider options for restructuring to meet new student and public needs.

- Expand the work of ECS' initiative on state policy for community colleges through a continuing series of policy briefs, a national policy forum, information services and technical assistance, and an offer to provide tailored in-state workshops.
- Work directly with networks of states at the forefront in advancing innovations in higher education—particularly those related to access, financing, performance assessment and accountability, uses of technology, and connecting learning and work.

♦ Promote the scale-up of effective K-12 education reform.
- Work with states where there is high interest in creating policy environments that support innovative, high-performance schools. Major continuing projects will include:
  - The ECS/Annenberg project, in partnership with New American Schools;
  - The State Leadership of Learning Initiative; and
  - The Building State-Level Reform Infrastructure Initiative.
- Focus ECS K-12 policy research, analysis, and development efforts on issues crucial to the success and scale-up of education reform; resource reallocation; standards implementation issues, including assessment, accountability and the professional development of educators; and the array of policies that promote flexibility and diversity in the education system, thereby providing more choices for parents and students.
- Continue work on a new ECS initiative, Governing America's Schools by producing research on current and alternative governance models; documenting the effects of governance on student achievement; supporting deliberations of a national commission; identifying key principles of effective governance; and, ultimately, offering technical assistance to states where there is interest in governance innovation.
- Initiate a new phase of ECS work on reform of teacher education and professional development.
- Support early development of the Compact for Learning and Citizenship, a project designed to increase K-12 students' involvement in public and community service, and to help schools make better use of volunteers.

- Increase the depth and rigor of information available to policymakers regarding what works in education reform and the impact of policy on improvement efforts.
  - Expand work of the Alliance for Best Practices in Education, an ECS partnership with the American Productivity and Quality Center, through new consortium benchmarking studies aimed at identifying and sharing best practices in education policy.
  - Strengthen ECS efforts, both independent and collaborative, to collect and share evidence regarding both the performance of restructured schools, colleges and universities, and the impact of policy on that performance. Revise and strengthen the annual ECS report on the progress of education reform.
- Provide leadership in defining leading-edge issues in education policy, and assist states in organizing discussion and initiating action on these issues. For example:
  - As the next phase in the ECS initiative on Harnessing Technology to Improve Teaching and Learning, support and facilitate state-based workshops, focusing on policy issues regarding technology infrastructure, funding, classroom methods and materials, and professional development.
  - Promote awareness of the implications of emerging brain research for education policy and practices by working with key state policymakers and education leaders to design and offer in-state seminars.

Contact

Education Commission of the States
707 17th Street, Suite 2700
Denver, Colorado 80202-3427
Voice: (303) 299-3600
Fax: (303) 296-8332
ecs@ecs.org
www.ecs.org

The Holmes Partnership

The Holmes Partnership is a consortium of nearly 100 American universities committed to making programs of teacher preparation more rigorous and connected to liberal arts education, to research on learning and teaching, and to wise practice in the schools. The Holmes Partnership incorporated in 1986 as a nonprofit organization "to enhance the quality of schooling through research and development and the preparation of career professionals in teaching." The Holmes Partnership focuses on:

- Sound arts and science curriculum—imparting deep understanding of the disciplines to teachers and their students;

- On-campus studies of the critical knowledge about learning and teaching—coherently organized, and integrated with

- In-school practice teaching, well-coached and gradually increasing in responsibility—in several settings, but especially in schools enrolling diverse students and those who are at-risk of academic failure; and

- Research in which university and school faculties collaborate—examining questions arising at the school, and trying out new approaches to learning, teaching, and the organization of schools.

At the core of the initiative are the Professional Development Schools. Professional Development Schools are regular elementary, middle, or high schools that work in partnership with a university to develop and demonstrate fine learning programs for diverse students; practical, thought-provoking preparation for novice teachers; new understandings and professional responsibilities for experienced educators; and research projects that add to all educators' knowledge about how to make schools more productive.

A Professional Development School is a center of responsible innovation where new programs and technologies can be tried out and evaluated. It is a place where faculty of the school and of the university both experience the *white water* feeling of working at the edge of their knowledge.

It is a place where new teachers, just forming their knowledge and technique, taste the reality of classrooms similar to those where they're likely to get their first jobs, and where they also see the skill, hear the counsel, and feel the support of expert teachers.

Each Professional Development School is invented through conversations and negotiations among university and public school faculties. Holmes Partnership Group staff advance their vision at the beginning of a process—conversations, actions; conversations, revisions—that are worked out over time into enduring organizations. (While a number of schools similar to the Partnership's conception are being developed in different parts of the nation, there are none that yet stand as models.)

University schools of education and public schools all over the country are beginning such conversations about long-term directions, cumulative change, and collaborative work. It is vital and renewing to think and talk seriously about creating a Professional Development School. Instead of reacting to each new hummock on the school reform landscape, educators in schools of education and school districts can play a leading role. The Holmes Partnership Group is the one to start building tomorrow's schools—today.

As starting points, The Holmes Partnership offers six principles for mutual efforts to design a Professional Development School. The six principles for mutual efforts follow:

- Teach for understanding so that students learn for a lifetime.

    Staff work to ensure that students become active producers of thought, not passive consumers. They work to involve students in learning tasks and programs in which students make sense of their own experiences, the world near and far, and their future.

- Organize the school and its classrooms as a community of learning.

    Both words—*community* and *learning*— have equal weight. Without the life of the mind, community lacks intellectual purpose. Without community, academic work may lack useful meaning.

    Students learn about democracy—both democratic discipline and free expression—by living it in a community together. Passive learners will rarely think powerfully, nor will they make strong citizens of a free republic. In a learning community, all children, not just a few, learn to work together to achieve intellectual and social understandings and to create an embracing culture. These arts of participation are themselves habits and skills to be learned in school.

    Schools should be public democratic spaces where young citizens learn critical thinking and civic courage; where knowledge operates in the service of values; where students, under adult guidance, begin to assume responsibility for their thought and action.

- Hold these ambitious learning goals for everybody's children.

  It is difficult to create such schools in a society whose families live on very unequal terms. Unlike a traditional laboratory school, a Professional Development School will grapple with problems that have been seen as roots of failure—the poverty of students' families, the paucity of resources in the school, the disconnection, in students' minds, between school now and their lives in the future.

- Teach adults as well as children.

  A Professional Development School is a regular school where teachers, administrators, and professors collaborate in giving prospective teachers practical experiences in how schools run and how teachers work. These experiences are integrated with both the professional course of study at the university and the instructional program of the school. Student teachers are emboldened to take up difficult problems because they can do so with the help of wise, veteran teachers. The focus of their professional preparation is on how to reach the children who are not succeeding in today's schools. University educators will learn too, gaining new understandings about the realities of schooling.

- Make reflection and inquiry a central feature of the school.

  A Professional Development School will not be simply the university's clinic or lab. It will be a center of inquiry with its own agenda, dealing with the school's tough questions. Mindful practice, critical reflection, collegial discourse and study, and continuing inquiry and experimentation will be normal ways of working, not exceptional events. Thus the school will teach student teachers habits of thinking back on their work, questioning it, trying out and evaluating new ways of teaching—by themselves and with colleagues.

- Invent a new organizational structure for the school.

  The school will fashion new, flexible roles and rotating assignments for teachers, based not on specializations but rather on how to improve the school's learning and teaching throughout the grades —taking the vantage point of a student's whole career in the school. Thus, the faculty may design alternative ways of organizing subjects and staff—interdisciplinary studies, for instance, and grouping students by characteristics other than age or narrowly conceived measurers of ability. Expert teachers will take formal or informal leadership roles.

The school will create strong connections with parents and community organizations—bridges for students between home, school, and their life beyond school. It will strive to ambitiously shape the way young people think about work, how they anticipate their future and link themselves to the broader world. Youth are hungry for adult attention. Teachers do not succeed by themselves alone. They need allies and coalitions in the community. The school's connections with the community will also create different roles for teachers.

The Holmes Partnership organizes its work around a multilevel series of interacting networks at the local, state, regional, national and international levels. An explanation of the interacting networks follows:

- Local networks will "enable leadership to make education schools better places for professional study and learning" while enhancing the quality and presence of professional development schools.

- State networks will focus on important policy issues to evaluate and complete reform agendas.

- Regional networks will provide formal opportunities for interaction and exchange among proximate local partnerships.

- National networks will provide strategic opportunities to work with other influential national organizations both for advocacy and for informing the public about this important work.

- International networks will help educators realize the global nature of improving professional practice.

The Process

Inventing and starting a Professional Development School is not just a design process; it's also a negotiation process. It's a back-and-forth dialogue between people in a university and people in a school district, and between principles and actions. It's a steady push toward intertwined transformations:

- Teachers becoming practical intellectuals, able to help all children learn with lasting understanding;

- The school becoming a democratic community in which all children belong, participate, and progress;

- Professional education becoming both a meld—practical experiences with theoretical understandings—and a continuum throughout a career; and

- Educational research becoming a joint investigation of questions vital to the school—professors, teachers, and administrators collaborating.

The New Holmes Partnership Goals

- Goal 1: High Quality Professional Preparation

  Provide exemplary professional preparation and development programs for public school educators. These programs must demonstrate rigor, innovation, and attention to the needs of diverse children and youth. Their design, content, and delivery must reflect research and best practice.

- Goal 2: Simultaneous Renewal

  Engage in the simultaneous renewal of public K-12 schools and the education of beginning and experienced educators by establishing strong partnerships of universities, schools and professional organizations and associations.

- Goal 3: Equity, Diversity, and Cultural Competence

  Actively work on equity, diversity and cultural competence in the programs of K-12 schools, higher education, and the education profession by recruiting, preparing, and sustaining faculty and students who reflect the rich diversity of cultural perspectives in this country and in our global community.

- Goal 4: Scholarly Inquiry and Programs of Research

  Conduct and disseminate educational research and engage in other scholarly activities that advance knowledge, improve teaching and learning for all children and youth, inform the preparation and development of educators, and influence educational policy and practice.

- Goal 5: Faculty Development

  Provide high quality doctoral programs for the future education professors and for advanced professional development of school-based educators. Redesign the work of both university and school faculty to enable accomplishment of The Holmes Partnership goals—better preparing educators in improving learning for children and youth and promoting conditions that recognize and reward education professionals who better serve the needs of all learners.

- Goal 6: Policy Initiation

    Engage in policy analysis and development related to public K-12 schools and the preparation of educators. Advocate policies that improve teaching and learning for all students, promote school improvement and enhance the preparation and continuing professional development of all educators.

Contact

Richard Kunkel, Ph.D., Executive Director
The Holmes Partnership
College of Education
Auburn University
Auburn, AL 36849-5218
Voice: (334) 844-4446
Fax: (334) 844-5785
kunkerc@mail.auburn.edu
www.udel.edu/holmes

The Institute for Urban and Minority Education (IUME)

The Institute for Urban and Minority Education (IUME) conducts research for better understanding the diversity of urban and minority group populations, and their experiences in the different institutions and situations that influence their social, psychological, and economic development. The Institute for Urban and Minority Education provides the knowledge necessary to develop governmental policies and design educational programs that support the development of ethnically and linguistically diverse groups.

Specifically, the Institute for Urban and Minority Education:

- Conducts research and analyzes policies;
- Provides technical assistance and professional development opportunities;
- Convenes educators and the public;
- Organizes programs for urban and minority youth; and
- Serves as a source of information.

The work of the Institute is supported by Teachers College, Columbia University, governmental agencies, and foundations. The staff consists of researchers and educators from many disciplines and fields.

Research and Policy Analysis

The Institute conducts research in such areas as the educational and economic circumstances of African-American, Hispanic, and newly arrived immigrant students; urban and minority families; the organizational, curricular, and instructional requirements of urban schooling; resource allocation in urban schools; and, generally, strategies for the psychological and social development of urban and minority youth.

Technical Assistance and Professional Development

The Institute assists schools in designing and implementing equitable programs and practices, provides multicultural and antibias training to educators and human service professionals, and helps communities design and maintain social programs and human services to foster the development of urban and minority youth.

Convening Authority

The Institute organizes forums for educators and the public, including opinion makers, to consider how the education system and the greater society can be organized to be more equitable, just, and civil for all groups.

Youth Programs

The Institute provides leadership training to minority youth through seminars, workshops, and fellowships, and also provides education in the use of electronic technology.

Information Services

The Institute publishes monographs, policy analyses, and research reports on topics of current importance to professionals and the public, briefs summarizing research or practice knowledge, and a newsletter describing current Institute activities and publications.

The ERIC Clearinghouse on Urban Education is part of IUME. The Clearinghouse hosts the ERIC/CUE Urban Education Web and the National Parent Education Network on the Internet.

Contact

Erwin Flaxman, Ph.D.
Institute for Urban and Minority Education
Teachers College, Columbia University
525 West 120 Street, Box 75
New York, NY 10027-6696
Voice: (212) 678-3780
Fax: (212) 678-4137
ef29@columbia.edu
iume.tc.columbia.edu

The National Center on Education and the Economy (NCEE)

The National Center on Education and the Economy (NCEE) is the manager of New Standards, which has produced the nation's most comprehensive and integrated internationally benchmarked performance standards for the schools. New Standards has also developed a set of performance assessments in Mathematics and English Language Arts that are matched to the standards. Assessments in science and applied learning are being developed.

Building on these standards and assessments, the National Center provides tools and technical assistance to support standards-based school reform in large urban centers, suburban districts, and rural towns. It draws on its strategic alliances with other organizations to help its partners accomplish the following:

- Implement New Standards and other state-of-the art systems of performance standards and assessments;

- Develop curricula and instructional environments for students that are aligned with the standards;

- Create school-to-work transition systems that help all students develop solid academic skills and the technical skills they will need to have rewarding careers;

- Build community supports and services for students who would otherwise have a hard time succeeding in school;

- Engage parents and other community members in the education of their children; and

- Redesign the organization and management of schools and districts for high performance.

The NCEE's America's Choice Program (formerly the National Alliance for Restructuring Education) provides an intensive program of technical assistance and professional development designed to help states and districts implement a comprehensive program of standards-based reform embracing all the previously described components.

In the job training and labor market systems arena, the NCEE's Workforce Development Program provides assistance to states and communities interested in building comprehensive school-to-work, job training, and labor market systems, built around systems of internationally benchmarked academic and occupational standards. The Workforce Development Program has also benchmarked occupational skill standards and skill standards systems worldwide, and is providing technical assistance to the National Skill Standards Board of the United States as that body develops a skill standards system for this country.

Program Offerings

- Comprehensive standards-based school design that focuses relentlessly on results, using assessments, curriculum, and instructional program, and a planning, management and organizational system, all aligned with standards.

- Continuous technical assistance from an NCEE staff member, delivered in your area.

- High quality professional development in all the areas of standards-based education, from one of the most experienced teams in the nation.

- Widely admired, completely aligned tools for standards-setting, assessment, curriculum, planning, managing and organizing.

- Access to the annual national America's Choice Conference, for new developments in standards-based education around the world; networking with other America's Choice schools from around the country.

- Systemwide program from the nation's leader in standards-based education.

Standards and Assessments

New York City School's chancellor Rudy Crew called America's Choice Performance Standards (formerly New Standards) "the best available national standards" in the United States, when his district adopted them. Because the standards are based on examples of student work that meet the standards, teachers, students, and parents know just what is needed to succeed. Whether the client uses these standards or develops their own performance standards, the client will be using the America's Choice Reference Examinations in English language arts and mathematics, administered in the fourth, eighth and tenth grades. America's Choice professional development programs introduces performance standards and assessments, shows student performance against identified standards and helps educators evaluate curriculum in terms of its fit with the standards.

Curriculum and Instruction

In the early grades, staff concentrate heavily on literacy, using proven research-based methods that emphasize phonics, oral language, guided reading and writing, and independent reading and writing. Currently, they provide resources designed to help match curriculum to the standards, using America's Choice materials, widely used commercial materials, and units that staff trains clients to create. America's Choice curriculum materials are designed to support student understanding of the concepts underlying the material, thereby providing a solid foundation for rapid progress. A key feature of the curriculum materials is that they enable students who are functioning below grade level in mathematics and English language arts to catch up.

Planning and Organization

America's Choice staff use a planning system that focuses on analyzing student performance, identifying weak spots and building programs to correct them. They assist clients in redesigning the master schedule and extending the school day and week to give students the time and program they need to reach high standards. America's Choice staff will also help clients organize their school staff into an effective leadership team and involve parents to support the learning of their children.

Key Program Features for All Schools

- Five design tasks
  - Standards and assessments
  - Instructional systems
  - Community services and supports
  - High performance management
  - Parent and public engagement
- New Standards Performance Standards

- New Standards Reference Exams
- Unique, powerful curriculum design, aligned to the standards
- Comprehensive safety net for students
- Class teacher who follows student for 3 years
- Planning and management system focused on results
- Onsite, continuous technical assistance
- Comprehensive professional development program

Key Program Features for K-8 Schools

- A 2½-hour literacy block and a 1-hour math block every day
- Teachers specialize in literacy and social studies or math and science

Key Program Features for 9-12 Schools

- Small school, "house" system
- Curriculum focused on academic core
- Strong college preparatory program
- Strong work-based technical preparatory program
- All students prepared for college

Key Program Features for Districts (Optional Package)

- School monitoring and review system
- Decentralized resource allocation system
- Full support system for low-performing schools
- Comprehensive accountability system design

New Standards: A New Process for Measuring Student Progress

New Standards represents the most extensive collaboration ever undertaken to measure student progress toward meeting higher, internationally benchmarked national standards. The joint effort to create these standards included educators whose jurisdictions enroll nearly half of the nation's students. New Standards began as a partnership between the Learning Research and Development Center (LRDC) of the University of Pittsburgh and the National Center on Education and the Economy. States and urban school districts also were key players in this partnership. The Governing Board included chief state school officers, governors and their representatives and numerous other educators and officials.

New Standards was founded by Lauren Resnick, Director of LRDC, and Marc Tucker, President of the NCEE. The Executive Director is Phil Daro. New Standards staff is based at the LRDC and NCEE as well as at the American Association for the Advancement of Science, the Fort Worth Independent School District, and the University of California Office of the President. Technical studies are based at LRDC with an advisory committee of leading psychometricians from across the nation.

Materials Available from the NCEE

- The New Standards Performance Standards

    The performance standards are the result of a two-year effort to make standards operational. The performance standards not only provide clear expectations for student achievement, but also include numerous examples of student work that show what work that meets the standards looks like. These standards are the basis of the New Standards assessment system. The reference examinations and portfolio system are based on these standards.

    - The performance standards are published in three volumes—elementary, middle, and high school. The elementary school performance standards are targeted around the end of 4th grade. The middle school standards are targeted around the end of 8th grade, and the high school standards are targeted around the end of 10th grade. Each volume contains performance standards for English language arts, mathematics, science, and applied learning.

- The performance standards contain more than 150 examples of student work to illustrate what standard-setting work looks like. All of the work samples are genuine student work. The work shows the efforts of students in diverse settings across America. Each work sample is linked to the standards and comes with an explanation of how the student's work illustrates the standard. The performance standards build upon the consensus content standards developed by the national professional associations, including the National Council of Teachers of Mathematics, National Research Council, and the American Association for the Advancement of Science's Project 2061. The applied learning performance standards are built upon the SCANS framework and comparable work in other countries.

- The performance standards have been progressively refined through extensive processes of consultation and review. They have been reviewed by subject experts and practitioners in the U.S. and many other countries. The standards were also reviewed by parents and community members through focus groups held in diverse communities. A unique feature of the standards is a video showing standard-setting work for the "speaking and listening" standard. The video shows how each student performance is linked to the standards and why that performance counts as standard setting.

♦ The New Standards Portfolio System

The New Standards Portfolio System provides evidence of achievement of the performance standards that depends on extended pieces of work (especially those that show revision) and accumulation of evidence over time. In 1995-96, 3,000 teachers and almost 60,000 students participated in a field trial of the Portfolio System. The New Standards Portfolio System is available in English language arts, mathematics and science at the elementary, middle and high school levels. The New Standards Portfolio System includes:

- One copy of the 1997 New Standards Performance Standards for the grade level(s) ordered.

- A black-line master book with teacher and student instructions and masters of all the entry slips that are needed for students to identify their work.

District, State, and National Systemic Initiatives

- A classroom set (25) of student accordion folders with legal-size folders for each of the exhibits required by the New Standards Portfolio System. Instructions for assembling exhibits are printed directly on the folders.

♦ New Standards Reference Examinations

The examinations represent a new and exciting way to measure student achievement. The New Standards Reference Examination system includes reference examinations in mathematics and English language arts. These examinations include a mix of traditional test items and performance tasks that ask students to use their knowledge to solve complex problems.

♦ New Standards Practice Tests

These tests parallel the Reference Examinations in format and type of task. They can help students become familiar with the type of questions and tasks found in the Reference Examinations. Three levels of the practice examinations are available in English language arts and mathematics.

♦ New Standards Released Tasks

These provide an economical way to introduce the New Standards tasks and scoring rubrics into the classroom. They include black-line masters for reproducing individual tasks, as well as examples of student responses to those tasks that illustrate "how good is good enough."

♦ New Standards Videos

The Public Reaction? Yes! In this video, focus groups are solicited to determine what the participants—including parents, teachers, students, and taxpayers—think of high national standards and the agenda of the New Standards.

Only Our Best is Good Enough. This video emphasizes that it is no longer appropriate for a small portion of our students to be expected to reach high standards while the rest graduate from college with the equivalent of a seventh-grade education.

♦ The Certificate of Initial Mastery: A Primer

A Certificate of Initial Mastery redefines accomplishment. Whether a student receives a Certificate at age 16 or 21, the Certificate signifies that the student has developed the knowledge and skills necessary to pass, much in the same way law students are expected to pass the bar exam or medical students need to pass their medical boards.

- States begin developing the Certificate of Initial Mastery

    The SAT and ACT are commonly thought of as the closest thing to school-leaving exams we offer in the United States. But these tests are designed primarily for the college-bound and do not necessarily measure what all students know and are able to do using a relevant, challenging format.

- *The International Experience with School Leaving Examinations*

    This document can help educators learn how other countries are changing their focus on the university-bound to the exclusion of front-line workers. What systems are being put in place to help students learn to think and understand new material quickly? Are their lowest standards of achievement among the highest standards we're setting for our students?

- *A School-to-Work Transition System for the United States*

    This report describes different approaches to designing a new education and training system to help young people transition from school to work, and suggests that a consensus on key elements of a new system is emerging. The author describes these key elements and how a system of academic and occupational skill standards are a critical part of that design.

- *On Occupational Clusters: Early Thoughts on Organizing the Work of the National Skill Standards Board* (with a commentary on the papers commissioned by the U.S. Department of Labor on Occupational Clusters)

    In the spring of 1994, the United States Congress passed the Goals 2000: Educate America Act, which, among other things, authorizes the establishment of a National Skill Standards Board. One of the Board's first tasks was to identify the occupational clusters in which standards will be set.

    Sixteen experts prepared papers addressing the principles that might be used by the Board to establish occupational clusters. Marc Tucker, National Center for Education and the Economy President, was asked to read these papers and bring forward the issues and salient points that would allow him to build upon, extend, or amend the argument advanced in his own paper. Marc Tucker's paper, along with his commentary on the other papers commissioned by the U.S. Department of Labor on Occupational Clusters, presents a wealth of insight put forth by some of the most innovative thinkers in the field.

- *Thinking for a Living: Education and the Wealth of Nations*

This document presents the timely and compelling report on the current state of education, employment and training systems, and on the enormous chasm that needs to be crossed between students' preparedness and their abilities to function in a new economy.

- *Standards for Our Schools: How to Set Them, Measure Them, and Reach Them*, by Marc S. Tucker and Judy B. Codding (San Francisco: Jossey-Bass, 1998).

- *Measure Up: Standards, Assessment, and School Reform*, by Robert Rothman (San Francisco: Jossey-Bass, 1995).

Contact

Susan Sullivan
National Center on Education and the Economy
700 Eleventh Street, NW, Suite 750
Washington, DC 20001
Voice: (888) 361-NCEE (6233) or (202) 783-3668
Fax: (716) 482-1284 or (202) 783-3672
schooldesign@ncee.org
www.ncee.org

The National Coalition of Advocates for Students (NCAS)

The National Coalition of Advocates for Students (NCAS) began in 1975 as a voluntary network of education advocates concerned about rising suspension and expulsion rates in public schools. Since then, NCAS has grown into a national advocacy organization with 22 member groups in 14 states.

The National Coalition of Advocates for Students works to achieve equal access to a quality public education for the most vulnerable students—those who are poor, children of color, recently immigrated, and children with disabilities. Rooted in the civil rights movement of the 1960s, NCAS reflects over 25 years of advocacy experience on the part of its member groups.

Focusing on kindergarten through grade 12, NCAS informs and mobilizes parents, concerned educators, and communities to help resolve critical education issues. Utilizing national projects and studies, public hearings and outreach through publications and the media, NCAS raises concerns that might otherwise not be heard.

The National Coalition of Advocates for Students plays a unique role. No other national coalition works full-time on public school issues from the perspective of meeting the needs of students who are not well served by the public schools.

This vantage point leads NCAS to conclude that fundamental structural changes are needed within schools and school systems. Without such changes, the majority of schools will remain unable to serve their increasingly diverse student populations well.

When a significant percentage of students fail academically or leave school before graduation, NCAS holds the school accountable. Because some schools serve all of their students well, the coalition believes that all schools can do so. Accordingly, NCAS seeks stronger governance roles for parents, who, in turn, press for needed changes in school policy and practice.

Advocating for improved opportunity for these vulnerable constituents draws NCAS into challenging and sometimes controversial areas. The National Coalition of Advocates for Students seeks answers to complex questions facing students, parents, and educators, such as:

- How to assess student achievement in ways that are both useful and fair?

- How to challenge damaging school practices such as ability grouping, tracking, labeling, grade retention, suspension, expulsion, and corporal punishment?

- How to provide special education services without relegating students to inferior classrooms from which they cannot escape?

- How to reduce drugs and violence in schools while acknowledging individual dignity and human rights?

- How to affirm and address the issues resulting from the many languages and cultures that immigrant students bring into the classroom?

- How to provide school-based support services to students facing youth unemployment, drug and alcohol abuse, HIV and AIDS infection, teenage pregnancy, street violence, suicide, and racial and cultural discrimination?

Contact

Jan Buettner, Resource Center Coordinator
National Coalition of Advocates for Students
100 Boylston St., Suite 737
Boston, MA 02116
Voice: (617) 357-8507
Fax: (617) 357-9549
NCASMFE@aol.com
www.ncas1.org

New American Schools (NAS)

New American Schools (NAS) is a dynamic coalition of teachers, administrators, parents, policymakers, community and business leaders, and experts from around the country committed to improving academic achievement for all students.

NAS works to change American classrooms, schools, and school systems using *designs*—blueprints for reorganizing an entire school rather than a single program or grade level within it—and by providing assistance to help schools implement these designs successfully. All NAS designs have been validated through extensive research and testing.

Currently, over 1,000 schools in 27 states throughout the county are using NAS designs. Eleven school districts and groups of districts have made a commitment to put NAS designs in place in at least 30 percent of their schools by year 2000. Most partners are on track to meet and exceed this goal by year three. New American Schools reflect one of the eight designs described below.

- ATLAS Communities

    The ATLAS design centers on *pathways*—groups of schools made up of high schools and the elementary and middle schools that feed into them. Teams of teachers from each pathway work together to design curriculum and assessments based on locally defined standards. The teachers in each pathway collaborate with parents and administrators to set and maintain sound management and academic policies, ultimately resulting in improved student performance.

    - Contact
        - Voice: (617) 969-7100
        - Atlas@edc.org
        - www.edc.org/FSC/ATLAS

- Co-NECT Schools

    Co-NECT gives K-12 educators the tools, skills, and support they need for comprehensive school reform focused on results. The goals are to boost academic achievement for all students, connect academics with the real world, and promote community accountability and involvement. The Internet and other technologies are used as a common thread to mobilize the school community in pursuit of these goals. The model is flexible, allowing schools to build on existing reform initiatives. Co-NECT does not require a new curriculum or espouse a particular instructional methodology. Rather the organization helps schools identify what works well, fix or replace what doesn't, and fill in missing pieces.

- Contact
    - Voice: (617) 873-5612
    - info@co-nect.com
    - www.co-nect.com

♦ Expeditionary Learning Outward Bound

Expeditionary Learning is a comprehensive K-12 design that aims at high achievement for all students as well as improvements in instruction and school culture. It draws on the philosophy and pedagogical principles of Outward Bound to *do school* in a way that is both adventurous and hands-on. Most teaching is done through learning expeditions, long-term, in-depth studies of a single topic that incorporate high academic and character standards, involve authentic projects, fieldwork, service and adventure, and culminate in a final product, performance or presentation to an audience beyond the classroom. In Expeditionary Learning Schools, students and teachers stay together for more than one year, teachers work in teams, and tracking is eliminated.

- Contact
    - Voice: (617) 576-1260
    - info@elob.org
    - www.elob.org

♦ Modern Red Schoolhouse Institute

This design strives to help all students achieve high standards through the construction of a standards-driven curriculum; use of traditional and performance-based assessments; establishment of effective organizational patterns and professional development programs; and implementation of effective community involvement strategies. Students master a rigorous curriculum, develop character, and promote the principles of democratic government. These elements of the traditional red schoolhouse are combined with a high level of flexibility in organizing instruction and deploying resources; use of innovative teaching methodologies; student groupings for continuous progress; and advanced technology as a learning and instructional management tool.

- Contact
  - Voice: (888) 275-6774
  - prandall@mrsh.org
  - www.mrsh.org

♦ National Alliance for Restructuring Education

This partnership of schools, districts, states, and leading national organizations works to change the education system from classroom to state house through a five-point set of priorities. Known as *design tasks*, these priorities are standards and assessments, learning environments, high-performance management, community services and supports, and public engagement. The National Alliance seeks to enable all graduating high school students to attain the Certificate of Initial Mastery, a credential representing a high standard of academic accomplishment.

- Contact
  - Voice: (202) 783-3668
  - nareinfo@ncee.org
  - www.ncee.org/OurPrograms/narePage.html

♦ Purposed-Centered Education: Audrey Cohen College

The Audrey Cohen College system of education focuses student learning on the study and achievement of meaningful *purposes* for each semester's academic goals. Students achieve their purpose by using their knowledge and skills to plan, carry out, and evaluate a constructive action to benefit the community and the larger world. Leadership is emphasized and students are expected to meet high academic standards.

- Contact
  - Voice: (212) 343-1234
  - JanithJ@aol.com
  - www.audrey-cohen.edu

♦ Roots and Wings

This elementary school design builds on the widely used Success for All reading program and incorporates science, history, and mathematics to achieve a comprehensive academic program. The premise of the design is that schools must do whatever it takes to make sure all students succeed. To this end, Roots and Wings schools provide at-risk students with tutors, family support, and a variety of other services. While the *roots* of the design refer to mastery of basics, the *wings* represent advanced accomplishments that students achieve through interdisciplinary projects and a challenging curriculum provided by the design.

- Contact
  - Voice: (410) 516-0274
  - rslavin@inet.ed.gov
  - scov.csos.jhu.edu/sfa

♦ Urban Learning Centers

The Urban Learning Centers design (formerly the Los Angeles Learning Centers) is a comprehensive Pre-K–12 model for urban schools. The curriculum and instruction are designed with research-based strategies which hold students to high standards and performance goals. Barriers to learning are addressed by building links to health, social service and referral agencies as well as on-campus support for parents and families. Governance and management are restructured to engage community members in decision making. Urban Learning Centers also incorporate the extensive use of advanced technology as an essential element for implementation of the design.

- Contact
  - Voice: (213)622-5237
  - gpruitt@laedu.lalc.PreK-12.ca.us
  - www.lalc.k12.ca.us/lalc/

Contact

New American Schools
1000 Wilson Boulevard, Suite 2710
Arlington, VA 22209
Voice: (703) 908-9500
Fax: (703) 908-0622
info@hq.nasdc.org
www.naschools.org

The Panasonic Foundation

Background

The Panasonic Foundation is a corporate foundation established in 1984 by a $10 million endowment from the Matsushita Electric Corporation of America (MECA)—known in the United States by its brand names Panasonic, Technics, and Quasar. Matsushita Electric Industrial, MECA's parent company, later strengthened the foundation with an additional endowment of $10 million. The foundation's endowment now stands at $24 million. The Panasonic Foundation's current annual program budget of approximately $1.7 million is dedicated entirely to the improvement of public elementary and secondary education in the United States.

Using its Framework for School System Success as a guide, the Panasonic Foundation works with public school districts to redesign their education systems by enhancing their capability to change as society's needs change. The Foundation does this by providing direct technical assistance through the Panasonic Partnership Program, which establishes 5- to 10-year partnerships with the districts. The Panasonic Foundation does not award grants.

The Foundation custom-builds assistance to meet the needs of each partnership district through a collaborative discussion with all district stakeholders. The technical assistance takes many forms, depending on the particular purpose it is designed to serve, for example:

- Providing on-site consultations with schools and districts to develop and implement their plans for instructional improvement and organizational change;

- Conducting retreats for school boards, school staffs, central offices, community groups, and others;

- Holding forums and focus groups to help communities determine their beliefs and perspectives on various educational issues, and to increase their support for education reform;

- Conducting workshops, seminars, and conferences on such topics as student learning standards and assessments, management-labor relations, site-based budgeting, and collaboration and coalition-building among key stakeholders within and outside the school system;

- Linking school and district personnel from partnership districts with other reform-minded individuals and districts around the country;

- Helping schools and districts forge closer ties with their communities;

- Taking teachers, administrators, and parents from partnership districts on site visits to exemplary schools or districts, and

- Helping districts and state departments of education assess their effectiveness in supporting local change.

Mission

The Panasonic Foundation's mission is to help public school systems that serve high percentages of children in poverty to improve learning for all students so that they may use their minds well and become productive, responsible citizens.

Beliefs

The Panasonic Foundation's underlying beliefs and guiding principles are:

- All children can learn.

- All students can achieve significantly higher levels of learning than they currently are achieving.

Operationally, the Foundation's beliefs are:

- For all students to learn at higher levels, schools as a whole need to fundamentally change.

- Decisions affecting student learning must be made in a shared, participatory manner by those closest to the students, that is, by parents and the school staff.

- State and local education systems must be restructured to support and promote school-level reform.

- All stakeholder groups need to take responsibility for and be engaged in the reform process.

Program Rationale

Schools have remained essentially the same over the last 100 years, while almost everything else about our society has undergone enormous changes. Just as yesterday's factories cannot meet the challenges of today's industries, the schools of yesterday are not able to meet today's need to prepare all students to lead productive lives in a multicultural, high-technology world.

At the same time, public schools are not independent entities; they are parts of local school districts and state systems of education under whose financial and other policies they operate. Unless these systems transform themselves into organizations that nurture positive school change, individual schools will not improve significantly or in large enough numbers.

Components of a Successful System

A successful school system is driven by the belief that all students can learn at challenging levels and actively enables each school to realize that belief. A successful system, as outlined in the Panasonic Foundation's Framework for School System Success, is characterized by these attributes:

- A vision focused on equity and learning for all;
- A strategic direction based on learning and the centrality of the school as the place of learning;
- Clear delineation of roles, authority, and responsibilities;
- An infrastructure that enhances professional and organizational capacity;
- Assessment and evaluation practices aligned with learning standards and strategic direction;
- An accountability system focused on results;
- Effective use of well-managed data;
- An effective communications system;
- Teachers unions and other professional associations seen as important system components; and
- Meaningful engagement of system constituents and the broader community.

The Technical Assistance Process

The foundation works with a core group of 15 senior consultants who provide ongoing consultation and technical assistance to the foundation's partner school systems. Additionally, the foundation draws on a network of more than 250 consultants as needed. Most of the foundation's consultants are or have been practicing teachers and administrators in exemplary restructuring schools and districts across the country.

In addition to the technical assistance provided through the Partnership Program, the foundation provides the following resources:

- *p3*, which is a newsletter that primarily highlights the ongoing reform efforts in Panasonic Partnership schools and school districts;

- *Strategies*, which is an issues series for school system leaders on district-level change, published in collaboration with the American Association of School Administrators; and

- *Learning by Doing: Panasonic Partnerships and Systemic School Reform* by Terry Clark and Richard Lacey (Delray Beach, FL: St. Lucie Press (800-272-7737)), which is a book about the Panasonic Partnership Program.

Program Participation

Prospective partner districts must serve large numbers of disadvantaged youth. In addition, the Foundation looks for districts that exhibit the following:

- Agreement with the foundation's underlying and operational beliefs about systemic, school-based, whole-school reform;

- Commitment and willingness to develop a serious restructuring agenda, including allocation of time and resources;

- Capability to make substantial changes in policy, authority, and allocation of resources to achieve the restructuring agenda;

- Congruence between the district vision for reform and its plan, and coherence across reform initiatives; and

- Stable financial and political environments.

The results the Foundation hopes to achieve include:

- All students learning at high levels;
- Reflective and informed practitioners and policymakers at all levels of the education system;
- Systems policies and practices that actively stimulate and support school-based improvement efforts; and
- School systems that have the capability to sustain and deepen ongoing school-based, whole-school reform.

Application Procedure

The Panasonic Foundation does not accept applications. Districts interested in exploring a partnership with the foundation are invited to write to them directly.

Contact

Sophie Sa, Executive Director
Panasonic Foundation
1 Panasonic Way, 1F-5
Secaucus, NJ 07094
Voice: (201) 392-4132
Fax: (201) 392-4126
info@foundation.panasonic.com
www.panasonic.com/foundation

The Urban Education Web

Eric Clearinghouse on Urban Education

The ERIC Clearinghouse on Urban Education (ERIC/CUE) maintains a Web site—the Urban Education Web (UEweb)—to foster the positive development and education of urban and minority children and youth. The Urban Education Web provides an array of information and other resources about these youth, their education, development, families, and communities. It also contains information about historically Black colleges and universities. The ERIC Clearinghouse on Urban Education also provides education professionals, policymakers, families, and the public with a wide range of materials and services. The Clearinghouse is a component of the U.S. Department of Education's ERIC (Educational Resources Information Center) system, which maintains the largest education database in the world and offers a variety of education information services. Through UEweb, users can learn about other ERIC/CUE resources and can contact ERIC/CUE.

ERIC/CUE activities include:

- Collecting reports and journal articles for the ERIC database;
- Answering questions about urban education, in English and Spanish;
- Training in use of the ERIC database and the Internet at conferences; and
- Publishing monographs, digests, bibliographies, parent guides, and other materials for dissemination to individuals and at conferences. These publications are also included in the ERIC database and UEweb.

Organization of UEweb

UEweb allows users to find information easily. UEweb is organized by sections, and by type of material within each section. Users can also fill in the form that appears after clicking on *SEARCH UEweb* to find information on a specific topic.

The contents of UEweb are hypertext; that is, they contain *hot links* on key phrases that lead to other resources such as an abstract or ordering information. There are also links to the entire ERIC database, the database of all the ERIC digests, and to the U.S. Department of Education Web sites.

Education Topics of UEweb

UEweb contains publications and information on many urban education subjects: Urban and Minority Families; Curriculum and Instruction; Equity and Cultural Diversity; School Reform and School Safety; Urban and Minority Youth Development; Urban and Minority Community Services; Teachers in Urban and Minority Schools; Technology in Urban Education; and Administration and Finance.

Types of Publications on UEweb

UEweb contains nearly 2,000 informational items, and new works are added frequently. Most of them are produced by ERIC/CUE, but UEweb also contains publications prepared by the U.S. Department of Education and other organizations with expertise on urban student issues. Types of publications include:

- Books: full-length publications produced by government agencies and community organizations
- ERIC/CUE Monographs: state-of the-art literature, research, and practice reviews, with extensive bibliographies
- ERIC/CUE Digests: summaries of information on key urban education issues
- ERIC/CUE Information Alerts: annotated bibliographies of works in the ERIC database
- ERIC/CUE Parent Guides: pocket-sized resources that help parents help their children learn and develop
- ERIC/CUE Directories: profiles of model urban education programs and descriptions of related exemplary materials
- ERIC/CUE Pathways: guides to Internet resources on particular urban education issues

National Parent Information Network (NPIN)

One section of UEweb, Urban/Minority Families, is also a part of the National Parent Information Network (NPIN). National Parent Information Network provides a wealth of resources for parents and the people who help them raise their children. It is jointly sponsored by the ERIC Clearinghouse on Elementary and Early Childhood Education (ERIC/EECE) at the University of Illinois and the ERIC Clearinghouse on Urban Education at Teachers College. The National Parent Information Network offers the following information and services:

- Short articles for parents on topics such as child rearing and development, health, talents, disabilities, testing, working with schools, and home activities;

- PARENTS-Ask-ERIC, a question answering service for parents, teachers, parenting specialists, and administrators;

- Listings of free or inexpensive materials published commercially;

- Forums about shared concerns for parents, teachers, and parent educators; and

- Descriptions of innovative parent programs in schools and communities.

Getting Online

You can also get assistance from ACCESS/ERIC by telephone at: 1-800-LET-ERIC or 1-800-538-3742

ACCESS/ERIC has prepared a pamphlet, *Getting Online: A Friendly Guide for Teachers, Students, and Parents,* that provides instructions for using the Internet and describes resources available online. Call ACCESS/ERIC for a free copy.

Contact

ERIC Clearing House on Urban Education
Institute for Urban and Minority Education
Teachers College, Columbia University
525 West 120th Street, Box 40
New York, NY 10027
Voice: (800) 601-4868
Fax: (212) 678-4012
eric-cue@columbia.edu
eric-web.tc.columbia.edu

6
Epilogue

Epilogue

Educators across the United States are looking for programs and curricula that will help students at risk to think critically, be socially responsible, and perform academically at or above grade-level expectancies (Bell, Meza, and Williams, 1995). Thomas (1997) suggested that educators who seek to sculpture a program to produce desired results need to rethink curricular goals with a clearer focus on bottom-line results. For years, educators have been working diligently to improve curricular and programmatic offerings. Nonetheless, based on the high numbers of students who leave school prematurely, there is much room for improvement.

Too often, decision makers implement more of the same and fail to realize that if what they have already done, didn't work well the first time, there is a very high probability that what they plan to do again will not work either. This section presents background information related to best practices from America's schools and offers suggestions for administrators, teachers, parents, and board members on how to begin to think strategically about implementing the best practices possible in their respective schools.

The programs in this book describe a small fraction of the exemplary programs currently in use in today's schools. The programs are designed to meet the educational needs of students, parents, and staff. In many cases, they suggest the course that should be followed and they recommend a process for implementation. That notwithstanding, programs do not fix schools. People do! Solving the problem of meeting the needs of students at risk lies in hiring and employing the right people to do the right job and giving them the support and resources they need to do it.

However, simply implementing an exemplary program does not ensure that a higher percentage of students at risk will graduate from high school. In addition to focusing on programs, educators must focus on results. Thomas (1997) stated that there is a need to more sharply focus instructional and organizational planning on improved student performance. To do that, we need to be very clear about what students need to know. Then we need to organize our systems to achieve that knowledge. Further, Thomas posits that education leaders need to be preparing for the inevitability of standards by thinking strategically about results. There are a number of habits of the mind that need to be cultivated in relation to standards and results. Following are just a few of those habits:

- Examine student achievement data closely.
- Read the research.

    There needs to be a renewed appreciation for the importance of research, and of connecting practice to research.

- Involve and inform the public.

  Lack of attention to improving public engagement has undermined many a laudable effort.

- Narrow the focus of staff development efforts.

  The good news is that professional development opportunities are on the increase. The bad news is that fragmented and poorly focused efforts are of marginal assistance to teachers.

- Use staff development monies strategically.

  Have both a school-level and a districtwide master plan that is focused on the assessed needs of teachers and administrators, that reflects the priorities for students achievement, and that addresses student achievement gaps that have been identified.

- Avoid the *buy a program/solve that curriculum problem* mentality at all costs.

  If parents are complaining that spelling is not being taught, don't succumb to simply buying a student spelling book and hoping the problem is fixed.

- Focus on the end product.

The *new* way of looking at curriculum is through the analysis of the results of student achievement and how it informs teaching and learning to ensure that all students are performing at higher levels. The three key stages are curriculum design, curriculum delivery, and results analysis (Thomas, 1997).

Too often, discussions of programs and practices that meet the needs of students at risk have been ignored. Educating students at risk is our collective responsibility and it must be given a high priority on our personal agendas. It is up to each of us to do our share. We must expose students at risk to programs, practices, strategies and policies that address their academic, social, and psychological needs—*the whole child*. The challenge is enormous, but not impossible. This book broadens the database available to educators and parents related to enhancing the successes of students at risk. Additionally, it provides a framework to make this possible.

Bibliography

Adenika-Morrow, T. J. (1996). A lifeline to science careers for African-American females. *Educational Leadership, 53*(8), 80–83.

Armstrong, T. (1998). *Awakening genius in the classroom*. Alexandria, VA: Association for Supervision and Curriculum Development.

Bell, J., Meza, A., & Williams, T. (1995). *Promising Practices and Programs for Improving Student Achievement*. Sacramento, CA: California Department of Education.

Black, S. (1998a). Parent support. *The American School Board Journal, 185* (4), 50–53.

Black, S. (1998b). Research: Facts of life. *The American School Board Journal, 185*(8), 33–36.

Berliner, B., & Bernard, B. (1995). More than a message of hope: A district-level policy-maker's guide to understanding resiliency (Clearinghouse No. EA 027 147). Portland, OR: Western Regional Center for Drug-Free School and Communities. (Eric Document Reproduction Service No. ED 387 946).

Clark, R.M. (1990, Spring). Why disadvantaged students succeed: What happens outside school is critical. *Public Welfare*, 17–23.

Council of Chief State School Officers. (1988). *School success for students at-risk: Analysis and recommendations of the council of chief state school officers*. Orlando, FL: Harcourt Brace Jovanovich.

Du Four, R., & Eaker, R. (1992). *Creating the new American school: A principal's guide to school improvement*. Bloomington, IN: National Educational Service.

Edmonds, R. (1979). Effective schools for the urban poor. *Educational Leadership*, 15–23.

Epstein J., & Dauber, S. (1991). School programs and teaches practices of parent involvement in inner-city elementary and middle schools. *The Elementary School Journal, 91*(3), 289–305.

Fulton, M. (1998). Investing in performance. *The American School Board Journal, 185*(4), 33.

Goodlad, J. (1984). *A Place Called School*. New York: McGraw-Hill.

Harvey, T. R., & Drolet, B. (1994). *Building teams, building people: Expanding the fifth resource*. Lancaster, PA: Technomic.

Hatch, T. (1998). How community action contributes to achievement. *Educational Leadership, 55*(8), 16–19.

Henderson, A. T., & Berla, N. (Eds). (1996). *A new generation of evidence: The family is critical to student achievement.* Washington, DC: National Committee for Citizens in Education.

Hill, H. D. (1989). *Effective strategies for teaching minority students.* Bloomington, IN: National Educational Service.

Johnson, R. S. (1996). *Setting our sights: Measuring equity in school change* Los Angeles: The Achievement Council.

Jones, R. (1998). What works: Researchers tell what schools must do to improve student achievement. *The American School Board Journal, 185*(4), 29–33.

Kellaghan, T. Sloane, K., Alvarez, B., & Bloom, B. (1993). *The home environment and school learning: Promoting parental involvement in the education of children.* San Francisco: Jossey-Bass.

Kuykendall, C. (1992). From rage to hope: Strategies for reclaiming black and Hispanic students. Bloomington, IN: National Education Service.

Lewis, R., & Morris, J. (1998). Communities for children. *Educational Leadership, 55*(8), 36.

Marzano, R. J. (1992). *A different kind of classroom.* Alexandria, VA: Association for Supervision and Curriculum Development.

Mobilization for equity partner organizations. (1998, February). *National Coalition of Advocates for Students,* 4.

National Institute of Education. (1985). *Becoming a nation of readers: The report of the commission on reading.* Champaign, IL: Author.

National Commission on Excellence in Education. (1983). *A nation at risk: The imperative for educational reform.* Washington, DC: U.S. Government Printing Office.

Ogden, E. H., & Germinario, V. (1988) . *The At-risk student: Answers for educators.* Lancaster, PA: Technomic.

Peters, T., & Waterman, R. (1982). *In search of excellence: Lessons from America's best-run companies.* New York: Harper & Row.

Pikes, T., Burrell, B., & Holliday, C. (1998). Using academic strategies to build resilience: Reaching today's youth. *The Community of Caring Journal, 2*(3), 44–47.

Purkey, S., & Smith M. (1983). Effective schools: A review. *Elementary School Journal, 83*(4), 427–452.

Rich, D. (1998). What parents want from teachers. *Educational Leadership, 55*(8), 37–39.

Rousell, M. (1996). Helping kids believe in themselves. *Educational Leadership, 53*(8), 86–87.

Sangor, R. (1996). Building resiliency in students. *Educational Leadership, 54*(1), 38–41.

Schlechty, P.C. (1990). *Schools of the 21st Century.* San Francisco: Jossey-Bass

School Choice Resources. (1998, February). *National Coalition of Advocates for Students,* 4.

Sokoloff, H. (1998). Creating miracles. *The American School Board Journal, 185*(4), 33.

Sullivan, P. (1998). The PTA's national standards. *Educational Leadership, 55*(8), 43–44.

Thomas, G. (1997). Focusing on results. *Thrust for Educational Leadership, 26*(4), 24–27.

U.S. Department of Education, National Center for Education Statistics. (1997). *Dropout rates in the United States: 1996.* (NCES 98-250). Washington, DC: U.S. Government Printing Office.

U.S. Department of Commerce, Bureau of the Census, *October 1996 Current population survey* (1996) . Unpublished data.

U.S. Department of Commerce, National Center for Education Statistics. *National education longitudinal study of 1988 base year, first, second, and third follow-up survey, 1988, 1990, 1992, and 1994.* Unpublished data.

Why it says to be rich—it's great for your health. (1998, July 30). *The Sacramento Bee,* p. A5.

Wong Fillmore, L. (1990). Now or later? Issues related to the early education of minority-group children. Cited in *Early childhood and family education: Analysis and recommendation of the council of chief state officers* (pp. 122–145). New York: Harcourt Brace Jovanovich.

Appendices

Appendix A: High School Completion Rates

High school completion rates of 18- through 24-year-olds not currently enrolled in high school or below, by state: October 1991-93 and 1994-96

State		1991-93	1994-96
TOTAL		85.7	85.8
NORTHEAST	Connecticut	90.9	96.1
	Maine	93.4	91.8
	Massachusetts	90.5	92.0
	New Hampshire	89.0	87.7
	New Jersey	89.8	87.0
	New York	87.6	90.9
	Pennsylvania	90.5	89.6
	Rhode Island	90.4	87.5
	Vermont	89.6	87.0
MIDWEST	Illinois	86.0	89.3
	Indiana	87.4	88.3
	Iowa	94.0	91.6
	Kansas	91.4	91.6
	Michigan	88.3	89.1
	Minnesota	91.7	95.3
	Missouri	88.3	88.0
	Nebraska	92.5	93.3
	North Dakota	95.7	93.0
	Ohio	89.7	87.7
	South Dakota	91.2	89.6
	Wisconsin	92.4	92.5
SOUTH	Alabama	81.0	86.8
	Arkansas	87.7	86.7
	Delaware	90.3	88.8
	Florida	84.5	80.1
	Georgia	81.9	81.3
	Kentucky	82.6	82.2
	Louisiana	82.5	82.2
	Maryland	91.0	93.4
	Mississippi	88.6	83.9
	North Carolina	84.2	87.2
	Oklahoma	81.8	87.0

State		1991-93	1994-96
	South Carolina	85.5	88.4
	Tennessee	77.5	83.3
	Texas	81.2	79.3
	Virginia	89.8	86.6
	Washington, DC	87.2	87.8
	West Virginia	84.6	89.3
WEST	Alaska	89.0	87.8
	Arizona	81.1	85.8
	California	78.2	78.6
	Colorado	87.2	87.9
	Hawaii	92.8	92.6
	Idaho	89.0	85.2
	Montana	91.6	89.8
	Nevada	83.3	81.4
	New Mexico	84.3	82.7
	Oregon	85.5	81.1
	Utah	94.6	91.3
	Washington	89.2	86.8
	Wyoming	92.1	89.4

SOURCE: U.S. Department of Commerce, Bureau of the Census, Current Population Survey, October (various years), unpublished data (as cited in National Center for Educational Statistics, 1996).

Appendix B: Membership, Dropout Counts, and Event Dropout Rates

Membership, dropout counts, and event dropout rates for grades 9-12: 1994-95

State	Dropout count	Membership	Dropout rate (%)
Alabama	12,525	201,157	6.2
Arkansas	6,248	128,052	4.9
California	63,881	1,449,436	4.4
Connecticut	6,290	128,561	4.9
Delaware	1,389	29,994	4.6
District of Columbia	1,879	17,752	10.6
Georgia	30,158	335,372	9.0
Hawaii	2,465	50,105	4.9
Indiana	13,183	288,370	4.6
Iowa	5,115	151,348	3.4
Kansas	6,594	130,789	5.0
Louisiana	7,549	213,337	3.5
Maine	1,863	56,764	3.3
Massachusetts	8,351	236,801	3.5
Minnesota	12,219	235,428	5.2
Mississippi	8,700	136,558	6.4
Missouri	17,637	250,168	7.1
Nebraska	3,737	83,958	4.5
Nevada	6,703	65,383	10.3
New Mexico	7,826	91,784	8.5
New York	31,992	777,488	4.1
North Dakota	906	36,120	2.5
Ohio	28,281	529,864	5.3
Oregon	10,656	149,309	7.1
Pennsylvania	20,992	514,633	4.1
Rhode Island	1,852	40,181	4.6
Texas	26,039	956,023	2.7
Utah	5,107	144,967	3.5
West Virginia	4,091	97,104	4.2
Wyoming	2,010	30,184	6.7

NOTE: All states except for Alaska, Kentucky, Michigan, Montana, New Hampshire, and Washington reported data. However, among the 44 states and the District of Columbia that reported dropouts, 29 states and the District of Columbia said they adhered exactly to the standard definition and collection procedures. The states that followed NCES definitions were: Alabama, Arkansas, California, Connecticut, Delaware, District of Columbia, Georgia, Hawaii, Indiana, Iowa, Kansas, Louisiana, Maine, Massachusetts, Minnesota, Mississippi, Missouri, Nebraska, Nevada, New Mexico, New York, North Dakota, Ohio, Oregon, Pennsylvania, Rhode Island, Texas, Utah, West Virginia, and Wyoming.

SOURCE: 1994-95 membership counts were obtained from the 1994-95 Public Elementary/Secondary School Universe Survey, Common Core of Data, National Center for Education Statistics. 1994-95 dropout counts were obtained from the 1995-96 Public Elementary/Secondary Agency Universe Survey, Common Core of Data, National Center for Education Statistics (as cited in National Center for Educational Statistics, 1996).

Appendix C:
Race-Ethnicity and Income

Percentage of persons, ages 16–24, by race-ethnicity and income: October 1996

	Race-ethnicity[1]		
Family income	White non-Hispanic	Black non-Hispanic	Hispanic
Family income[2]	13.3	35.7	31.5
Low income level	58.1	54.6	60.7
Middle income level	28.6	9.7	7.9
High income level			

[1] Due to relatively small sample sizes, American Indian/Alaskan Natives and Asian/Pacific Islanders are included in the total but are not shown separately.

[2] Low income is defined as the bottom 20 percent of all family incomes for 1996; middle income is between 20 and 80 percent of all family incomes; and high income is the top 20 percent of all family incomes.

SOURCE: U.S. Department of Commerce, Bureau of the Census, Current Population Survey, October 1996, unpublished data (as cited in National Center for Educational Statistics, 1996).

Appendix D: Event Dropout and Persistence Rates

Event dropout and persistence rates and number and distribution of dropouts from grades 10–12, ages 15–24, by background characteristics: October 1996.

Characteristics	Event Dropout Rate (%)	School Persistence Rate (%)	Number of dropouts (thousands)	Percent of all dropouts
Total	5.0	95.0	485	100.0
Sex				
Male	5.0	95.0	241	49.6
Female	5.1	94.9	245	50.4
Race-ethnicity[1]				
White, non-Hispanic	4.1	95.9	267	54.9
Black, non-Hispanic	6.7	93.3	103	21.1
Hispanic	9.0	91.0	100	20.6
Family income[2]				
Low income level	11.1	88.9	145	29.8
Middle income level	5.1	94.9	282	58.1
High income level	2.1	97.9	59	12.1
Region				
Northwest	3.4	96.6	61	12.6
Midwest	4.6	95.4	109	22.5
South	5.5	94.5	180	37.0
West	6.2	93.8	135	27.9

[1] Due to relatively small sample sizes, American Indian/Alaskan Natives and Asian/Pacific Islanders are included in the total but are not shown separately.

[2] Low income is defined as the bottom 20 percent of all family incomes for 1996; middle income is between 20 and 80 percent of all family incomes; and high income is the top 20 percent of all family incomes.

NOTE: Because of rounding, details may not add to totals.

SOURCE: *U.S. Department of Commerce, Bureau of the Census, Current Population Survey, October 1996,* unpublished data (as cited in National Center for Educational Statistics, 1996).

Appendix E: Selected Web Sites

Almost every college and university has somebody studying the factors involved in student achievement. A good reference librarian can help you turn up reams of articles and reports on the subject. If you're looking for research on a specific topic (say, proven methods in reading instruction), try specific organizations (such as the National Council for Teachers of English or the International Reading Association). But if you're looking for more general information, here are a few of the many resources you can find on the Web:

American Educational Research Association. Washington, DC. www.aera.net.

American Federation of Teachers. Washington, DC. www.aft.org.

Appalachian Educational Laboratory, Inc. (provides links to nine other regional education laboratories). www.ael.org.

AskERIC. ERIC Clearinghouse on Information and Technology. Syracuse University. http://ericir.syr.edu.

Association for Supervision and Curriculum Development. Alexandria, VA. www.ascd.org.

Center for Social Organization of Schools. John Hopkins University. http://scov.csos.jhu.edu.

Consortium for Policy Research Center. University of Wisconsin at Madison. www.wcer.wisc.edu/cpre.

Education Commission of the States. Denver. www.ecs.org.

Education Testing Service. Princeton, NJ. www.ets.org.

High/Scope Educational Research Foundation. Ypsilanti, MI. www.highscope.org.

National Commission on Teaching and America's Future. Teachers College, Columbia University. www.tc.columbia.edu/~teachcomm.

National Education Association. Washington, DC. www.nea.org.

Parents as Teachers National Center. St. Louis. www.patnc.org.

Source: *The American School Board Journal.* (April 1998, p. 31).

Appendix F: Information About Parental Involvement

Casanova, Ursula. "Parent Involvement: A Call for Prudence." *Educational Researcher*, November 1996, 25, pp. 30–32, 46.

Daniels, Harvey. "The Best Practice Project: Building Partnerships in Chicago." *Educational Leadership*, April 1996, 53, pp. 38–43.

Epstein, Joyce L. "School/Family/Community Partnerships: 'Caring for the Children We Share.'" *Phi Delta Kappan*, 1995, 76, pp. 705–707.

Epstein, Joyce L. "School Programs and Teacher Practices of Parent Involvement in Inner-City Elementary and Middle Schools." *The Elementary School Journal*, January 1991, 91, pp. 289–305.

Hoover-Dempsey, Kathleen, and Sandler, Howard. "Why Do Parents Become Involved in Their Children's Education? A New Look at the Research Evidence." *Review of Educational Research*, Spring 1997, 67, pp. 3–42.

Miller, Amy, and Narrett, Carla. "Does Parent Involvement and Parent Feedback about Reading Progress Influence Students' Reading Progress?" Paper presented at the Annual Meeting of the American Psychological Association, New York, August 1995, ED398336.

Yap, Kim, and Enoki, Donald. "In Search of the Elusive Magic Bullet: Parent Involvement and Student Outcomes." ERIC Document, 1994. ED381228.

Organizations

Alliance for Parental Involvement in Education, PO Box 59, East Chatham, NY 12060-0059; (518) 392-6900.

Center on Families, Communities, Schools, and Children's Learning, Johns Hopkins University, 3505 N. Charles St., Baltimore, MD 21218; (410) 516-8800.

Home and School Institute, MegaSkills Education Center, 1500 Massachusetts Ave. N.W., Washington, DC 20005; (202) 466-3633.

Institute for Responsive Education, 605 Commonwealth Ave., Boston, MA 02215; (617) 373-2595.

National Parent Information Network, ERIC Clearinghouse on Elementary and Early Childhood Education, University of Illinois, 805 W. Pennsylvania Ave. Urbana, IL 61801-4897; (800) 583-4135.

Parents as Teachers National Center, 10176 Corporate Square Drive, Suite 230, St. Louis, MO 63132; (314) 432-4330.

Web Sites

"Family Involvement in Children's Education; Successful Local Approaches." U.S. Department of Education. www.ed.gov/pubs/FamInvolve

"National Standards for Parent/Family Involvement Programs." National PTA. www.pta.org/programspfistand. html

"Parental Rights; An Infobrief Synopsis." *Educational Issues 1997*, Association for Supervision and Curriculum Development. www.ascd.org/issue/par.html

Source: *The American School Board Journal*. (1998, April, p. 52.)

Appendix G: New Report Documents Public Engagement

The Annenberg Institute for School Reform recently unveiled the findings of an 18-month study on what the group calls "public engagement"—efforts to bring parents, educators, and business and community leaders together as partners to reshape their local schools. The report, "Reasons for Hope, Voices for Change," documents what the institute views as a grassroots movement that is changing the relationship between the public and public schools, building a powerful local constituency for school change.

Researchers from the Institute, based at Brown University in Providence, Rhode Island, examined 175 public engagement projects across the United States, seeking to better understand their origins, leadership, focus, and objectives. Their conclusions may help to influence the effectiveness and potential of public engagement. The report found that:

1. most engagement efforts work in isolation;
2. few engagement efforts have gone to "scale," as traditionally defined;
3. "process" outcomes are powerful but hard to measure. In other words, the process of engaging a broad group of people to discuss education issues has its own value beyond the product;
4. community-driven efforts are more readily apparent, but education leaders are driving some significant efforts;
5. teachers are not yet a significant force in public engagement;
6. the potential of students is largely untapped;
7. the use of technology to support engagement is growing but not yet widespread;
8. the work of engagement is difficult to do and to sustain;
9. engagement challenges traditional notions of power, and
10. engagement is often born from crisis.

Erik Robelen

Appendix H: The PTA's National Standards

Generally speaking, schools are becoming more involved in noninstructional issues—particularly those related to the child's home life. To be successful in this venture, school personnel have to have a plan—a well-devised plan which capitalizes on the strengths of the community's human and fiscal resources. They have to engage school staff and community members in activities which address all of the various types of parental involvement. By using the Parent Teacher Association's (PTA) National Standards (Sullivan, 1998) as a model of excellence, schools, parents, and concerned citizens will be better able to improve the performance of students at risk and better enable them to have healthier, more positive attitudes toward learning and school. To emphasize the belief that parents are a child's first teachers, the National PTA has developed new guidelines that support family involvement in schools.

The National PTA recommends that parents, educators and community leaders work together in a cohesive way to implement the standards. The following steps outline the process for improving family involvement—and student success.

- Create an action plan team. Involve representatives from each group—parents educators, administrators, and others—in reaching a common understanding and in setting mutual goals.

- Examine current practice. Survey school staff, community leaders, and parents to ensure a clear understanding of the current status of parent and family involvement.

- Develop a plan of improvement. Based on the evaluation of current practice, identify first steps and priority issues, including developing a parent/family involvement policy. A comprehensive, well-balanced plan should include activities that relate to each standard.

- Develop a written parent/family involvement policy. A written policy establishes the vision, mission, and foundation for the future.

- Secure support. Keep stakeholders aware of the plan and its progress. Stakeholders include those responsible for implementation and those who will be affected.

- Provide professional development for school/program staff. Effective training is essential. The best models of adult education provide staff and volunteers with several opportunities to explore the issues, work together, and monitor and evaluate progress.

- Evaluate and revise the plan. Parent and family involvement is not a one-time goal. It merits a process of continuous improvement and commitment to long-term success (Sullivan, 1998).

Appendix I: Schools of Promise

"We're not experimenting; we know what it takes to save a child. Either we start building all our children, or we'll have to build more jails. America's Promise shakes things up, opens doors for you." Last February, United States retired General Colin Powell announced "a crusade to create partnerships that focus on the school," through America's Promise—The Alliance for Youth.

One such partnership connects Powell's America's Promise organization with Communities in Schools, Quest International, the American Association of School Administrators, and other groups, including the Association for Supervision and Curriculum (ASCD). American's Promise has identified five resources that every child must have for health, success, and well-being:

1. An ongoing relationship with a caring adult.
2. Safe places and structured activities during nonschool hours.
3. A healthy start with a potential for a healthy future.
4. Marketable skills through effective education.
5. The opportunity to give back through community service.

Through national, state, and local forums and summits, Powell hopes to lead schools and communities to work together for the children. The Association for Supervision and Curriculum and other educational organizations that comprise the Learning First Alliance are making plans to collaborate with the program.

Carolyn R. Pool

For information on how to become a School of Promise, visit the Web site of Communities in Schools (http://cisnet.org) or America's Promise (http://www.americaspromise.org/).

Source: Annenberg Institute for School Reform. (1998). Reasons for hope, voices for change. Providence, R. I.: Author. (as cited in Lewis, R., & Morris, J. (1998). Communities for children. Educational Leadership, 55(8), 36).

Appendix J:
Listen, Discuss, and Act: Recommendations from the Education Commission of the States

1. Listen to people first, talk later.
2. Expect to fail if you do not communicate well with teachers.
3. Make involving parents and the community a top priority.
4. Be clear about what it means to set high standards for all students, and what it will take to meet them.
5. Show how new ideas enhance, rather than replace, the old ones.
6. Educate parents about the choices available to them.
7. Help parents and other community members understand how students are assessed and what the results mean.

Source: Education Commission of the States (1996a), Listen, Discuss, and Act, pp. 15–17.

Appendix K: Resources for Change Schools

Accelerated Schools Project
402 S. Ceras
School of Education
Stanford University
Stanford, CA 94305-3084
Phone: (650) 725-1676
Fax: (415) 725-6140

The Achievement Council
3460 Wilshire Blvd., Site 420
Los Angeles, CA 90010
Phone: (213) 487-3194
Fax: (213) 487-0879

Annenberg Institute for School Reform
Brown University
Box 1985
Providence, RI 02912
Phone: (401) 863-7990
Fax: (401) 863-1290

Anti-Defamation League
(A World of Difference)
720 Market Street, Suite 800
San Francisco, CA 94102-2501
Phone: (415) 981-3500
Fax: (415) 981-8933
or
10495 Santa Monica Blvd.
Los Angeles, CA 90025
Phone: (310) 446-8000
Fax: (310) 470-8712

California Tomorrow
436 14th Street Suite 820
Oakland, CA 94612
Phone: (510) 496-0220
Fax: (510) 496-0225

Center for Education Reform
1001 Connecticut Ave. NW,
Suite 204
Washington, DC 20036
Phone: (202) 822-9000
Fax: (202) 822-5077

Center for Leadership in School Reform (CLSR)
950 Breckenridge Lane, Suite 200
Louisville, KY 40207
Phone: (502) 895-1942
Fax: (502) 895-7901

Center for Research on Education, Diversity & Excellence (CREDE)
University of California, Santa Cruz
1156 High Street
College 8, Rm. 201
Santa Cruz, CA 95064
Phone: (831)459-3500
Fax: (831) 459-3502

The Children's Defense Fund
25 E Street, NW
Washington, DC 20001
Phone: (202) 628-8787
Fax: (202) 628-3510

Clearinghouse for Immigrant Education (CHIME)
    100 Boylston Street, Suite 737
    Boston, MA 02116-4610
    Phone: (800) 441-7192 or
    (617) 357-8507
    Fax: (617) 357-9549

Coalition of Essential Schools
    1814 Franklin Street, Suite 700
    Oakland, CA 94606-5300
    Phone: (510) 433-1451
    Fax: (510) 433-1455

The College Board
    45 Columbus Ave.
    New York, NY 10023
    Phone: (212) 713-8000

The College Board—Equity 2000
    1233 20th Street, NW, Suite 600
    Washington, DC 20036-2304
    Phone: (202) 822-5900
    Fax: (202) 822-5939

The Education Trust
    1725 K Street, NW, Suite 200
    Washington, DC 20006
    Phone: (202) 293-1217
    Fax: (202) 293-2605

Educators for Social Responsibility
    23 Garden Street
    Cambridge, MA 02138
    Phone: (617) 492-1764
    Fax: (617) 864-5164

ERIC Clearinghouse on Educational Management
    University of Oregon
    5207 University of Oregon
    Eugene, OR 97403-5207
    Phone: (800) 438-8841
    Fax: (541) 346-2334

Facing History and Ourselves
    16 Hurd Road
    Brookline, MA 02445
    Phone: (617) 232-1595
    Fax: (617) 232-0281

Intercultural Development Research Association
    5835 Callaghan Road, Suite 350
    San Antonio, TX 78228
    Phone: (210) 684-8180
    Fax: (210) 684-5389

Institute for Educational Leadership (IEL)
    1001 Connecticut Ave., NW, Suite 310
    Washington, DC 20036
    Phone: (202) 822-8405
    Fax: (202) 872-4050

Institute for Responsive Education
    Northeastern University
    50 Nightingale Hall
    Boston, MA 02115
    Phone: (617) 373-2595
    Fax: (617) 373-8924

National Alliance of Black School
Educators
    2816 Georgia Avenue, NW
    Washington, DC 20001
    Phone: (202) 483-1549
    Fax: (202) 483-8323

National Association for Asian and
Pacific American Education
(NAAPAE)
    ARC Associates, Inc.
    1212 Broadway Street, Suite 400
    Oakland, CA 94612
    Phone: (510) 834-9455
    Fax: (510) 763-1490

National Center for Restructuring
Education, Schools, and Teaching
    Teachers College,
    Columbia University
    Box 110
    525 W. 120th Street
    New York, NY 10027
    Phone: (212) 678-3432
    Fax: (212) 678-4170

National Center on Educational
Outcomes for Students
With Disabilities
    University of Minnesota
    350 Elliott Hall
    75 East River Road
    Minneapolis, MN 55455
    Phone: (612) 626-1530
    Fax: (612) 624-0879

National Coalition of Advocates
for Students
    100 Boylston St., Suite 737
    Boston, MA 02116-4610
    Phone: (617) 357-8507
    Fax: (617) 357-9549

National Council of La Raza (NCLR)
    1111 19th Street NW, Suite 1000
    Washington, DC 20036
    Phone: (202) 785-1670
    Fax: (202) 785-0851
    or
    523 W. 6th Street, Suite 301
    Los Angeles, CA 90014
    Phone: (213) 489-3428
    Fax: (213) 489-1167

The NETWORK, Inc.
    136 Fenno Drive
    Rowley, MA 01969
    Phone: (800) 877-5400
    Fax: (978) 948-7836

New England Association of
Schools and Colleges
    The Office of School/College
    Relations
    "Rural Partnership Project for
    Student Success"
    209 Burlington Rd.
    Bedford, MA 01703-1433
    Phone: (781) 271-0022
    Fax: (781) 271-0950

National Center on Education and the Economy
   700 11th Street NW, Suite 750
   Washington, DC 20001
   Phone: (202) 783-3668
   Fax:(202) 783-3672

Yale Child Study Center
   School Development Program, Dept. A
   53 College Street
   New Haven, CT 06510
   Phone: (203) 737-1020
   Fax: (203) 737-1023

Success for All (SFA)
   Success For All Foundation, Inc.
   200 West Towsontown Blvd.
   Baltimore, MD 21204-5200
   Phone: (800) 548-4998
   Fax: (410) 324-4444

Teachers of English to Speakers of Other Languages (TESOL)
   1600 Cameron Street, Suite 300
   Alexandria, VA 22314-2751
   Phone: (703) 836-0774
   Fax: (703) 836-6447

Source: Johnson, R. S. (1996). *Setting our sights: Measuring equity in school change.* Los Angeles: The Achievement Council. (List was revised by author with permission January 1999.)

Appendix L: Mobilization for Equity Partner Organizations

Mobilization for Equity (MFE) is a multilevel project designed to address school equity concerns at national, state, and local levels. State and local activities are spearheaded by 16 National Coalition of Advocates for Students (NCAS) members groups. Working with the 16 MFE partner organizations, NCAS national staff help to support and coordinate local efforts to realize the MFE agenda. For further information regarding local MFE activities, please contact:

Advocates for Children of New York
    105 Court Street, 4th Floor
    Brooklyn, NY 11201
    Phone: 718-624-8450
    Fax: 718-624-1260
    E-mail: advocatl@idt.net
    Contact: Sonia Mendez-Castro

Arkansas Advocates for Children & Families
    931 Donaghey Building
    Little Rock, AR 72201
    Phone: 501-371-9678
    Fax: 501-371-9681
    E-mail: hn3302@handsnet.org
    Contact: Amy Rossi/
    Connie Whitfield

ASPIRLA Association, Inc.
    1444 I Street N.W., Suite 800
    Washington, DC 20005
    Phone: 202-835-3600
    Fax: 202-835-3613
    E-mail: aspira1@aol.com
    Contact: Hilda Crespo

California Tomorrow
    Fort Mason Center, Building B
    San Francisco, CA 94123-1380
    Phone: 415-441-7631
    Fax: 415-441-7635
    E-mail: 6549633@mcimail.com
    Contact: Laurie Olsen

Center for Law & Education
    1875 Connecticut Avenue N.W.,
    Suite 510
    Washington, DC 20009
    Phone: 202-986-3000
    Fax: 202-986-6648
    E-mail: cledc@erols.com
    Contact: Paul Weckstein

Coalition for Quality Education
    1702 Upton Avenue
    Toledo, OH 43607
    Phone: 419-537-9246
    Fax: 419-537-7102
    E-mail: mfecqe@aol.com
    Contact: Lola Glover

Education Law Center—NJ
155 Washington Street, Suite 205
Newark, NJ 07102
Phone: 973-624-1815
Fax: 973-624-7339
E-rnail: educlawctr@aol.com
Contact: Wilbur Haddock

Education Law Center—PA
801 Arch Street, Suite 610
Philadelphia, PA 19107
Phone: 215-238-6970
Fax: 215-625-9589
E-mail: elc@elc-pa.org
Contact: Janet Stotland

Intercultural Development Research Association (IDRA)
5835 Callaghan Road, Suite 350
San Antonio, TX 78228-1125
Phone: 210-684-8180
Fax: 210-684-5389
E-rnail: amontmyr@idra.org
Contact: Aurelio Montemayor

Massachusetts Advocacy Center
100 Boylston Street, Suite 200
Boston, MA 02116
Phone: 617-357-8431
Fax: 617-357-8438
E-mail: massadvctr@aol.com
Contact: John Mudd

Mississippi Human Services
P.O. Box 1684
Jackson, MS 39215-1684
Phone: 601-355-7495
Fax: 601-355-1506
E-mail: hn0137@handsnet.org
Contact: Rims Barber

Multicultural Education, Training & Advocacy
240-A Elm Street, Suite 22
Somerville, MA 02144
Phone: 617-628-2226
Fax: 617-628-0322
E-mail: rlr@shore.net
Contact: Roger Rice

National Council of La Raza
1111 19th Street N.W., Suite 1000
Washington, D.C. 20036
Phone: (202) 785-1670
Fax: (202) 776-1794
Contact: Charles Kamasaki

North Carolina Education & Law Project
P.O. Box 28068
Raleigh, NC 27611
Phone: (919) 856-2150
Fax: (919) 856-2175
E-mail: hn1020@handsnet.org
Contact: Stephen Bowens

Parents Union for Public Schools
311 South Juniper Street, Suite 200
Philadelphia, PA 19107
Phone: 215-546-1166
Fax: 215-731-1688
E-mail: ParentsU@aol.com
Contact: Sarah Gilliam

Student Advocacy Center
2301 Platt Road
Ann Arbor, MI 48104
Phone: (313) 973-7860
Fax: (313) 973-7894
E-mail: sacinmi!aol.com
Contact: Ruth Sweifler

Associate Partner:
Statewide Parent Advocacy
Network, Inc. (SPAN)
    35 Halsey Street, 4th Floor
    Newark, NJ 07102
    Phone: 201-642-8100
    Fax: 201-642-8080
    E-mail: AutinD@aol.com
    Contact: Diana AutinFax:

Source: Mobilization for equity partner organizations. (1998, February). *National Coalition of Advocates for Students,* 4.

Appendix M: School Choice Resources

Rethinking Schools
   1001 E. Keefe Avenue
   Milwaukee, WI 53212
   Phone: (414) 964-9646
   Fax: (414) 964-7220
   Web Page: www.rethinkingschools.org

Center for Law and Education
   1875 Connecticut Avenue, NW, Suite 51
   Washington, DC 20009
   Phone: (202) 986-3000
   Fax: (202) 986-6648
   E-mail: ciedc@erols.com

Parents for Public Schools
   National Office
   P.O. Box 12807
   Jackson, MS 39236-2897
   Phone: 1-800-880-1222
   Fax: (601) 982-0002
   Web Page: www.pps.net

Source: School choice resources. (1998, February). *National Coalition of Advocates for Students*, 4.

Appendix N: Programs At-a-Glance (In Alphabetical Order)

Accelerated Schools Project
  Ceras Bldg.
  School of Education
  Stanford University
  Stanford, CA 94305-3084
  Voice: (650) 725-1676
  Fax: (650 725-6140
  www.leland.stanford.edu/
  group/ASP

Advancement Via Individual Determination (AVID)
  AVID Center
  McConaughy House
  2490 Heritage Park Row
  San Diego, CA 92110
  Voice: (619) 682-5050
  Fax: (619) 682-5060
  mcsavid@sdcoe.k-12.ca.us
  www.avidcenter.org

The California Mini-Corps
  510 Bercut Drive, Suite Q
  Sacramento, CA 95814
  Voice: (916) 446-4603
  Fax: (916) 446-9271
  Mavila@bcoe.butte.k12.ca.us

The Center for Educational Renewal
  College of Education
  Box 353600
  University of Washington
  Seattle, WA 98195-3600
  Voice: (206) 543-6230
  Fax: (206) 543-8439
  weber.u.washington.edu/cedren

The Center for Leadership in School Reform
  950 Brekenridge Lane, Suite 200
  Louisville, KY 40207
  Voice: (502) 895-1942
  Fax: (502) 895-7901
  infor@clsr.org
  www.clsr.org

The Center for Research in Human Development and Education (CRHDE)
  Temple University
  1301 Cecil B. Moore Avenue
  Philadelphia, PA 19122-6091
  Voice: (800) 892-5550
  Fax: (215) 204-5130
  lss@vm.temple.edu
  www.temple.edu/LSS

The Center for the Study and Teaching of At-Risk Students
  4725 30th Avenue NE
  Seattle, WA 98105-4021
  Voice: (206) 543-3815
  Fax: (206) 685-4722
  alsmith@u.washington.edu

The Clearinghouse for Immigrant Education (CHIME)
  The National Coalition of Advocates for Students
  100 Boylston St., Suite 737
  Boston, MA 02116-4610
  Voice: (800) 441-7192
  Voice: (617) 357-8507
  Fax: (617) 357-9549
  NCASMFE@aol.com
  www.ncasl.org

Coalition of Essential Schools (CES)
  Coalition of Essential Schools National Office
  1814 Franklin Street, Suite 700
  Oakland, CA 94612
  Voice: (510) 433-1451
  Fax: (510) 433-1455
  www.essentialschools.org

Core Knowledge
  Core Knowledge Foundation
  801 East High Street
  Charlottesville, VA 22902
  Voice: (804) 977-7550
  Fax: (804) 977-0021
  coreknow@coreknowledge.org
  www.coreknowledge.org

The Development Studies Center—Child Development Project
  2000 Embarcadero, Suite 305
  Oakland, CA 94606-5300
  (800) 666-7270
  Voice: (510) 533-0213 ext. 239
  Fax: (510) 464-3670
  info@devstu.org
  www.devstu.org

Different Ways of Knowing—The Galef Institute
  11050 Santa Monica Blvd.
  Third Floor
  Los Angeles, CA 90025
  Voice: (310) 479-8883
  Fax: (310) 473-9720
  sue@galef.org
  www.dwoknet.galef.org

The Edison Project
  521 Fifth Avenue, 15th Floor
  New York, NY 10175
  Voice: (212) 419-1600
  Fax: (212) 419-1604
  sabrown@newyork.edison project.com
  www.edisonproject.com

The Education Commission of the States
  707 17th Street, Suite 2700
  Denver, CO 80202-3427
  Voice: (303) 299-3600
  Fax: (303) 296-8332
  ecs@ecs.org
  www.ecs.org

Appendices

Effective Schools
    Effective Schools Products, Ltd.
    2199 Jolly Road, Suite #160
    Okemos, MI 48864
    Voice: (800) 827-8041 or
    (517) 349-8841
    Fax: (517) 349-8852
    staff@effectiveschools.com
    www.effectiveschools.com

Efficacy
    The Efficacy Institute
    128 Spring Street
    Lexington, MA 02421
    Voice: (781) 862-4390
    Fax: (781) 862-2580
    Efficacy@tiac.net

EQUITY 2000
    The College Board
    1233 20th Street, NW, Suite 600
    Washington, DC 20036-2304
    Voice: (202) 822-5930
    Fax: (202) 822-5939
    Equity@collegeboard.org
    www.collegeboard.org

Foxfire
    The Foxfire Fund, Inc.
    P.O. Box 541
    Mountain City, GA 30562-0541
    Voice: (706) 746-5828
    Fax: (706) 746-5829
    foxfire@foxfire.org
    www.foxfire.org

Helping One Student to Succeed (HOSTS)
    The HOSTS Corporation
    1349 Empire Central, Suite 520
    Dallas, TX 75247
    Voice: (214) 905-1308 or
    (888) 380-9117
    Fax: (214) 905-1176
    cwoolery@hostscorp.com
    www.hostscorp.com

Higher Order Thinking Skills Program (HOTS)
    Education Innovation
    P.O. Box 42620
    Tucson, AZ 85733
    Voice: (800) 999-0153 *or*
    (520) 795-2143
    Fax: (520) 795-8837
    Info@hots.org
    www.hots.org

The Holmes Partnership
    College of Education
    Auburn Unversity
    Auburn, AL 36849-5218
    Voice: (334) 844-4446
    Fax: (334) 844-5785
    kunkerc@mail.auburn.edu
    www.udel.edu/holmes

The Institute for Urban and Minority Education (IUME)
    Teachers College,
    Columbia University
    Box 75
    New York, NY 10027-6696
    Voice: (212) 678-3780
    Fax: (212) 678-4137
    ef29@columbia.edu
    iume.tc.columbia.edu/

The International Youth Leadership Institute (IYLI)
    Institute for Urban and Minority Education
    Box 11
    Teachers College,
    Columbia University
    New York City, NY 10027
    Voice: (212) 678-3295

The League of Professional Schools
    124 Aderhold Hall
    The University of Georgia
    Athens, GA 30602
    Voice: (706) 542-2516
    Fax: (706) 542-2502
    lps@coe.uga.edu
    http://www.coe.uga.edu/lps

Mathematics, Engineering, Science Achievement (MESA) Program
    University of California
    300 Lakeside Drive, 7th Floor
    Oakland, CA 94612-3550
    Voice: (510) 987-9337
    Fax: (510) 763-4704
    Michaelaldaco@ucop.edu
    www.mesa.edu

The (Ronald E.) McNair Program
    Division of Graduate Studies and Division of Student Affairs
    LAB School 137
    5048 No. Jackson
    Mail Stop LS44
    Fresno, CA 93740-8022
    Voice: (209) 278-2946
    Fax: (209) 278-7460
    or

The U.S. Department of Education
    600 Independence Avenue, SW
    The Portals Building, Suite 600D
    Washington, DC 20202-5249
    Voice: (202) 708-4804

MegaSkills
    The MegaSkills Education Center of the Home and School Institute
    1500 Massachusetts Avenue, NW
    Washington, DC 20005
    Voice: (202) 466-3633
    Fax: (202) 833-1400
    HSIDRA@erols.com
    www.MegaSkillsHSI.org

The National Center on Education and the Economy (NCEE)
    700 Eleventh Street, NW, Suite 750
    Washington, DC 20001
    Voice: (888) 361-NCEE (6233) *or*
    (202) 783-3668
    Fax: (716) 482-1284 *or*
    (202) 783-3672
    Schooldesighn@ncee.org
    www.ncas1.org

The National Coalition of Advocates for Students (NCAS)
    100 Boylston St., Suite 737
    Boston, MA 02116-4610
    Voice: (617) 357-8507
    Fax: (617) 357-9549
    NCASMFE@aol.com
    www.ncasl.org

Appendices

The National Writing Project
   University of California
   5511 Tolman Hall, #1670
   Berkeley, CA 94720-1670
   Voice: (510) 642-0963
   Fax: (510) 642-4545
   nwp@socrates.berkeley.edu
   wwwgse. berkeley.edu.nwp

New American Schools
   1000 Wilson Blvd., Suite 2710
   Arlington, VA 22209
   Voice: (703) 908-9500
   Fax: (703) 908-0622
   info@hq.nasdc.org
   www.naschools.org

The Paideia Program
   National Paideia Center
   School of Education
   P.O. Box 26171
   University of North Carolina, Greensboro
   Greensboro, NC 27402-6171
   Voice: (336) 334-3729
   Fax: (336) 334-3739
   troberts@email.unc.edu
   www.edu/depts/ed/ celpaideia.html

The Panasonic Foundation
   1 Panasonic Way, 1F-5
   Secaucus, NJ 07094
   Voice: (201) 392-4132
   Fax: (201) 392-4126
   info@foundation.panasonic. com
   www.pansonic.com/foundation

Parent Expectations Support Achievement (PESA) Program
   LA County Office of Education, Room 246
   9300 Imperial Highway
   Downey, CA 90242-2890
   Voice: (800) 566-6651 or
   (562) 922-6665
   Fax: (562) 922-6699
   Miller_Anita@1acoe. edu
   www.1acoe.edu/pesa_home.html
   or
   www.lacoe.edu/tesa

Project Zero
   Project Zero Development Group
   Harvard Graduate School
   323 Longfellow Hall
   Cambridge, MA 02138
   Voice: (617) 495-4342
   Fax: (617) 495-9709
   info@pz.harvard.edu
   pzweb.harvard.edu

Reading Recovery
   Reading Recovery Council of North America
   1929 Kenny Road, Suite 100
   Columbus, Ohio 43210
   Voice: (614) 292-7111
   Fax: (614) 292-4404
   bussell.4@osu.edu
   www.readingrecovery.org

School Development Program
    Yale Child Study Center
    School Development Program, Dept. A
    53 College Street
    New Haven, CT 06510
    Voice: (203) 737-1020
    Fax: (203) 737-1023
    info@clsr.win.net
    info.med.yale.edu/comer

SCORE
    Educational Innovations/SCORE
    23706 Whale Cove
    Laguna Niguel, CA 92677
    Voice: (949) 363-6764
    Fax: (949) 363-6764
    sharonmarjo@earthlink.net
    www.scor.ed.com

Success For All (SFA)
    Success For All Foundation, Inc.
    200 West Towsontown Blvd.
    Baltimore, MD 21204-5200
    Voice: (800) 548-4998
    Fax: (410) 324-4444
    sfa@successforall.net
    www.successforall.net

Teach For America (TFA)
    315 W. 36th Street
    New York, NY 10018
    Voice: (800) 832-1230 *or*
    (212) 279-2080
    Fax: (212) 279-2081
    www.teachforamerica.org

Teacher Expectations and Student Achievement (TESA)
    Los Angeles County Office of Education,
    Room 246
    9300 Imperial Highway
    Downey, CA 90242-2890
    Voice: (800) 566-6651 *or*
    (562) 922-6665
    Fax: (562) 922-6699
    Miller_Anita@lacoe.edu
    www.lacoe.edu/tesa

Teachers of English to Speakers of Other Languages (TESOL)
    1600 Cameron Street, Suite 300
    Alexandria, VA 22314-2751
    Voice: (703) 836-0774
    Fax: (703) 836-6447
    tesol@tesol.edu
    www.tesol.edu

The Urban Education Web
    ERIC Clearing House on Urban Education
    Institute for Urban and Minority Education
    Teachers College, Columbia University
    525 West 120th Street, Box 40
    New York, NY 10027
    Voice: (800) 601-4868
    Fax: (212) 678-4012
    Ericcue@columbia.edu
    ericweb.tc.columbia.edu

For Product Safety Concerns and Information please contact our EU
representative GPSR@taylorandfrancis.com
Taylor & Francis Verlag GmbH, Kaufingerstraße 24, 80331 München, Germany

www.ingramcontent.com/pod-product-compliance
Lightning Source LLC
LaVergne TN
LVHW081450070426
835510LV00015B/1860